About the authors

Tessa Cooper teaches and lectures on nutrition and weight loss and has considerable experience in the nutrition and fitness fields.

Glenn Cooper, her husband, is a Harvard-trained physician and specialist in internal medicine.

Taking Charge of Cholesterol

Tessa & Dr Glenn Cooper

CORONET BOOKS
Hodder & Stoughton

First published in Great Britain in 1990 by New English Library paperbacks

Coronet edition 1993

The right of Tessa and Glenn Cooper to be identified as the authors of this work has been asserted by them in accordance with the Copyright, Designs and Patents Act 1988.

British Library C.I.P.

Cooper, Tessa
  Taking charge of cholesterol
  1. Man. Cardiovascular system. Diseases. Prevention. Role of low cholesterol diet
  I. Title. II. Cooper, Glenn
  616.105

ISBN 0 340 60176 0

Printed and bound in Great Britain for Hodder and Stoughton Paperbacks, a division of Hodder and Stoughton Ltd., Mill Road, Dunton Green, Sevenoaks, Kent TN13 2YA. (Editorial Office: 47 Bedford Square, London WC1B 3DP) by Cox & Wyman Ltd., Reading, Berks.

Acknowledgments

We have benefited from the help of several individuals in the course of researching and writing this book. Charles Wymer and Dr Rose Cooper provided useful research assistance. David Robson of the *Sunday Mirror* and John May of Magpie Research donated their valuable expertise and time to the analysis of our national cholesterol awareness survey. Dr Eleanor Carlson of Lifeline Nutritional Services developed the fabulous software program, Comp-Eat 3, which greatly eased the task of developing our cholesterol-lowering plan. And finally, we wish to thank our editor. Humphrey Price for his support and encouragement and our agent, Mary Clemmey for all her efforts on our behalf.

Contents

INTRODUCTION

Let's begin with a shocking statistic: every hour twenty-one people in Britain die from coronary heart disease. That's over 180,000 deaths per year, making coronary heart disease the largest single cause of death in the country – the number one killer. One third of all British men and one quarter of all British women die of this disease. For the sake of argument, suppose that twenty-one people were dying every hour from a clearly identifiable and preventable cause. To take a purposely ridiculous example, suppose the cause were exploding television sets. Imagine the reaction! Every newspaper in the land would publish screaming headlines. The House of Commons would be uncharacteristically united in action. Consumers would be urged to take immediate action to protect themselves and their families. In short, the problem would be dealt with swiftly and effectively.

We submit that the situation with coronary heart disease is altogether analogous with exploding televisions. There is now clear and unequivocal evidence that most heart attacks are preventable. However, the interval between cause and effect for an exploding TV is seconds; for heart disease it is decades. It is this long interval that makes it all too easy for educators, governments and consumers to become complacent about the problem. The Eat, Drink and Be Merry Syndrome is attractive in the short run but tomorrow inevitably comes.

THE COST OF HEART DISEASE

Of course, not everyone who has a heart attack dies. The majority of victims recover but in the process they incur lost productivity, lifestyle changes and sometimes lingering disabilities. The psychological cost of heart disease to the victim and his family is certainly high but difficult to quantify. The monetary cost of heart disease to the nation *can* be quantified and it is astronomical. The Department of Health and Social Security estimates that the National Health Service spends over 500 million pounds per year on hospital beds, medication and surgical treatment for coronary heart disease patients. About seventy million working days per year are lost as a result of heart disease and the annual cost in lost production is some 1.5 billion pounds. We believe we are dealing with a clear and very real national tragedy. Human lives and financial resources are being wasted to preventable disease. The time has come to do something about it. It's time to save lives and save money.

NOT JUST A BRITISH PROBLEM

Britain is certainly not the only country in the world experiencing an epidemic of coronary heart disease. Coronary disease is the leading killer in most industrialized countries. It is a disease of affluence and surfeit. During the Second World War food rationing in the UK limited choice and supply but many experts are of the opinion that the nation's diet was never healthier. After the war, deaths from heart disease in Britain rose dramatically for both men and women but especially for middle-aged men. Among men aged 35 − 44 years the mortality rate doubled between 1950 and 1965. Deaths from coronary disease peaked in the UK in the 1970s, plateau'ed for a decade and drifted down slightly during the 1980s. Isn't that good news? While it is clearly heartening that the mortality curve

2

is no longer pointing heavenwards we must look to our world neighbours for comparative statistics to gauge the real position.

The United States, for example, also experienced a dramatic rise in coronary disease after the war; between 1940 and 1960 deaths for men and women increased by 50 per cent. However, since 1960 the United States has reversed this trend and has achieved a 50 per cent reduction in mortality. (Despite this fall, half a million Americans die each year from the disease and a further 2.5 million are severely disabled.) During the same time interval, Britain has managed only a meagre 10 per cent reduction in mortality for men and a 2 per cent reduction for women.

These two charts graphically demonstrate the UK's league standings and performance in the coronary heart disease arena.

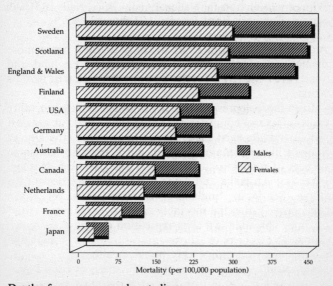

Deaths from coronary heart disease
a) Current death rates for men and women.

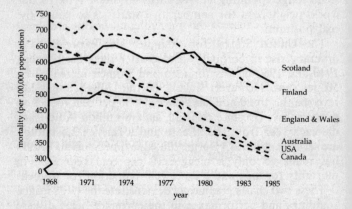

b) Death rates for men aged 40 to 69 during the last two decades. With permission from the National Audit Office, National Health Service: *Coronary Heart Disease*, 14 February 1989.

As you can see from chart a), only Sweden has a more dismal record of heart disease. Scotland, England and Wales are close rivals for the dubious distinction of world's worst.

Even more depressing is chart b) which depicts mortality rates in several countries for those individuals at greatest risk – middle-aged men. As we have noted, the United States still has a major problem but it has also had some success in reducing mortality over the past two decades. Likewise, Australia and Canada are on a nice downward slope. Scotland, England and wales, however, have experienced rather flat mortality curves over the same period of time. This data is a clear indication that as a nation we are not performing those necessary and achievable manoeuvres to resolve this public health crisis. As the government's Committee on Medical Aspects of Food Policy bluntly put it, ' . . . the United Kingdom's position in comparison with other countries is particularly conspicuous'.

THE HEART OF THE MATTER

What is the cause of this monumental health problem?

Coronary heart disease has its roots in many causes, but one of the deepest and strongest roots is cholesterol. Cholesterol is a fat-like substance which is present in everyone's blood and body tissues. Put simply: 1) elevated blood cholesterol increases the risk of heart attack and related diseases; 2) if one lowers blood cholesterol the risk of coronary heart disease diminishes; 3) a reduction in consumption of foods containing cholesterol, and especially one type of fat called saturated fat, can effectively lower blood cholesterol in most individuals. These fundamental premises are, of course, worthy of considerably more comment and we shall address them in detail later. For the moment, suffice it to say that this book is a practical guide to lowering cholesterol through simple, achievable dietary and lifestyle modifications − and thus lowering the risk of heart disease.

WHAT THE GOVERNMENT HAS DONE

Past and present governments cannot be accused of turning a blind eye to the problem of cholesterol and coronary heart disease. Over the past few years the government's health department had convened many expert panels and has issued many analyses and recommendations.

In 1974 the government commissioned a select group of academic expert advisers, the Committee on Medical Aspects of Food Policy, commonly referred to as COMA, to produce a report entitled 'Diet and Coronary Heart Disease'. In this report the committee attributed high rates of heart disease mortality to excessive fat in the British diet and recommended reductions, especially in saturated fat.

In 1980, the health department, the Health Education

Council and the British Nutrition Federation established a large multidisciplinary group called NACNE, the National Advisory Committee on Nutrition Education. The mission of this group was to analyse the existing scientific evidence and to issue recommendations for improving the nation's health by dietary modification. Three years later the NACNE report, called 'Proposals for Nutritional Guidelines for Health Education in Britain', was published. This report was critical of the state of the average British diet. It cited excessive consumption of fat, sugar and salt and low consumption of fibre as causative factors in our high incidence of heart disease and cancer. The report suggested a number of practical, albeit fairly non-specific, short-term and long-term corrective dietary goals.

The NACNE report received wide publicity upon its release and its central themes were further promulgated by the Learning Resources branch of the Inner London Education Authority which used the report as a basis for an attractively designed book called *Nutrition Guidelines*. The book, published in 1985, has been widely used in national secondary school curricula.

Another important government milestone was the publication in 1984 of a new report from COMA entitled 'Diet and Cardiovascular Disease'. This booklet, widely known as the COMA Report, is to date the most specific set of government recommendations on dietary manoeuvres to combat heart disease. Building on the recommendations of the NACNE Report, the COMA Report advocated specific reductions in the levels of total fat, saturated fat and cholesterol in the diet.

Since the COMA Report was of a technical nature, the Health Education Council was given the task of producing for the public a practical guide for implementing the recommendations at home and in the community. A useful booklet called *Guide to Healthy Eating* was published by the Council in 1986.

Furthermore, the COMA recommendations have been made widely available to an important audience, namely practising doctors, in the pages of our most prestigious and widely read medical journals, the *British Medical Journal* and *The Lancet*.

General practitioners have been specifically targeted and their own professional society, the Royal College of General Practitioners, produced a practical manual called *The Prevention of Coronary Heart Disease* in 1988.

How do the most recent UK government recommendations on diet and heart disease compare with official views from other countries?

It is perhaps comforting that every national and international scientific panel which has examined the issue has come to similar conclusions. The COMA Report is somewhat conservative in its recommendations regarding dietary guidelines for the general population but it is nevertheless in broad agreement with comparable recent reports issued by the World Health Organization, the European Atherosclerosis Society, the National Research Council in America and multiple other national health authorities throughout the world.

There is, it seems, a worldwide consensus of opinion on dietary goals for the prevention of coronary heart disease and the official position of the UK health authorities is in line with world opinion. Yet we have seen data that British mortality figures are not declining nearly as rapidly as in other countries, which suggests that government recommendations are not being put into practice. There seems to be a real gap between theory and practice.

THE NUTRITIONAL GAP

Let's take a closer look at this gap between official recommendations for a healthy diet and the actual average diet in Britain.

The COMA Report calls for a national diet for older children and adults in which no more than 35 per cent of total calories are derived from fat. Furthermore, no more than 15 per cent of total calories should come from saturated fat. For people who are at particular risk of developing heart disease, such as those with a strong familial history of heart attacks, the recommendations are stricter: saturated fat should contribute no more than 10 per cent and total fat no more than 30 per cent of total calories. Also, for these individuals, total daily cholesterol should not exceed 300 milligrams.

Currently in Britain the typical diet misses these recommendations by a long way. On average, 42 per cent of our calories are derived from fat and saturated fat accounts for 20 per cent of our total caloric intake.

It may be illustrative to do a nutritional analysis of a 'typical' British menu for one day. As you look at the menu, ask yourself if it differs substantially from your normal meals.

BREAKFAST

orange juice
1 fried egg
2 slices bacon
1 piece of toast with butter and jam
tea with milk

MORNING SNACK

tea with milk
2 chocolate digestives

LUNCH

corn beef sandwich
fruit
coffee with milk

DINNER

2 pork sausages
mashed potatoes
peas
roll with butter
apple pie with whipped cream
coffee with milk

BEDTIME SNACK

1 cup cocoa

The total number of calories for this menu is approximately 2,400 which is average for a normal, moderately active man. However, a massive 48 per cent of the calories come from fat and half of that (24 per cent of the total) comes from saturated fat. If this diet is in any way similar to your own or to anyone's dear to you, read on.

THE PROBLEMS OF PUTTING GUIDELINES INTO PRACTICE

The desirability of putting existing government guidelines into practice is clear. Professor Phillip James, who chaired the NACNE committee, recently asserted in an interview that 50,000 lives in Britain would be saved each year if people adhered to current recommendations on dietary fat reduction. Yet, the message does not seem to have reached its mark. There are three possible explanations: people may not have heard the message, they may have heard it but have not been persuaded by it, or they may have heard it but not understood it. Most probably all three have played a part.

Who is to blame? The government? Educators? The medical community? Food manufacturers? Consumers?

We honestly do not believe that it is worthwhile spending a great deal of time dishing out blame and criticism. There have certainly been shortcomings and failures on all levels; otherwise we would be winning the battle against coronary heart disease.

As we have seen, past and present governments have not ignored the problem but it can be strongly argued that the level of commitment and the financial resources needed to get the message across have not been adequate for the task.

Some educational authorities have had the interest and resources to teach children and teenagers about good nutrition and to put theory into practice in the school lunch room; others have not.

Doctors must surely shoulder some responsibility. Less than three years after the NACNE report was published a survey of general practitioners conducted to find out their attitudes towards healthy eating and the kind of dietary advice they gave to their patients found that 70 per cent of GPs had never heard of the NACNE report. Of those who had heard of it only 8 per cent could recall its principal recommendations. A third of the doctors thought it was important to give their patients dietary counselling but fewer than a third actually did so with any regularity.

Commenting on this survey in the *British Medical Journal*, Professor Philip James said, 'The importance of diet in relation to health has never received much attention in medical schools, with only a few minutes devoted to it during the entire course of an average doctor's training. It's hardly surprising then to find such a low level of awareness about our recommendations.'

Food manufacturers have had a variable record. Those with products high in saturated fat and cholesterol have not enthusiastically embraced consumer-oriented nutritional labelling. On the other hand purveyors of intrinsically healthy foods have realized that it makes good commercial sense to promote their products on their nutritional virtues. As long as the promotion is clear and truthful we believe that this is a reasonable way for consumers to learn about good nutrition.

And finally there is us, the consumers. Are we to blame also? There are those who would argue that consumers are blameless, that failures in the prevention of heart disease rest with these other groups. We cannot completely agree with this assessment. We believe that consumers would generally benefit from an attitude shift regarding health care and disease prevention. We would like to see people exercise the same amount of care and consideration in their purchase and preparation of foods and acquisition of medical advice as they exercise in the choice and purchase of their video recorders and motor cars. People often pride themselves on being smart consumers when it comes to durable goods but they may be ignorant and neglectful of the ultimate durable possession: their own body.

Enough said about blame. Now we move on to making coronary disease prevention work. And we would remind you that indeed it can work. As we have noted, across the Atlantic Americans have orchestrated a dramatic turnabout since the 1960s and have slashed mortality from heart disease in half. Over there the campaign against heart disease has had many standard bearers − cardiologists, family doctors, medical educators, politicians, consumer groups, the media. And despite the successes of the past two decades the country is redoubling its efforts now, with massive publicly and privately-funded programmes of cholesterol awareness and reduction.

We believe that a similar effort is required in Britain if we are to win the battle against heart disease. Up until recently coronary prevention was ' . . . everybody's business but no one's responsibility', as Julian Hart, a GP in Wales, aptly wrote in the *British Medical Journal* a couple of years ago. The time has come to exercise shared responsibility on all levels. Politicians, doctors, educators, the media, the food industry and consumers all need to take charge of this massive health care problem and wrestle it to the ground.

Lately there have been some encouraging signs that the

country is on the threshold of a cholesterol revolution. Hardly a week goes by without some newspaper, magazine or television show doing a piece on cholesterol. More and more advertising campaigns for healthy food products are highlighting cholesterol. Doctors and health economists are publicly debating appropriate strategies for screening the population to detect individuals with elevated cholesterol. And, most importantly, the topic of cholesterol and heart disease is starting to creep into everyday, commonplace conversation at work and at home.

PERSONAL RESPONSIBILITY

The core philosophy of this book is that we, as health care consumers, need not and should not sit back complacently and apathetically until our government or our teachers or our general practitioners are able to get the cholesterol message across to us in a palatable and understandable form. We all have a responsibility for our own health and the health of our loved ones. We can delegate this responsibility to others or take the responsibility on our own shoulders. *Taking Charge of Cholesterol* is for individuals who are willing and eager to deal with personal responsibility and influence the course of their own lives and the lives of their families.

We think it important to state at the outset for whom this book is intended and for whom it is not intended. It is *not* for food faddists, or people who favour extreme or radical dietary approaches. It *is* for people who want to learn more about cholesterol and heart disease, people who want the tools to assess their personal risk of heart disease, people who love to eat and dine out, and people who want a practical, sensible dietary approach to lowering cholesterol.

The traditional British diet is not a healthy diet but it is delicious! In this book we do not intend to throw the baby out with the bath water. Relatively minor changes in our eating habits can substantially decrease our risk of heart disease. This book is not about deprivation and austerity. It is about enjoying food and enjoying good health.

Finally, if you are going to be taking personal responsibility for coronary disease prevention the first thing you should do is satisfy yourself that the advice you are receiving is being delivered by qualified individuals! Glenn Cooper is an American physician who trained at Harvard University and qualified in Boston as a specialist in Internal Medicine (medical diseases of adults). He is involved in medical research and is the author of numerous scientific papers. He is now a permanent resident of Britain. Tessa Cooper was brought up in England and went to college and graduate school in the United States where she received an undergraduate degree in physical education and exercise physiology from Northeastern University in Boston and a masters degree in nutrition from Tufts University. She teaches, writes and gives dietary counselling to groups and individuals in Berkshire and Surrey. We have previously written a practical popular book on weight reduction (*The Two-Day Diet*, Pan Books, 1989).

HOW TO USE THIS BOOK

There is a wide gulf between nutritional recommendations and nutritional practice. We may be told: reduce your fat consumption to about 30 per cent of total calories, decrease saturated fats, increase polyunsaturated fats, watch your polyunsaturated/saturated fat ratio, limit cholesterol intake, increase fibre, etc, etc, but then what do we do after we've been told these things? One of the authors (GLC) freely admits that before writing this book he didn't have a clue how to put these recommendations into practice, and he has been a medical doctor for quite a long time. *Taking Charge of Cholesterol* offers a newly-designed, uniquely understandable method for putting theory into everyday use. We're genuinely excited about this method because it is extremely easy to use and actually teaches you about the fat and cholesterol content of foods as you go along. After a few weeks the method becomes second nature and you will be self-reliant and armed with a good deal of nutritional knowledge.

If you wish, you may skip straight to Chapters 5 and 6 and start getting into the plan. However, in the spirit of becoming a better consumer of medical care and taking a degree of personal responsibility for your coronary heart disease prevention programme we would encourage you use the book sequentially to measure your personal knowledge about cholesterol and compare your responses to thousands of Britons who participated in our national survey; to learn how cholesterol causes heart disease and how lowering it can prevent its development; to find out about the importance of tackling cholesterol in children; to learn how to get a cholesterol blood test and how to interpret the results and to discover all the practical tools at your immediate disposal for reducing your risk and your family's risk of coronary heart disease.

1

CHOLESTEROL AWARENESS: A NATIONAL SURVEY

The first step required in taking charge of cholesterol is personal awareness of the subject. That is why we were keenly interested to learn how knowledgeable and aware people are about the food they eat and their risk of developing coronary heart disease.

With the cooperation of the *Sunday Mirror*, we conducted a major national survey in October 1989 to find out the answers to these questions.

The response to the survey was overwhelming. Within days of its publication we received over 16,000 replies, an indication of the considerable interest that exists in the subject matter. In this chapter we present the interesting and provocative results of our analysis.

Before you read the results, take a few minutes to answer the questionnaire yourself to see how your knowledge and awareness compares to that of others.

CHOLESTEROL AWARENESS SURVEY

Please tick how many times each week, on average, you yourself eat each of the following foods. PLEASE TICK ONE BOX ONLY UNDER EACH FOOD.

	Chips	Fish in batter	Biscuits
Never	☐	☐	☐
Less than once a week	☐	☐	☐
Once a week	☐	☐	☐
Twice a week	☐	☐	☐
3 times a week	☐	☐	☐
4 times a week	☐	☐	☐
5 times a week	☐	☐	☐
6 times a week	☐	☐	☐
7 times a week	☐	☐	☐
8 times a week	☐	☐	☐
9 + times a week	☐	☐	☐

	Cakes & pastries	Chocolate
Never	☐	☐
Less than once a week	☐	☐
Once a week	☐	☐
Twice a week	☐	☐
3 times a week	☐	☐
4 times a week	☐	☐
5 times a week	☐	☐
6 times a week	☐	☐
7 times a week	☐	☐
8 times a week	☐	☐
9 + times a week	☐	☐

Similarly in the case of the following foods, please tick below how many times each week, on average, you yourself eat each of the following foods. PLEASE TICK ONE BOX ONLY UNDER EACH FOOD.

	Red meat or meat products like sausages, bacon, burgers or pies	Fish (not fried fish in batter)
Never	☐	☐
Less than once a week	☐	☐
Once a week	☐	☐
Twice a week	☐	☐
3 times a week	☐	☐
4 times a week	☐	☐
5 times a week	☐	☐
6 times a week	☐	☐
7 times a week	☐	☐
8 times a week	☐	☐
9+ times a week	☐	☐

	Fresh Poultry	Fresh fruit	vegetables
Never	☐	☐	☐
Less than once a week	☐	☐	☐
Once a week	☐	☐	☐
Twice a week	☐	☐	☐
3 times a week	☐	☐	☐
4 times a week	☐	☐	☐
5 times a week	☐	☐	☐
6 times a week	☐	☐	☐
7 times a week	☐	☐	☐
8 times a week	☐	☐	☐
9+ times a week	☐	☐	☐

Please tick in the appropriate box below how many whole eggs you personally eat each week, on average.

Never eat eggs..☐
Less than one a week...☐
One ....☐
Two...☐
Three ....☐
Four...☐
Five..☐
Six...☐
Seven..☐
Eight ....☐
Nine...☐
Ten or more..☐

Please tick in the appropriate box below the kind of milk you use *most frequently*

Never drink milk..☐
Channel Island (gold top).....................................☐
Whole fat (silver top)...☐
Semi-skimmed...☐
Skimmed ....☐

Please tick in box below any other kind of milk which you *also use* each week

Never drink milk..☐
Channel Island (gold top).....................................☐
Whole fat...☐
Semi-skimmed...☐
Skimmed ....☐

Please tick the kind of spreads which you use *most frequently* on bread, rolls, etc.

Butter..☐
Ordinary margarine...☐
Margarine labelled high in polyunsaturates.............☐
Low fat spread..☐
Other ....☐
Never eat spreads...☐

Please tick any other kind of spread which you yourself also *ever* eat nowadays

Butter..☐
Ordinary margarine...☐
Margarine labelled high in polyunsaturates.............☐
Low fat spread..☐
Other ....☐
Never eat spreads...☐

Please tick the kind of fat used *most frequently* in your household's cooking

Butter...☐
Lard...☐
Ordinary margarine..☐
Margarine labelled high in polyunsaturates.............☐
Ordinary vegetable oils..☐
Vegetable oils high in polyunsaturates...................☐
Other...☐
None...☐

Please tick any other kind of fat also *ever* used in your household's cooking

Butter...☐
Lard...☐
Ordinary margarine..☐
Margarine labelled high in polyunsaturates.............☐
Ordinary vegetable oils..☐
Vegetable oils high in polyunsaturates...................☐
Other...☐
None...☐

When you are shopping do you usually think about the amount of cholesterol and types of fats in the foods you purchase? PLEASE TICK AS APPROPRIATE

Yes...☐
No ....☐
Rarely go shopping...☐
Never go shopping...☐

And do you usually carefully examine the nutrition labels on food products to help you in your choice of what you buy? PLEASE TICK AS APPROPRIATE

Yes...☐
No ....☐
Rarely go shopping...☐
Never go shopping...☐

Please tick how much the subject of cholesterol interests you

Constantly...☐
Quite a lot...☐
Just a little...☐
Not at all..☐

Which *one* of the following foods in each separate group do you think has the *highest* cholesterol content? PLEASE TICK ONE BOX ONLY FOR (A) AND ONE FOR (B). IF YOU ARE NOT ABSOLUTELY SURE, PLEASE SELECT THE ONE YOU THINK IS MOST LIKELY.

Group A

4oz of lean beef..☐
4oz of lean pork..☐
4oz of calves liver..☐
One egg (uncooked)..☐
4oz of Cheddar cheese..☐

Group B

4oz of fresh prawns (no batter, uncooked)............☐
4oz of tuna (canned, in oil)..................................☐
4oz of cod (no batter, uncooked)........................☐
4oz of sardines (canned, in oil)...........................☐

Which *one* of the following foods in each separate group do you think has the *lowest* cholesterol content? PLEASE TICK ONE BOX ONLY FOR (A) AND ONE FOR (B). IF YOU ARE NOT ABSOLUTELY SURE, PLEASE SELECT THE ONE YOU THINK IS MOST LIKELY.

Group A

4oz of lean beef..☐
4oz of lean pork..☐
4oz of calves liver..☐
One egg (uncooked)..☐
4oz of Cheddar cheese.......................................☐

Group B

4oz of fresh prawns (no batter, uncooked)............☐
4oz of tuna (canned, in oil)..................................☐
4oz of cod (no batter, uncooked).........................☐
4oz of sardines (canned, in oil)............................☐

Which *one* of the following oils do you think is *highest* in polyunsaturated fats? PLEASE TICK ONE BOX ONLY IF NOT ABSOLUTEY SURE. PLEASE TICK THE ONE MOST LIKELY.

Olive oil...☐
Coconut oil..☐
Palm oil...☐
Sunflower oil..☐

Which *one* of the following oils do you think is *highest* in saturated fat? PLEASE TICK ONLY ONE BOX. IF NOT ABSOLUTELY SURE PLEASE TICK THE BOX MOST LIKELY.

Olive oil...☐
Coconut oil..☐
Palm oil...☐
Sunflower oil..☐

Which of the following foods do you think are completely free of cholesterol? PLEASE TICK ALL THAT APPLY.

Rice ....☐
Potatoes ....☐
Apples ....☐
Butter beans ....☐
Peanuts ....☐
None of these ....☐

Which of the following activities do you think will generally favourably affect blood cholesterol levels? PLEASE TICK ALL THAT APPLY.

Eating more high-fibre foods ....☐
Decreasing cigarette smoking ....☐
Decreasing coffee consumption ....☐
Increasing physical activity ....☐

Have you yourself ever had a blood test to check your own cholesterol level?

Yes...□
No...□
Don't know/cannot remember...............................□

If you answered YES at a please tick where you had the blood test.

Doctor's surgery...□
Nurse at work..□
State clinic..□
Private clinic...□
State hospital...□
Private hospital..□
Other..□

Do you know your own blood cholesterol level?

Yes...☐
No ....☐

Is your blood cholesterol level higher than normal?

Yes...☐
No ....☐
Don't know..☐

Have you ever been advised by anyone in the medical profession of the need to reduce your own cholesterol level?

Yes...☐
No ....☐

Have you ever been on a diet to reduce your cholesterol?

Yes...☐
No ....☐

Please tick which of the following statements apply to you?

I worry about my own risk from heart attack.........☐
I worry about other members of my family
having a heart attack..☐
I don't worry about heart attacks at all.................☐

Please tick below any of the statements which apply to you personally?

I smoke cigarettes..☐
I have high blood pressure.....................................☐
I have diabetes...☐
I am at least a stone overweight...........................☐
I have close blood relatives who have died
prematurely from heart attack/stroke...................☐

SOME TECHNICAL ASPECTS ABOUT THE SURVEY ANALYSIS

In any survey one tries to avoid biases creeping in to distort the results. If the goal is to determine the attitudes and factual knowledge of a cross-section of the general population, the survey would be one which selected people at random to answer the questions.

The survey we conducted had some biases naturally built in. First, the questionnaire only reached readers of the particular newspaper, who may or may not be representative of the population at large. Second, not all readers answered the questionnaire and sent it to be analysed. People who did so, again, may or may not be representative of the general population.

Having sounded these warnings, we are cautiously optimistic that our survey reflects the attitudes and knowledge of the general British public. We base this belief on the similar demographics (age, sex, locality and socio-economic grouping) of the survey respondents compared to the demographics of the country as a whole. The respondents to our survey tended to be more middle-aged and affluent than the general population but most differences were small, as you will see from the table.

We analysed the survey with the professional help and guidance of David Robson of the *Sunday Mirror* and John May of Magpie Research in London. Of the total sample of over 16,000 questionnaires returned to us, 80 per cent were from women and 20 per cent from men. Using a random sampling technique to balance the male and female respondents to reflect the population at large and to select a manageable but significant group for computer entry, 2,119 surveys were chosen for analysis (1,013 males, 1,106 females).

YOU ARE WHAT YOU EAT

In your battle against coronary heart disease you must deal with several risk factors that increase your chances for having a heart attack. This battle is a good news/bad news story. The bad news is that some risk factors are beyond your control. For example, being a male and having a strong

	Adult Population in Britain %	Cholesterol Survey Sample %
AGE		
15–24	20	10
25–34	17	23
35–44	17	25
45–54	14	17
55–64	14	14
65+	19	10
		(adjusted –
SEX		see p29)
Male	48	48
Female	52	52
REGION		
London	20	20
Midlands	15	14
Northwest	12	10
Yorkshire	10	8
Wales and West	8	6
South/Southeast	9	9
Anglia/East	6	4
Southwest	3	4
Northeast/Border	5	5
Central Scotland	6	14
North Scotland	2	4
Ulster	2	1
SOCIO-ECONOMIC CLASS		
Upper middle/middle	17	24
Lower middle	23	20
Skilled working	27	19
Working	32	34

family history for coronary heart disease places you at increased risk – and there is nothing you can do about that. The good news is that the other major risk factors are entirely within your control. Two of the most important controllable risk factors are cigarette smoking and elevated blood cholesterol. Almost everyone *knows* that cigarettes cause heart disease, lung disease and cancer. The course of action for you is therefore straightforward and understandable: STOP SMOKING! However, in this survey we have found that, unlike for smoking, there is a considerable knowledge and awareness gap on the subject of cholesterol.

In an attempt to discover how to narrow this gap we analysed your preferences for a variety of foods because when it comes to blood cholesterol levels, you are what you eat. As you will learn from this book, cholesterol can be lowered by eating *less* saturated fat, *less* cholesterol, *more* polyunsaturated fat and *more* fibre.

And lowering your cholesterol is one of your most powerful weapons against coronary heart disease.

Let's start with the great British love affair with fish and chips. We found that 83 per cent of you regularly eat chips and 64 per cent regularly eat fish in batter. Men are bigger consumers of fish and chips than women and there are strong regional differences as well. The Welsh, Northerners and Scots are the greatest fish and chip eaters while Londoners and Southerners eat the least. Sadly this is a dangerous love affair since these foods are very high in saturated fat.

Most people know that biscuits, cakes, pastries and chocolates are fattening but it is less well appreciated that they, too, are loaded with saturated fat. As a nation we are heavy consumers of these foods – according to the survey, approximately 85 per cent of men and women regularly eat them. The biscuit-eating capital in the UK is Scotland, where 25 per cent of respondents said they ate biscuits seven or more times a week. Wales and western England were a close second. People in the Anglia and Midlands region eat the fewest biscuits. Only 13 per cent of them indulge seven or more times a week.

As for cakes and pastries, there is a remarkable uniformity in the habits of the nation. We found no significant age, sex or regional differences. Everywhere, about a third of all people ate these at least twice a week. Some eye-catching differences appear, however, in chocolate consumption. Scots, Welsh and western Englanders are the greatest chocolate lovers but it is strikingly clear that chocolate-eating is a game for the young. About 70 per cent of 15 to 19-year-olds eat chocolate at least twice a week and 25 per cent of them indulge seven times a week or more. The older you are, the less chocolate you eat. Only about 30 per cent of those over age 35 unwrap chocolate bars more than twice a week and fewer than 2 per cent tuck in seven or more times a week.

As a nation we are also avid consumers of red meat and eggs, both high in cholesterol. No strong age, sex or regional differences here – about 90 per cent of Britons regularly eat meat and eggs. A half of the population eats meat two or more times a week. While many medical authorities think it prudent to limit egg consumption to about three per week, 20 per cent of people exceed this, a small percentage eating over ten a week!

We also asked about foods such as non-fried fish, poultry, fruits and vegetables – foods that are healthier for you and do not raise cholesterol. In fact the oils naturally found in fish and the soluble fibre in some fruits and vegetables can help to *lower* cholesterol. While over 90 per cent of all respondents eat non-fried fish and poultry on a regular basis, these choices are consumed less often than red meat products. Only 15 per cent of people choose these foods more than twice a week. We wondered whether the cost of healthy items might have an influence on their use. For expensive foods like fresh fish, this may be a factor. For example, upper middle-and middle-class people consume fish far more frequently than working-class people.

The news is better as far as fresh fruits and vegetables are concerned. Over 80 per cent of us take fresh produce more than twice a week and almost half have seven or more portions a week. However, teenagers eat fresh produce far less frequently than adults. And it appears that people who need them the most, the biggest consumers of high-fat, high-cholesterol foods, are the lightest consumers of healthy foods.

We were encouraged to find that people tend to make healthy choices in their use of milk, spreads and cooking fats. Consumption of whole-fat milk (which is high in saturated fat) is greatest among teenagers then declines as people grow older. Overall, 25 per cent of people buy whole milk most frequently, while 70 per cent buy the lower-fat semi-skimmed and skimmed varieties. As a nation, our love of butter has melted away over the past decade, and in our survey only 15 per cent of people use butter as their preferred spread. The message on the benefits of polyunsaturated fats seems to have been taken to heart since three-quarters of respondents choose margarine labelled high in polyunsaturates and low-fat spreads. The same holds true for cooking fats. Almost half of respondents primarily use vegetable oils labelled high in polyunsaturates. Next most common are ordinary vegetable oils. Butter is least used and lard is near the bottom of the list.

CHOLESTEROL QUIZ

We asked a few questions in the survey to test your knowledge about the cholesterol and fat content of specific foods. The results? Not too good!

We asked which of the following foods are highest and lowest in cholesterol: beef, pork, calves' liver, eggs and Cheddar cheese. Over half the respondents thought that

Cheddar cheese was highest in cholesterol. That is incorrect. Cheese is one of the lowest on this list. Only 9 per cent chose the correct answer, namely calves' liver. Organ meats are extremely high in cholesterol. Eggs come second here. Which is lowest? Only 19 per cent got this one correct – it's lean beef. In fact lean meats are low enough in cholesterol to fit, in moderation, into a low-cholesterol diet. Half of the respondents thought liver was lowest.

Cholesterol Content of Various Foods

Food	Cholesterol (milligrams)
125g/4oz calves liver	420
one egg (uncooked)	235
125g/4oz lean pork	125
125g/4oz Cheddar cheese	114
125g/4oz lean beef	67
125g/4oz uncooked prawns	227
125g/4oz sardines in oil	114
125g/4oz tuna in oil	74
125g/4oz cod (no batter)	68

Among seafood, shellfish has the highest cholesterol content by far. Only 17 per cent knew that prawns had the most cholesterol. Fifty per cent thought that sardines were tops. A third knew that cod was the lowest in cholesterol, but most thought the right answer was prawns.

The questions we asked on cooking oil were designed to make the point that vegetable oils differ widely in the kind of fat they contain.

The single most important dietary manoeuvre for lowering cholesterol is reducing saturated fat intake. Another important manoeuvre is to increase your intake of polyunsaturated fat, within limits of course.

Towards this end, your vegetable oils should be low in

saturated fat and relatively high in polyunsaturated fats. Of the following oils: olive, coconut, palm and sunflower, the highest in saturated fat is coconut oil, by a wide margin. Palm oil is second highest and olive oil and sunflower oil are the lowest. Most people mistakenly thought that olive oil was highest in saturated fat. In fact, olive oil is highest in another kind of fat — monounsaturated fat which, like polyunsaturated fats, has cholesterol-lowering properties. Only 18 per cent knew that the correct answer was coconut oil.

Sunflower oil is the highest in polyunsaturated fat, followed by olive oil, palm oil and coconut oil. In this instance, an impressive 62 per cent of people correctly identified sunflower oil as highest.

Saturated and Polyunsaturated Content of Various Oils

	Saturated Fat	Polyunsaturated Fat
	(grams per tablespoon)	
Coconut oil	11.1	0.2
Palm oil	5.9	1.1
Olive oil	1.8	1.4
Sunflower oil	1.7	6.5

The last question we asked was a bit sneaky. We wanted to find out if people knew that vegetables do not contain cholesterol. Rice, potatoes, apples, butter beans and peanuts are cholesterol-free. Most people knew that apples do not have cholesterol but only 5 per cent knew that peanuts were cholesterol-free. Very few people correctly responded that all of them lack cholesterol, a substance found only in animal tissues.

Finally, we asked whether certain activities had a favourable effect on blood cholesterol levels. A majority of people knew that eating more high-fibre foods, such as oat bran can lower cholesterol, but most people were unaware that decreasing cigarette smoking, decreasing coffee consumption and increasing physical activity also have beneficial effects on blood cholesterol. You can find out much more information on these topics in Chapter 5.

CHOLESTEROL AWARENESS

You cannot tackle a problem if you don't know you've got it or if you don't have the tools to deal with it. We were therefore very interested to learn whether people are aware of cholesterol and whether they act on their awareness.

Sixty-seven per cent of respondents said they think about the cholesterol and fat content of foods when they shop and 57 per cent of people claim to carefully examine nutrition labels of food they are buying. Women are more cholesterol- and label-conscious than men and, in general, people in their fourth and fifth decades of life pay the most attention to fat and cholesterol. We found no significant regional or class differences. Answering a related question, 17 per cent said that the subject of cholesterol interest them constantly, 49 per cent quite a lot, 28 per cent just a little and 5 per cent not at all.

As it turns out, interest and awareness of cholesterol go hand in hand with knowledge of the subject and sensible food choices. For example, people who think about cholesterol when they shop for food and who are quite interested in the subject scored better in the cholesterol quiz. They also eat high-cholesterol, high-fat foods less frequently and eat more fish, poultry, fresh fruit and vegetables than people who are uninterested in the subject.

Perhaps the highest level of cholesterol awareness comes from a knowledge of one's own cholesterol count. Only 24 per cent of survey respondents have had a blood test to check their cholesterol level. In contrast, it is estimated that six in ten Americans have had a cholesterol test. We found that twice as many men as women have been tested. Relatively few people below the age of 35 have been checked. Most are in their 40s to 60s. Unfortunately, much of the damage from high cholesterol has been done by this stage of life. The earlier one acts, the better.

The vast majority of people were tested at their doctor's surgery or an NHS hospital. A fair number (12 per cent) had their test done by a nurse at work or in a non-traditional site such as a high street chemist. Not everyone tested actually knew their cholesterol count. We think that's a pity. If you have the test, find out the result and ask your doctor, nurse or chemist what it means. About 40 per cent of people who were aware of their result know that their level is higher than it should be.

Once again, awareness and knowledge go hand in hand. People who have had a cholesterol test and especially those who know their count is too high have the greatest knowledge about the cholesterol and fat content of foods, and they also make the healthiest food choices.

And knowledge appears to lead to action. Over 90 per cent of people who know their cholesterol counts are too high have been advised by a medical professional to lower their cholesterol and have been on a cholesterol-reducing diet. Medical experts estimate that 60 per cent of Britons have cholesterol levels that are higher than desirable and could benefit from cholesterol lowering. However, only 14 per cent of the total survey population have been advised by a medical professional to reduce their cholesterol and only 19 per cent have been on a cholesterol-lowering diet.

THE WORRY FACTOR

Worrying about one's health is a productive thing to do only if it translates into positive action. We wanted to know how worried people are about their risk of heart attacks and whether they act on their worries.

We found a huge worry factor in Britain. Almost 70 per cent of respondents worry about their own risk for heart attacks, the risk of another family member or both. Typically, men worry more about themselves and women worry more about their men! Unfortunately, worry alone does not seem to have a big impact on healthy food choices or nutritional knowledge. People who worry about their own risk of heart attack make similar food choices to the general survey population but scored a bit better on the cholesterol quiz than non-worriers.

Those who have the most reason to worry are people with other major risk factors for heart attack. In this survey 23 per cent of people smoked cigarettes, 23 per cent had a close blood relative who died of a heart attack, 38 per cent were significantly overweight and 12 per cent have either diabetes or high blood pressure. Many individuals had multiple factors which dramatically increase their risk for heart attack. We found that people with other risk factors, especially smokers, seem to have a head-in-the-sand attitude. They tend to worry less than everyone else about heart attacks, are less interested in the subject of cholesterol, pay less attention to fat and cholesterol when shopping and make less healthy food choices.

ACTION FOR A HEALTHY HEART

In the survey we discovered that the traditional high-fat, high-cholesterol British diet is still much enjoyed. We found a heavy consumption of fish and chips, red meat and meat products, eggs, cakes, pastries, biscuits and chocolate. But there were a few signs that healthy eating is coming into its own as judged by the frequency with which people choose fresh fruits and vegetables, fish, poultry, low-fat milk and polyunsaturated margarines and oils. We were surprised to find such a high degree of awareness and interest in cholesterol and we were encouraged that cholesterol awareness is clearly associated with healthy eating choices and nutritional knowledge.

As a nation, we still have a long way to go if we are to shed the dubious distinction of having one of the worst records in the world for deaths from coronary heart disease. You owe it to yourself and your family to take positive action right now to increase your knowledge of cholesterol and choose a healthier diet. We hope this book will help in these efforts.

2

KILLER CHOLESTEROL

One of the longest 'jury trials' in modern medical history is over. Standing trial was cholesterol, accused of being a major cause of coronary heart disease and killing and incapacitating millions of men and women every year. The jury was composed of international medical and scientific experts, many of whom devoted their entire careers to conducting research and sifting through reams of evidence. The courtroom was large and diffuse – universities and research laboratories all over the world, medical clinics, national health offices, the pages of medical journals and the meeting halls of the medical establishment.

It may be argued that the trial of cholesterol was called into session over half a century ago, when, in 1933, the scientist Nicholai Anitschkow published an article which proposed that cholesterol in our food is transported in the bloodstream and deposited in the walls of the arteries of the heart, ultimately causing heart attacks. He based this radical assertion on twenty rears of his own experiments into the effect of a variety of diets on rabbits and the accumulated experience of other doctors of his day. Anitschkow's visionary hypothesis became known over the years as the diet – heart idea, the notion that the food we eat, through its effect on blood cholesterol, influences the occurrence of coronary heart disease.

The trial of cholesterol in the court of medical opinion was intricate and complex. We will necessarily touch on only some of the most important highlights of the evidence presented to aid in the understanding of the issues and the debate surrounding this fascinating medical saga.

The Charge

Elevated blood cholesterol is accused of clogging the arteries of the heart and other organs, leading to heart attack and other killing diseases.

The Defendant

Cholesterol is a natural substance, an odourless, colourless powder which is like a fat in that it does not mix with water. Present in all animals, it has a vital and beneficial role. It is a key component in the delicate protective covering of every cell in the body and is a principle building block for many of the body's hormones. It is also an important ingredient of the digestive juice, bile. However, in excess, cholesterol is alleged to turn from hero to villain.

Our bodies actually produce most of the cholesterol that circulates in our bloodstreams. The main site of production is the liver, which in man produces 800–1,000 milligrams of cholesterol every day, about 75 per cent of the amount that circulates in most people.

The rest of our blood cholesterol comes from the food we eat. Yet, cholesterol in our diets is not really essential. A strict vegetarian, who avoids all foods of animal origin and thus consumes no dietary cholesterol, is able to make sufficient cholesterol to fully satisfy his body's requirements.

Furthermore, the body has some capacity for regulating the amount of cholesterol in the blood. It can reduce blood cholesterol by decreasing the amount produced by the liver, by slowing the absorption of dietary cholesterol through the intestinal tract and by increasing the amount of cholesterol eliminated from the body via the bile juices.

Some individuals have genetic deficiencies which interfere with normal cholesterol-regulating mechanisms and they naturally have anything from mild to severe elevations in blood cholesterol. Try as they might through dietary measures many of these individuals will never be able to get their cholesterols into a safe range. These people require drug therapy.

At the other end of the spectrum are those people who can seemingly eat whatever they like and stay out of the danger range.

However, the great majority of individuals who have elevated blood cholesterol have natural tendencies towards lower cholesterol counts. Too much cholesterol and, more importantly, too much saturated fat in their diets simply overwhelms their body's ability to keep cholesterol levels in a safe zone.

Fats and cholesterol are distributed to all the cells of the body via the bloodstream. Since blood is mostly water and since fats and cholesterol cannot mix with water, nature has devised clever transport vehicles called lipoproteins to ferry them about.

Lipoproteins are minute bundles of fat and cholesterol, covered by proteins. The protein blanket makes the bundles water-soluble and allows the fatty cargo to be efficiently carried throughout the system. In our crime story, lipoproteins are like microscopic getaway vehicles. There are three major types of lipoproteins: very low density lipoproteins (VLDL), low density lipoproteins (LDL) and high density lipoproteins (HDL).

Bad Cholesterol versus Good Choesterol

VLDL particles are the main carriers of fats (also known as triglycerides). They also contain lesser amounts of cholesterol. After a meal, the fat ingested is carried to the liver which produces large numbers of VLDLs to transport the triglyceride for use as a major energy source for the body.

When the cells extract the triglycerides they need, the VLDLs, now depleted of fat, become known as LDLs. Without the triglyceride cargo, cholesterol now constitutes a major component of this new lipoproteins. LDL is commonly referred to as 'bad cholesterol' since this is the form of cholesterol most implicated in the development of coronary heart disease. The higher the LDL cholesterol levels the more cholesterol is available to clog the walls of arteries. LDL cholesterol is the real villain in our tale.

On the other hand, another type of lipoprotein, the HDL particle actually appears to be protective *against* coronary heart disease. These smallest of all lipoproteins circulate in the blood and literally extract cholesterol from the dangerous LDL particles and from the cells of the body. Then they carry the pirated cholesterol back to the liver where it is broken down and eliminated. HDL cholesterol has been dubbed the 'good cholesterol'. It is claimed that the higher the HDL levels, the lower the risk of heart disease. The most dramatic evidence for this assertion comes from certain families which have a genetic tendency to have very high levels of HDL cholesterol. In these families successive generations of men and women live free from coronary heart disease into their 80s and 90s. If LDL cholesterol is our alleged villain, then HDL cholesterol is our Good Samaritan. It goes to show you that you can't judge a whole family by the actions of one of it's members!

The Crime

Coronary heart disease is not primarily a disease of the heart muscle. Rather, it is a disease of the arteries which supply blood to the heart muscle.

The heart is by necessity a durable organ. In a span of seventy years the human heart will contract and relax over

2,500,000,000 times, pumping life-sustaining blood laden with oxygen and nutrients throughout the body. Since the heart muscle is continuously exercising it is a particularly avid user of its own effluent. Oxygen-rich blood is supplied to the heart muscle by a network of coronary arteries which originate from the top of the heart and branch out in three main networks to cover the whole organ.

The underlying cause of coronary heart disease is a condition known as atherosclerosis – an insidious process which develops over a lifetime. In its advanced state the arteries of the heart become hardened and narrowed by fatty cholesterol-rich deposits called atheroma or plaque which restrict the flow of blood through the internal channels.

Atherosclerosis ordinarily takes decades to become severe enough to cause symptoms of disease or life-threatening consequences. The earliest manifestations of atherosclerosis are slightly raised greasy lines on the insides of arteries, called fatty streaks.

Incredibly, the process which typically culminates in a heart attack in the fifth to seventh decade begins shortly after birth. One study of infants aged one month to one year who died from a variety of causes showed that almost half of them had fatty streaks in their major blood vessels!

Over the years fatty streaks may be converted to the immediate forerunner of full-blown atherosclerosis, the fibrous plaque. A plaque is a thick lump on the inside of arteries which has a greasy base of fat and cholesterol, covered by a pearly-white cap of dense fibrous tissue. In some individuals these raised lumps are ubiquitous in the blood vessels of the heart and other organs by the third and fourth decades of life.

In the final stage of atherosclerosis, plaques become larger, coalesce and become hardened by calcium deposits. Arteries which in their normal state are rubbery and pliant become thick and stiff, like lengths of lead pipe.

When the coronary arteries become so blocked by atherosclerotic plaques that the flow of blood is critically diminished the symptoms of coronary heart disease begin. When the heart is deprived of the oxygen it lets the rest of the body know it. Angina pectoris, the chest pain associated with coronary heart disease, is often described as a pressure or heaviness in the centre of the chest, sometimes with a radiation into the neck, jaw or left shoulder. It usually occurs with stress or physical exertion and goes away with rest. Attacks may be rare or strikingly frequent and predictable. Angina is a disturbingly ominous symptom which demands immediate medical attention. It is a sure and certain warning that serious trouble is on the horizon.

Atherosclerosis also commonly affects organs other than the heart. When it blocks the arteries carrying blood to the legs crampy pains may occur with walking. When the neck arteries become clogged with plaques, the flow of blood to the brain may be diminished enough to cause symptoms such as transient weakness or numbness of arms or legs or slurring of speech. These symptoms are warning signs of an impending stroke, a condition in which parts of the brain become seriously damaged by blockage of blood flow.

Heart attack is the term commonly used to describe what happens to the heart muscle when its blood supply is so severely restricted that a portion of the muscle actually dies for want of oxygen. The technical term for this malady is myocardial infarction. Heart attacks kill and cripple and represent the ultimate crime of cholesterol.

Many heart attacks strike in the early hours of the morning while their victims lie in bed. Others occur following heavy exertion such as running to catch a bus or shovelling snow. The victim is more likely to be male than female. In Britain, among the 45 to 54-year age group, men are five times more likely than women to die from a heart attack. In fact, two of every five deaths in British men of this age are caused by heart disease.

The gender gap narrows with advancing age. The overall incidence of coronary disease increases dramatically as people grow older. However, in the 65 to 74 age group men are only about two times as likely to have a fatal heart attack as women. It is likely that female sex hormones have a protective effect on the development of atherosclerosis and coronary heart disease. With menopause, hormone levels fall and the protection wears off.

The victim, a coronary artery, already narrowed and hardened by years of atherosclerosis, may at once become further narrowed or completely blocked by a gelatinous blood clot. Alternatively the trickle of blood through a chronically narrowed channel may simply be insufficient to supply the needs of a heavily exercising heart.

Whatever the immediate precipitant, blood-starved portions of the heart muscle literally start dying within a few minutes. The victim experiences chest pain and discomfort far worse than angina pectoris. Words like 'crushing' and 'suffocating' and 'it feels like an elephant sitting on my chest' are often used in description.

Unfortunately, many victims never get a chance to describe their symptoms. When the heart attack is massive enough or if it hits a critical region of the organ, the nerve circuits controlling the beating action of the heart may go haywire. The normal rhythmical contraction of the muscle ceases and the heart is plunged into a final few minutes of wild uncoordinated fluttering. Unconsciousness comes quickly as the brain is denied freshly pumped blood and the end comes shortly thereafter unless immediate advanced medical help happens to be available. Doctors cryptically call this sad state of affairs sudden death. It is a tragedy that for some individuals sudden death is the very first sign of heart disease.

Fortunately, most heart attack victims survive and make it to hospital for treatment. Some will recover completely with medicines and/or surgery, although many of them will have more heart attacks later on. Others will have permanent problems and disabilities, manifested by irregular heart beats, chest pains and breathing difficulties. The worst off will literally become coronary invalids, living a bed-to-chair existence.

Elevated blood cholesterol is not the only culprit standing accused in this crime story. There are other co-conspirators which have already been firmly implicated. Without a doubt, gender and age are important risk factors for the development of heart disease. Men are more likely than women to have heart attacks and the same is true for older people versus younger people. There is not, however, a great deal to be done about one's gender or age.

But there are two other prime villainous risk factors, as we have mentioned, namely cigarette smoking and high blood pressure. The gang of three: elevated cholesterol, cigarettes and high blood pressure, are thought to be the modifiable major risk factors for the development of coronary heart disease.

People with diabetes are also at increased risk as are children of parents with coronary heart disease. Other lesser factors may include obesity, lack of physical activity, stress, and personality type. Furthermore, a combination of the above major and minor factors probably increases one's overall risk of heart disease.

The crime is atherosclerosis and heart attack, the victims are ourselves, our families, our friends and our neighbours. What, then, is the evidence against cholesterol?

The Evidence

There are three lines of evidence which can be argued in the case linking elevated cholesterol with coronary heart disease. The first involves animal experiments, the second, epidemiologic, or observational studies on large numbers of individuals in various countries around the world and the third, intervention studies where cholesterol-lowering therapies have been employed.

The Animal Evidence

Animal studies on the relationship between cholesterol, atherosclerosis and coronary heart disease date back to the early part of the century, when Anitschkow began his work on rabbits. Over the years a large number of experiments on animals have corroborated and expanded upon his pioneering work. To summarize the current state of knowledge:

1. Many species of animals including rodents, dogs and monkeys develop atherosclerosis when fed diets which raise their blood cholesterol levels.

2. When animals such as monkeys, which have high blood cholesterol, are observed for long periods of time they are seen to develop fatty streaks in their arteries which progress to raised plaques and finally full-blown atherosclerosis, resembling the process seen in humans with coronary heart disease.

3. Severe progressive atherosclerosis in rhesus monkeys can be reversed when their blood cholesterol is lowered by dietary changes or drug therapy.

As an aggregate, animal experiments offer substantial evidence supporting the association between blood cholesterol and atherosclerosis.

Epidemiologic Evidence

Epidemiology is the study of disease occurrence and control within a population. In a typical epidemiologic study of coronary heart disease, researchers observe people who are clinically free of the disease for long periods of time. Over the years, some of those people will develop coronary heart disease. Since much is known about all the people in the study it is possible to determine associations between factors such as age, sex, cholesterol levels, blood pressure, smoking habits, etc on the development of coronary disease.

The oldest and largest such study in the world is the Framingham study. For forty years, American researchers have been intensively studying the population of an entire town, Framingham, Massachusetts. Investigators have gathered a host of data, including the blood cholesterol values of thousands of men and women and have periodically remeasured these values over the years. All heart attacks which have occurred among the population have been carefully investigated and recorded. The study is still ongoing and the children of the original participants are now being studied. Because of its enormous size and scope, the Framingham study is of enormous scientific value. A great deal of what we know about the risk factors for coronary heart disease originates from this typical New England town.

With respect to cholesterol, the findings of the Framingham study are clear and conclusive: **blood cholesterol values predict one's chance of developing coronary heart disease later in life.** The relationship is typically striking for middle-aged men of 35−44 years. For men with cholesterol levels below 190 (4.9)*, the risk of developing coronary heart disease over the next ten years is 17 per cent. For those with higher cholesterol levels, in the 235-249 (6.1-6.4) range there is a 34 per cent ten-year risk. Those with the highest cholesterols, 295-309 (7.6-8.0) have an alarming 65 per cent chance of heart attack within ten years. Cholesterol levels in the 235-249 (6.1-6.4) range have traditionally been thought to be on the high side of normal for industrialized countries. Yet fully one-third of men in this so-called high-normal range were struck by heart

* There are two ways in which cholesterol levels are commonly expressed. The larger number refers to the number of milligrams of cholesterol contained in a decilitre of blood plasma. The smaller number refers to the number of millimoles of cholesterol in a litre of plasma. The smaller number when multiplied by 38.7 will always equal the larger number. Since both methods of expressing blood cholesterol are currently used in the UK, this book will provide both values for any given cholesterol level.

attacks during ten years of observation! If this is 'normal' we should all strive for abnormality.

The Framingham study showed that the risk of heart attack was directly related to blood cholesterol – the higher the total cholesterol levels or the LDL cholesterol levels, the greater the risk. However, the study could not exclude the possibility that there were certain threshold levels for blood cholesterol, above and below which the risk of heart disease is dramatically different. For example, one might well imagine a kind of step-like plateau effect; as illustrated in the diagram.

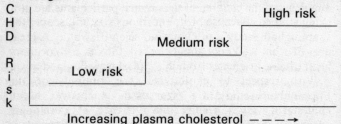

The risk of heart disease from elevated cholesterol is step-like

It is certainly important to know if these kinds of thresholds exist, for if they do, small reductions in blood cholesterol could lead to large reductions in the risk of heart disease.

The answer to this kind of question could only be provided by an incredibly large epidemiologic study, involving hundreds of thousands of volunteers. In 1986, the results of just such a study were revealed. The Multiple Risk Factor Intervention Trial (MRFIT) screened more than 350,000 healthy American men aged 35–57 and observed them for six years for the development of coronary heart disease. During those six years, over 5,000 of these men died of heart attacks and related illness. The graph derived from this study, shows that the relationship between cholesterol levels and coronary disease is smooth and continuous, not rising in steps. There is *no* absolute threshold of protection from

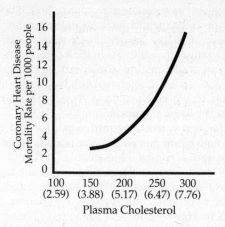

The risk of heart disease from elevated cholesterol is continuous. Based on Stanler et al., *Journal of the American Medical Association*, volume 256, p 2823, 1986.

heart disease. The message is simple: **the lower the blood cholesterol, the lower the risk; the higher the cholesterol, the higher the risk.**

Multiple epidemiologic studies conducted in Britain and many other countries during the past forty years have come to similar conclusions. All reveal a direct correlation between cholesterol levels and occurrence of coronary disease. Indeed a population has not been found with high rates of coronary heart disease with low levels of blood cholesterol.

The case for a relationship between elevated cholesterol and coronary heart disease is further strengthened by observations of groups of people with diets that are radically different from the standard Western diet or who have undergone radical dietary changes during their lives.

The Japanese are an interesting group to consider. Several studies (including the Framingham and MRFIT studies) have clearly demonstrated that cigarette smoking and high blood pressure are strong risk factors for developing coronary heart disease. The Japanese are prone to high blood pressure and are notorious for their avid cigarette consumption. Yet, Japan has a very low incidence of coronary heart disease. The explanation probably lies in their diet. Because of their ultra-low saturated fat/low-cholesterol diets, Japanese tend to have low serum cholesterol levels. In the absence of significant cholesterol problems their other coronary risk factors seem to be minimized.

Likewise, many other countries in Asia and Africa are rife with high blood pressure, cigarette smoking and diabetes but have low levels of blood cholesterol and very little coronary heart disease. This kind of evidence suggests that cholesterol is a risk factor of paramount importance.

Studies have been conducted on Japanese who have migrated to Hawaii and San Francisco. Those who have settled in Hawaii have generally adopted a diet higher in fat than the typical Japanese diet but lower in fat than the typical American diet. These Japanese tend to have cholesterol levels and rates of coronary heart disease greater than their countrymen back home but still lower than Americans.

However, Japanese who settle further afield in San Francisco often adopt a diet similar to Americans. With time, these Japanese develop cholesterol elevations and heart disease rates depressingly similar to native Americans.

These kinds of observations provide strong evidence that people such as the Japanese do not have genetic protective mechanisms against heart disease. The explanation is more fundamental: dietary and perhaps lifestyle change seem to raise cholesterol and bring on heart disease.

Just as a high-fat diet seems to raise a group's cholesterol levels, a low-fat diet seems to lower cholesterol. Numerous studies of people who eat very low-fat diets by choice (vegetarian Seventh Day Adventists) or by circumstances (victims of war and famine) demonstrate that these individuals have very low cholesterols and very low rates of heart disease.

Intervention Evidence

The strongest way to prove the case against cholesterol is to perform an experiment which demonstrates that lowering blood cholesterol actually decreases the risk of coronary heart disease and, most importantly, the risk of death from heart disease. For thirty years researchers in England, Scandinavia, Europe and America conducted studies in which one group of patients with elevated cholesterol was given diet or drug therapy to lower cholesterol while another group of similar patients received no therapy or sham (placebo) treatments. Unfortunately, virtually all these trials had serious flaws in the way they were designed and most yielded inconclusive results. Also, most studied too few patients and observed them for too short a time to reach significant results. While all studies suggest that lowering cholesterol was beneficial, none of them absolutely proved that this manoeuvre prevented heart attacks and deaths.

The debate on cholesterol raged on through the 1960s, 1970s and into the 1980s. Many researchers were convinced that cholesterol was the root of the problem but they lacked the definitive hard proof.

The proof came to light in 1984 when an American study called the 'Lipid Research Clinic's Coronary Primary Prevention Trial' was published. No clinical trial is perfect but the Lipid Research Clinic's study was impeccably designed and well poised to answer the cholesterol question once and for all. Over 3,800 middle-aged men with moderate to severe elevations in cholesterol but without any evidence of coronary heart disease were randomly assigned to receive a cholesterol-lowering drug called cholestyramine or an identical-tasting sham (placebo) powder. Neither the doctors not the patients knew the identity of their treatment. In addition all men were placed on an identical modest cholesterol-lowering diet. The patients were carefully followed by the investigators for seven to ten years for evidence of the development of coronary heart disease.

At the end of the study the group receiving the cholesterol-lowering drug was found to have cholesterol counts an average of 8.5 per cent lower than the group receiving the sham therapy. This cholesterol reduction was associated with a significant 19 per cent reduction in the incidence of fatal and nonfatal heart attacks. Also the occurrence of angina, electrocardiogram abnormalities and coronary bypass surgery was significantly lower in the group which received the drug treatment.

The core findings of the Lipid Research Clinic's study deserve to be highlighted because they are so significant: FOR EVERY 1 PER CENT FALL IN BLOOD CHOLESTEROL THERE WAS A 2 PER CENT FALL IN SUBSEQUENT CORONARY HEART DISEASE (HEART ATTACK AND HEART ATTACK DEATH). Thus, some men who achieved a 25 per cent reduction in their cholesterol counts had a 50 per cent reduction in their risk of heart attacks!

Although this was a study of a drug therapy, experts agree that there is every reason to believe that cholesterol reductions achieved through diet would have the same effect on coronary heart disease. In fact, a number of placebo-treated patients in the Lipid Research Clinic's study who achieved significant reductions in cholesterol through diet alone had the same degree of risk reduction as drug-treated patients. Changes in diet can easily lower blood cholesterols by 25 per cent or more. THIS MEANS THAT YOU CAN CUT YOUR RISK OF HEART ATTACK IN HALF OR EVEN MORE BY FOLLOWING THE PLAN IN THIS BOOK.

Since the Lipid Research Clinic's trial two other particularly exciting studies have become available. In one study (the NHLBI Type II Coronary Intervention Study) cardiologists at the US National Institute of Health studied patients with elevated cholesterols and atherosclerotic narrowing of their coronary arteries, confirmed and documented by an x-ray dye test called coronary arteriography.

One group of patients was treated with a cholesterol-lowering drug and the other received sham medication. After five years of treatment patients underwent another coronary arteriogram. In the course of the study total cholesterol levels fell 1 per cent in the sham group and 17 per cent in the active medication group. LDL cholesterol levels in this group fell even further − 26 per cent.

But the exciting finding was this: the group of patients who experienced reductions in their total and LDL cholesterols had significantly less progression of atherosclerosis within their coronary arteries. The disease process was slowed down or halted.

A second study confirmed these findings and went even further. In the US Cholesterol-Lowering Atherosclerosis Study (CLAS), coronary arteriograms were also employed to track the progression of atherosclerosis in two groups of patients, one of which received an intensive regimen of diet and drugs.

After two years of study the treated group had markedly lower total cholesterols (26 per cent lower) and LDL cholesterols (43 per cent lower) than the untreated group. This degree of cholesterol reduction translated into dramatic differences in the actual amount of atherosclerosis within the coronary arteries. Not only was there significantly less disease progression in the cholesterol-reduced group but there was actually clear improvement in coronary atherosclerosis in 16 per cent of patients who received diet and drug therapy. The disease process was actually rolled back, a unique and highly exciting finding.

Let us now summarize the evidence gathered against cholesterol:

* Animals with diet-induced elevations in blood cholesterol develop atherosclerosis

* In man, the higher the blood cholesterol, the higher the risk of heart attack later in life

* Blood cholesterol levels can be raised or lowered by the foods we eat

* Lowering cholesterol lowers the risk of fatal and nonfatal heart attacks

* Reducing cholesterol in people who have coronary heart disease can halt the progression of the disease and may even reverse it

The evidence is strong and persuasive. However, one may well ask whether there are any risks associated with lowering cholesterol. The question is a fair one since some, though not all, epidemiologic studies have suggested that people who have the lowest cholesterol levels in a population have a higher occurrence of cancer deaths. It is, however, a well-known phenomenon that some types of cancer cells cause blood cholesterol levels to fall. Careful analysis of the data leads the majority of experts to conclude that certain individuals with low cholesterols have early cancers which have not yet grown to a stage where they are detectable. In these people low blood cholesterol is not the cause of cancer. On the contrary, cancer may predate and cause low blood cholesterol.

The Verdict

After more than fifty years of research and deliberation, the world medical and scientific community has come to an almost unanimous verdict: elevated blood cholesterol stands convicted of being a major public health threat through its causative rôle in atherosclerosis and coronary heart disease. Cholesterol is clearly a killer.

The Sentence

Immediate action is needed to render this villain harmless. Elevated cholesterol is sentenced to be lowered. That's what this book is about.

3

YOUR CHOLESTEROL COUNT

At this point you are probably asking yourself: is *my* cholesterol count normal?

Assuming you are in possession of your blood test result, the question seems straightforward. Yet the answer is surprisingly difficult since there is active debate about the definition of a 'normal' cholesterol level.

NORMAL VERSUS DESIRABLE

The arbitrary rule of thumb applied to the interpretation of medical blood tests is that the 'normal range' encompasses the results of 95 per cent of the population. Thus, only 5 per cent of the population would be considered 'abnormal'. While this concept of normality works well for most blood tests it fails miserably for cholesterol testing.

For example, it would be completely unreasonable to claim that only 5 per cent of Britons have abnormal cholesterol levels when coronary heart disease is the number one cause of death in the society. Further complicating the definition of normality is the idea that what is 'normal' in one society may be terribly 'abnormal' in another. A blood cholesterol value considered quite average in a Western country would be viewed as alarmingly high in an African or Asian country.

Put simply, average blood cholesterol values within Britain and other Western countries are too high and far too many people have cholesterol levels that place them at risk of coronary heart disease. Rather than wrestling with the thorny issues of normality, it is more practical to talk about *desirable* levels of cholesterol.

As discussed in the previous chapter, epidemiological studies demonstrate that there is no threshold of risk for blood cholesterol levels. The risk of heart disease rises smoothly and continuously with rising cholesterol. As a guiding principle, the lower the cholesterol, the better.

Numerous scientific groups around the world have studied the available evidence and have arrived at similar opinions about desirable cholesterol levels. The expert consensus in Europe is that it is 'desirable' to have a cholesterol level below 200 (5.2). Levels between 200 and 250 (5.2–6.5) are considered 'moderately-high' and levels above 250 (6.5) represent 'high' blood cholesterol.

TOTAL BLOOD CHOLESTEROL LEVELS

Desirable Cholesterol	Moderately High Cholesterol	High Cholesterol
	200 (5.2)	250 (6.5)

It is important to emphasize that these three ranges – desirable, moderately high and high – have somewhat arbitrary cut-off points. The difference in risk between a cholesterol level of 249 and 250 is virtually nil. However, at a cholesterol level of 250 (6.5) the risk for coronary heart disease is twice as great as at 200 (5.2). Above 250 (6.5) the risk rises steeply.

In Britain the average blood cholesterol level is about 230 (5.9) which means that the population as a whole has a cholesterol problem. About six out of every ten people have a cholesterol level above the desirable range! The chances are that *you* have a cholesterol problem.

TOTAL CHOLESTEROL AND CHOLESTEROL RATIOS

So far, we have concentrated on desirable levels of total blood cholesterol. As mentioned in Chapter 2, the major component of total blood cholesterol is LDL cholesterol, the so-called bad cholesterol. LDLs comprise 60–70 per cent of total cholesterol. The second largest component is HDL cholesterol (good cholesterol) which comprises 20–30 per cent of the total. VLDLs, which are largely fat-carriers, make up most of the rest.

Since good cholesterol and bad cholesterol have opposing actions it appears to be desirable to have low levels of bad cholesterol and high levels of good cholesterol. Measuring only the total cholesterol may obscure the nature of the balance between LDL and HDL cholesterol. Some scientists argue that the ratio between total cholesterol and HDL cholesterol is even more important than the total cholesterol level. A ratio of less than 4.5 is regarded as desirable but the lower the ratio the better.

Two examples illustrate the potential difficulties in relying exclusively on total cholesterol levels.

In the first case, consider R.S., a 46-year-old man I first saw in the coronary care unit where he was admitted following a massive heart attack. He was not a smoker and his blood pressure was fine. His total cholesterol was 180 (4.6), well within the desirable range. Why did he have a heart attack? We had our probable answer when the result of his HDL test came back from the laboratory. It was only 25, so his ratio (180/25) was 7.2. Too much of his blood cholesterol was LDL or bad cholesterol and further tests revealed extensive coronary atherosclerosis.

Also consider the case of D.E., a 53-year-old avid runner,

who had a routine cholesterol screening test which was moderately high – 235 (6.1). It is not uncommon for runners to have high levels of good cholesterol so we checked his HDL. It was 70, which is very high, and his ratio of 3.4 was excellent. As he lacked other risk factors we were able to assure him that he was not a likely candidate for coronary heart disease.

It is fair to say that these cases represent exceptions rather than the rule. In the great majority of individuals the total cholesterol count is a good gauge of the risk of coronary heart disease, since so much of the total is composed of the deleterious LDLs. While LDL cholesterol is the target of efforts to lower cholesterol, total cholesterol can be used in its place as a screening test.

Total cholesterol is also a better screening test than the cholesterol ratio since it is less expensive to perform, more readily available and does not require an overnight fast. Occasionally it is advisable to measure HDL cholesterol and calculate the ratio but a practical approach for identifying those at risk of coronary heart disease and monitoring a cholesterol-lowering programme can be based largely on measuring total cholesterol levels.

HOW TO GET A CHOLESTEROL TEST

Obtaining a cholesterol blood test is simple and painless but we hasten to add that it does take some personal initiative to get it done. While more and more general practitioners are routinely measuring cholesterol in their surgeries, this practice is still not commonplace. However, most GPs will respond quite favourably to a request to do a cholesterol test. A small sample of blood is drawn with a needle from the arm and sent to a laboratory for analysis. The result is typically available in a day or two.

A routine total cholesterol test can be drawn at any time of the day, before or after meals. The more specialized

60

measurement of HDL cholesterol requires an overnight fast for accurate results.

When the results of your cholesterol test are ready you will want to discuss them with your doctor. Here are some questions you should ask: What is my cholesterol count? Is it in the desirable range or is it elevated? If it is elevated what should I do to lower it? What about my other risk factors for heart attack? Is my blood pressure normal? Can I get help to stop cigarette smoking (if you smoke)? While this book provides practical answers to many of these questions, there is no substitute for the powerful partnership of a doctor and patient working together towards common goals of good health.

Other options for cholesterol testing are becoming increasingly available. One option for those who can afford it is a private medical check-up. On a physician's order, a private laboratory will charge about £4 for a total cholesterol test. BUPA medical centres also offer cholesterol testing in the context of a comprehensive Heart Risk Assessment. This programme includes a medical history, blood pressure check, electrocardiogram, measurements of height and weight, urine test, diabetes test and blood cholesterol test. At the conclusion, you receive an assessment of your heart disease risk and advice on what, if anything, you should do to lower your risk.

If you are interested in just checking your cholesterol level, a new, accessible and inexpensive option is the pinprick cholesterol test. A variety of relatively affordable desktop machines are now available which measure total blood cholesterol from a few drops of blood from a pinprick. One of the most widely used machines is the Reflotron system which cost about £3,600. putting it in the financial reach of chemists, GP clinics, and occupational health centres. In participating pharmacies, for a fee of £6, you can walk in and a few minutes later walk out with your cholesterol count in hand.

Pinprick cholesterol testing in the community has been

criticized by some on the grounds that it is not accurate and that providing cholesterol counts without proper counselling is inadvisable. On the first point, a recent study at the Queen Elizabeth Medical Centre in Birmingham showed that most Reflotron tests in general practices and occupational health departments were fairly accurate. However, almost 9 per cent of results were considerably higher or lower than the actual cholesterol value of the samples. The source of the problem was largely limited to a few testing centres which had poor operator technique and out-of-date testing strips. The performance of chemists which operate Reflotrons is not yet known.

On the second point, chemists which perform cholesterol screening do give their customers some interpretation of their result. People with cholesterol values under 200 (5.2) are advised to adopt and maintain a healthy lifestyle. Those between 200 (5.2) and 260 (6.5) are given more specific advice on diet, lifestyle and smoking and those above 250 (6.5) are advised to get in touch with their GP. With permission, the chemist will send the test result directly to the doctor's surgery.

While we are concerned about potential inaccuracies in community/based pinprick cholesterol testing, on balance we support the initiative. It is clearly the responsibility of operators of pinprick testing units to assure the ongoing quality of their measurements.

The consumer must be aware, however, that the gold standard for cholesterol measurement is a traditional blood test drawn from the arm with a needle. We would advise anyone whose fingerprick test is above 200 (5.2) to have the result confirmed by traditional tests before embarking on a course of action.

We are also concerned about the possible harm that can come from giving someone a result of a medical test without proper interpretation. We have seen many patients who have suffered needless anxiety over a laboratory result delivered without adequate explanation. However, we oppose using this concern as an argument for keeping people in the dark about their own health. The health care profession has a duty to educate and inform people. With clear information and balanced arguments, most individuals are capable of making informed decisions about their own health. The kind of information offered by cholesterol-testing pharmacies at the present seems adequate and sensible.

However, if pinprick cholesterol-testing is to spread even more widely, to shopping precincts and supermarkets as it has in America, the practice will have to be monitored very carefully to insure against inaccuracies and abuses.

TO SCREEN OR NOT TO SCREEN

The increasing availability of cholesterol blood testing raises an important and difficult question: should everyone in the country be targeted for cholesterol screening or only certain individuals? This question is central to an ongoing debate on the best strategies for approaching the prevention of coronary heart disease. The first approach is called population screening and as the name implies a national goal would be the comprehensive screening of the entire population. The second approach is high-risk screening, involving those who have already suffered a heart attack, those with a family history of heart disease and those with a personal history of one or more known coronary risk factors. Both strategies have advocates and detractors.

Those who advocate mass screening of the whole population argue that this is the best way to identify all individuals whose elevated cholesterol places them at risk of coronary heart disease. Efforts at lowering cholesterol can be concentrated on those who test high. People with cholesterol levels in the desirable range can be safely exempted from cholesterol-lowering measures. Furthermore, if screening starts early enough in life, the process of atherosclerosis can be arrested before it becomes significant later on.

It is interesting to note that the United States has embraced population screening with a goal of testing all Americans over 20 years of age and repeating tests every five years. Childhood testing is also advocated by many American authorities.

In Britain, various working groups of professional medical societies have considered population screening. In 1987 the British Hyperlipidaemia Association and in 1988 the Royal College of General Practitioners advocated screening all adults. However, the most recent recommendation of the Working Group on Cardiovascular Disease of the Faculty of Community Medicine (1989) is a rejection of population screening. Commenting on the American approach to population testing in the journal *The Lancet*, the group argued that 'the implications for laboratories, nutritionists, and clinicians would be enormous if similar recommendations were adopted in the UK . . .' and that 'major developments in the National Health Service are needed before a blood cholesterol screening programme can be contemplated'. It may be argued that this is a resource-constrained approach. There simply may not be enough personnel and financial resources within the NHS to deal with the ramifications of mass cholesterol screening, when over 60 per cent of the population will require some form of advice, treatment and follow-up. This assessment may be correct but it is not heartening.

Proponents of high-risk cholesterol screening are largely those who have rejected mass screening. A strategy that concentrates on individuals who are known to be at risk of heart disease cuts down on the vast numbers of screening candidates and partly gets around the problem of limited medical resources. The problem with this approach is that metaphorically speaking the horse may be out of the barn already. Unless elevated cholesterol is detected relatively early in life, before other risk factors develop, the damage may be done by the fourth or fifth decade.

Population screening and high-risk screening are logically associated with two differing strategies for lowering cholesterol.

If one advocates screening the entire population then it is unnecessary to advise dietary change for everyone, since millions of people will have desirable levels of cholesterol. Why not concentrate cholesterol-lowering efforts on those who need it most?

On the other hand, if one supports targeted high-risk screening then it is logical to advocate dietary change for everyone in the country. High-risk screening will miss millions of individuals who would also benefit from cholesterol lowering. If it were possible to reduce the cholesterol of much of the population through dietary changes and lower the average national cholesterol level then tens of thousands of people each year would avoid death from coronary heart disease.

Admittedly, much of the foregoing discussion has been theoretical, since public health interest groups in this country are still wrestling with the relative advantages and disadvantages of high-risk versus population strategies and there is no unified national course of action. At present there is perhaps more momentum behind high-risk cholesterol screening and population-orientated mass dietary intervention (based on theCOMA nutritional guidelines described in our Introduction). However, what happens to you personally in the short term will most likely be based on your own general practitioner's bias, interest and expertise.

THE STRATEGY OF TAKING CHARGE

While public health officials, practising doctors, politicians and health economists debate the most cost-effective means of tackling the national problem of cholesterol and coronary heart disease there is someone who may be neglected in the process: YOU.

Public health strategies by necessity consider large populations, not individuals. We believe that you owe it to yourself and your family to become informed consumers of health services and personally take charge of your preventative health programme. One need not be a trained professional to direct a campaign against preventible diseases. Armed with the necessary facts about cholesterol control and coronary heart disease you can orchestrate personal and familial diet and lifestyle changes of proven benefit. We are *not* advocating actions that in any way interfere with the critical link that should exist between and individual and his or her general practitioner. We *are* advocating an informed partnership between doctor and patient where the patient has an awareness of important health care issues and knows what questions to ask.

Risk factor identification is an important part of an effective preventative health programme. One of the important modifiable risk factors is self-evident. Either you smoke cigarettes or you do not. If you do, your course of action is clear: GIVE UP!

Two other key modifiable risk factors, high blood pressure and elevated cholesterol, require identification. We think you should work with your doctor to make sure that you and your family are properly screened for blood pressure and cholesterol problems. Don't wait for public health strategies to trickle down to your awareness. Don't wait for someone to offer you a screening test. Don't get lost through the policy cracks in our health care system. Take charge of the cholesterol problem and start taking action.

YOUR PERSONAL ACTION PLAN

Do you have to know your cholesterol count before taking

action on cholesterol? In fact, it's not necessary but we believe it is highly desirable to possess this information. You and your family have nothing to lose and much to gain by making the kind of dietary changes that will reduce cholesterol. If your cholesterol happens to be above the desirable range then dietary change is certainly advisable. If, instead, it is in the desirable range there is still no harm and probably considerable benefit in lowering it further. Remember, the lower the cholesterol, the lower the risk. Furthermore, it makes a great deal of sense for all members of the family, not just one or two adults with an identified cholesterol problem to adopt a healthy style of eating. Finally, the kind of diet changes we are proposing have merits beyond the prevention of heart disease. A lower-fat and higher-fibre diet may be beneficial in preventing other diseases, such as cancer of the large intestine and breast.

So why bother with cholesterol testing? We think there are two important reasons why you should. First, in our experience, people are less likely to embark on a programme of diet and lifestyle change without first knowing their cholesterol counts. Knowing that a problem exists tends to focus one's commitment to action; having a target cholesterol count to work towards provides a tangible goal. Second, without knowledge of your initial cholesterol count you will not be able to monitor your progress, gauge your success or take appropriate further actions to achieve your cholesterol-lowering goal.

It is important to define the goals of your personal action plan. One of the fortunate aspects of cholesterol-lowering efforts is that any change in the downward direction translates into decreased risk of coronary heart disease. THE IDEAL SITUATION, HOWEVER, WOULD BE TO ACHIEVE A CHOLESTEROL LEVEL BELOW 200 (5.2). This goal is especially important for people who have other risk factors of coronary heart disease.

You may consider yourself at higher risk of heart disease if you have ONE of the following:

EITHER

Definite previous heart attack or angina symptoms indicative of coronary heart disease

OR

Two of the following risk factors:

Male sex
Heart attack before age 55 in a parent, brother or sister
Smoking over ten cigarettes per day
High blood pressure
Diabetes
Extreme obesity

If you fall into a higher risk category based on these criteria you should make every effort to reach a desirable cholesterol level. IF YOU ARE NOT IN A HIGHER RISK CATEGORY IT IS REASONABLE TO SET YOURSELF LESS STRINGENT GOALS, AIMING FOR A CHOLESTEROL LEVEL AT THE LOWER END OF THE 200–250 (5.2–6.5) RANGE. But again, the lower your cholesterol, the better.

Our overall recommendations for cholesterol testing and follow-up are as follows (details of these action plans can be found in Chapter 6):

* If you are over 20 years old check your total blood cholesterol. If the result is under 200 (5.2) simply follow the Basic healthy eating plan in this book and repeat a cholesterol test every five years

* If your cholesterol count is over 200 (5.2), confirm the value with two repeat tests done on separate occasions. Repeat tests should not be pinprick tests

* If repeat tests show moderately high cholesterol, 200–250 (5.2–6.5), we recommend that you follow our Basic eating plan for eight weeks then have another test.

If you have not achieved your goal, carry on with the Basic plan for another eight weeks. If a repeat test is still too high then move to our Strict plan

* If your initial cholesterol is in the high range, over 250 (6.5), we advise you to use our Basic plan, retest your cholesterol every eight weeks as above and progress to the Strict plan if necessary. It is important that you work closely with your doctor if your cholesterol is in this range, especially if you are already in the higher risk group for coronary heart disease. Your doctor may recommend a determination of your cholesterol ratio. While most people will have an excellent response to diet, your doctor may elect to refer you to a specialist clinic at some point or prescribe cholesterol-lowering medications

* Once you have achieved your cholesterol goal, repeat cholesterol testing once or twice a year to confirm that you have remained in your target range

LOWERING YOUR CHOLESTEROL COUNT

You can expect to achieve significant reductions in your cholesterol count by following the diet plans in this book. As a general rule, individuals with relatively high initial cholesterol levels will have greater responses than individuals with relatively low levels. Switching from the typical British diet to our Basic plan will achieve an average reduction of 30–40 (0.8–1) points. Thus, most people who start off in the moderately high range − 200–250 (5.2–6.5) − will drop into the desirable range. Advancing from the Basic plan to the Strict plan will cause a further decline of about 15 (0.4) points. Some people will experience even greater reductions on these plans while others will have lesser responses. It is important to note that the reductions achieved will be primarily in LDL or bad cholesterol so your cholesterol ratio will improve.

To place these numerical changes into the context of risk reduction, suppose you have an initial cholesterol count of 230 (6.0) and lower your cholesterol by 50 (1.3) points. This is a reduction of 22 per cent which means that your risk of future heart attack may be reduced by up to 44 per cent!

In our view, a chance to cut your heart attack risk virtually in half through simple dietary manoeuvres is too good a chance to pass up.

4

CHILDREN AND CHOLESTEROL

The food preferences we have as adults are formed to a large extent in childhood. Children develop their eating habits at the dinner table, influenced by cultural, regional and familial pressures. These eating habits are reinforced by interactions with other children, media advertising and the availability of foods at the school cafeteria and tuck shop. It is undeniable that most children have natural biological cravings for some foods, such as sweets. However, there are no natural cravings for the heavy use of salt, the use of butter instead of margarine or the use of whole milk instead of skimmed milk, to cite a few examples. These are learned preferences.

If we accept the assertion that the typical British diet is unhealthy and promotes coronary heart disease then we must critically examine the diets of our children to see how the problem starts.

In 1986, the Department of Health and Social Security and the Scottish Home and Health Department published a survey that comprehensively defined the eating habits of children aged 10–15.

Their report, *The Diets of British Schoolchildren*, makes interesting reading. For example, 93 per cent of children ate chips at least once a week and chips, bread, milk, biscuits, meat products, cake and puddings were the main sources of calories. High-fibre, vitamin-rich foods like fruits and vegetables were not popular items. On average children consumed 38 per cent of their calories as fat and a third had over 40 per cent of their total energy intake as fat, with chips and whole milk as the major contributors.

These findings are significant, given the recommendation of the COMA Panel on Diet and Cardiovascular Disease that no more than 35 per cent of calories should come from fat. Particularly alarming is the negative influence of school meals. Children obtained over half of all their chips, buns and pastries in school. Furthermore an analysis of the nutritional content of school meals showed that they were 39–45 per cent fat.

One obvious conclusion of the survey is that high-fat, low-fibre eating habits are already entrenched by age 10 and they persist into adolescence. Also, school meals seem to perpetuate the problem. The implication is clear: our national epidemic of coronary heart disease may have its origins in unhealthy eating in childhood.

THE START OF THE PROBLEM

A heart attack occurs in seconds but it takes decades for deadly deposits of atherosclerosis to build up inside the arteries. There is ample evidence that the process of atherosclerosis starts in childhood. A major insight into the origins of atherosclerosis comes from autopsy examinations of children and young adults who died from accidents or war injuries.

Fatty streaks, the earliest signs of atherosclerosis, have been found in the aortas (the main artery leading from the heart) of 8–10 year olds! A ten-year heart study in Bogalusa, Louisiana also found fatty streaks in the aortas and coronary arteries of teenagers and young adults who met untimely deaths mainly from accidents or suicides. Researchers found a strong relationship between elevated levels of total and LDL cholesterol in these young people and the presence of fatty streaks. Another study done during the Korean War showed that young American GIs killed in action had a surprisingly high incidence of early atherosclerosis and coronary heart disease. Many of the soldiers were only 18 years old. Thirty-five per cent had mild disease of their coronary arteries, 39 per cent had a moderate amount of disease and 3 per cent had complete obstruction of one or more coronary blood vessels. Only 23 per cent of these young men had no evidence at all of coronary disease.

These studies demonstrate that atherosclerosis can start very early in life and suggest strongly that efforts to control cholesterol and prevent atherosclerosis must likewise start early.

CHOLESTEROL LEVELS IN CHILDREN

Newborn infants have low cholesterol levels. In the first few months of life the levels rise rapidly and by the time a child is two they approach adult levels. During childhood the cholesterol count usually remains steady, only to dip slightly at puberty and rise again towards adult levels during adolescence. By the time a person reaches the second decade of life the adult cholesterol profile is generally established.

There are two main factors that determine a child's cholesterol count: inheritance and diet.

Without doubt, our lifelong tendencies towards low, middle or high cholesterol levels are inherited from our parents. This is not to say that they are *fixed* by inheritance, since one's cholesterol count can rise or fall with diet and lifestyle changes. But inheritance governs your cholesterol range throughout life and the degree to which it will change with intervention. An extreme example of the inheritance factor is the condition known as homozygous familial hypercholesterolemia, or FH. In this thankfully rare condition, a child inherits genes from both parents that interfere with the removal of LDL (bad cholesterol) from the bloodstream; consequently the child has extremely elevated cholesterol levels. By early childhood or adolescence the unfortunate child may have the circulatory system of an 80-year-old man. Riddled with severe atherosclerosis, a child may suffer a heart attack before his or her tenth birthday. Obviously, intensive and extraordinary treatment is needed for these children.

These cases are dramatic but they teach us that elevated cholesterol in children can cause problems at an early age. Less severe forms of FH occur with far greater frequency, affecting approximately one in 500 births. In a recent study from Utah, men who were afflicted with FH had their first heart attack at an average age of 42 and on average died at 45. If there is a parental history of severe cholesterol problems it is wise to check a child's cholesterol count very early in life so preventative therapy can be started immediately.

A child's diet also influences the cholesterol count. Data from the Bogalusa Heart Study show that infant fed on low-cholesterol, high-polyunsaturated fatty acid formulas have lower cholesterol levels than infants consuming cow's milk. Numerous studies have also demonstrated that childhood cholesterol levels can be lowered with low-fat, low-cholesterol diets. It would be ethically unacceptable to conduct an experiment to see the effects on deliberately feeding children on high-fat, high-cholesterol diets. However, few would doubt that the effect would be to raise cholesterol levels.

As previously mentioned, childhood cholesterol counts are generally lower than in adults. The desirable range for cholesterol in children is also lower. For adolescents in Western societies the average cholesterol count is approximately 160 (4.2). In Asian societies, where cardiovascular disease is rare, the average count is closer to 120 (3.1). Only 5 per cent of Western children have cholesterol levels over 200 (5.2). A childhood level over 200 would be a clear cause for concern as it could signal the presence of FH. A desirable range for children had not been well-defined but some authorities argue that a cutoff point around the 170 (4.4) mark would be appropriate.

THE CASE FOR A PRUDENT DIET IN CHILDHOOD

From the evidence presented, we can reasonably conclude that the consumption of excessive amounts of fat in childhood may set the scene for an unhealthy eating style in later life and may also contribute to the early progression of atherosclerosis and coronary heart disease. In order to tackle our national problem of heart disease we believe that the dietary habits of children need to be changed. The goal should be a shift towards the same kind of prudent diet we advocate for adults − lower in fat and cholesterol and higher in fibre. More specifically, the target is a diet in which no more than 30−35 per cent of calories come from fat, less than 10 per cent from saturated fat, with an average daily consumption of cholesterol of no more than 300−400 milligrams.

While we urge that children with suspected FH be tested for elevated cholesterol, we do not advocate routine cholesterol testing for all children. There is no reason to perform testing unless one is prepared to take corrective action. The implications of elevated cholesterol levels are clear in adults but this is not the case in children. If, for example, dietary manoeuvres failed to reduce a 10-year-old's cholesterol below the 190 (4.9) level, would a medical practitioner prescribe cholesterol-lowering medications? Very likely not. These drugs have not been well-tested in children and their long-term effects have yet to be determined. Furthermore, there is no data that enables one to predict the risk of future coronary heart disease from childhood cholesterol levels nor could anyone even say with much certainty that this particular 10-year-old would grow up to be an adult with a cholesterol count above the desirable range.

Our second reason for discouraging routine testing in children is even more important. Such testing would inevitably lead to unnecessary anxiety in parents and children when and if they are informed about a 'problem' or an 'elevation' or a 'condition'. Despite the best advice and counselling, some parents and children will believe they are facing a disease. This is a situation to be avoided at all costs especially if one child is put on a 'special diet'. We know of some extreme cases where anxiety over childhood cholesterol levels has lead well-meaning parents to deprive their children of essential nutrients in their effort to promote a cholesterol-lowering diet.

In our opinion, it makes much more sense to encourage all children to adopt a prudent diet, such as our Basic plan in this book. Such an approach sows the seeds for better adult nutrition and conforms with the desirable goal of a uniform healthy diet for the entire family — one set of meals for adults and children, no 'special diets' for anyone.

When should children be introduced to a prudent diet? Certainly not before age 2 and probably not before age 5. The unweaned infant who is breast-or bottle-fed has a fibre-free diet where 50 per cent of the calories come from milk fat. The composition of this diet is absolutely perfect for this stage of life and the transition to a lower fat, higher fibre diet should not occur too early or too precipitously. Whole milk is a critical nutritional source in infants and toddlers and the early use of skimmed or semi-skimmed milk and high-fibre foods may lead to nutritional deficiencies. Also low-fat, high-fibre meals are not particularly attractive to toddlers.

The fifth year is a reasonable and practical age to aim to make the transition to a prudent diet. A gradual transition may be accomplished by the progressive reduction in whole milk as a dietary staple between the ages of 2 and 5, increasing the use of vegetable fats rather than animal fats and introducing more fibre in the form of fresh fruits, vegetables and cereal grains.

Studies where adolescents have been urged to change to a prudent diet show conclusively that young people *can* achieve significant reductions in their cholesterol levels. The key is motivation. The notion of 'going on a diet' and sacrificing pleasurable foods must be avoided since the goal is lifelong dietary modification. We believe that no foods should be forbidden − this pertains to adults as well. The key is moderation and sensible substitution of healthier choices. In Chapter 6 we explain our approach in detail.

The prudent diet is a feasible diet for children and adolescents. Include your children in your overall strategy of taking charge of cholesterol and give them the tools to help them become healthier adults.

5

YOUR CHOLESTEROL TOOL KIT

In previous chapters we have discussed the risks associated with elevated cholesterol and the rôle you can play in protecting yourself and your family from coronary heart disease. Now it's time to give you the tools you need to take charge of cholesterol.

Your cholesterol tool kit is full of useful implements. You will find that the tools are not exotic or difficult to use. On the contrary, they are readily accessible to everyone. You will also find that the tools are not expensive. Healthy eating does not have to cost a lot. Your cholesterol tool kit contains a variety of foods and strategies that you can pick up and use immediately. Let's examine the contents of the tool kit.

TOOL 1

DECREASE YOUR CONSUMPTION OF SATURATED FATS AND INCREASE CONSUMPTION OF POLY-UNSATURATED AND MONOUNSATURATED FATS

It might strike you as odd that we begin our discussion of cholesterol-lowering tools with fats rather than cholesterol. It would seem logical that the best way to lower blood cholesterol would be to decrease the amount of cholesterol in your diet. That assumption is wrong. We will return to dietary cholesterol in the next section but it is clear that your most powerful tool for reducing cholesterol is cutting down on the amount of *saturated fat* in your diet.

There are three kinds of fat in the food we eat: saturated fat, polyunsaturated fat and monounsaturated fat. Foods containing fat usually have a mixture of all three kinds of fat but many foods have a predominance of one kind or another. It is important to distinguish between different types of fat, since each has a different effect on blood cholesterol levels.

As a rule of thumb, saturated fats tend to have undesirable effects on blood cholesterol and polyunsaturated and monounsaturated fats have desirable effects.

Saturated fat derives its name from the fact that each carbon atom in the long chemical chains that make the backbone of the fat molecule is saturated with hydrogen atoms. Most saturated fats are solid at room temperature. Foods high in saturated fat come from both animal and vegetable sources. Red meat, whole milk, cheese and butter are rich sources. Vegetables are usually low in saturated fat but there are four kinds of vegetable fats that are naturally high: coconut oil, palm oil, palm kernel oil, and cocoa butter (the main fat in chocolate). These high-saturated-fat vegetable oils may not be common items in your pantry but they are ubiquitous in prepared and packaged foods. With the exception of these vegetable oils it is safe to say that animal fats are high in saturated fat and vegetable fats are low.

Polyunsaturated fat has two or more carbon atoms in its chemical backbone that are not saturated with hydrogen atoms. This chemical difference causes most polyunsaturated fats to be liquid at room temperature. The main source of polyunsaturated fats in the diet are fish oils and vegetable oils. Once again, the exceptions are coconut oils, cocoa oils and palm oils. It is possible to chemically convert polyunsaturated fats into saturated fats through a process known as hydrogenation. Hydrogenation solidifies fats and is used commercially to convert less expensive oils such as cottonseed and soybean oil into fats with the physical characteristics of more expensive animal fats. It is therefore not surprising that hydrogenated vegetable oils are extensively used in processed food items. Foods may either be partially or completely hydrogenated. Once fully hydrogenated, the polyunsaturated fat behaves in the body like a saturated fat.

Vegetable oils high in polyunsaturates include sunflower, safflower, corn, soybean and cottonseed oils. Other sources are nuts, beans and whole grains.

Another important source of polyunsaturated fats is fish. Although both vegetable and fish polyunsaturated fats have a beneficial effect on blood cholesterol they have a different chemical structure. In most vegetable polyunsaturates the first area of unsaturation occurs in a certain position along the chemical backbone called the omega-6 position. However, fish oils are unsaturated in a different area, the omega-3 position. Fish oils are often referred to as omega-3 fatty acids. As we shall see, this simple chemical difference makes fish polyunsaturated fats particularly effective in lowering cholesterol. Deep water fish including herring, kipper, pilchard, mackerel, salmon and trout are especially good sources of omega-3 fatty acids. Other good sources are halibut, bluefish, sardines and bass.

Monounsaturated fat has only one carbon in its backbone not fully saturated with hydrogen atoms. It exists predominantly in liquid form. The richest source of monounsaturated fat is olive oil which contains about 75 per cent monounsaturates. Peanut oil is also a fairly rich source.

GOOD FAT AND BAD FAT

In the 1940s, Ancel Keys, a physiologist from the University of Minnesota, performed a series of experiments feeding human volunteers special diets carefully supplemented with varying amounts of cholesterol, saturated and poly-unsaturated fats. He found that dietary cholesterol had a fairly small effect in raising blood cholesterol levels. However, fat supplementation had a significant effect. The effects were predictable and reproducible and could be summarized in a mathematical equation:

Increase in Blood Cholesterol $= 2.7 \times$ amount of dietary saturated fat $- 1.3 \times$ amount of dietary polyunsaturated fat

This equation says two things. First, saturated fats raise and polyunsaturated fats lower blood cholesterol. Second, saturated fats are twice as effective in raising cholesterol as polyunsaturated fats are in lowering it. The Keys experiments and many others have led to the concept of good fat (poly and monounsaturates) and bad fat (saturates). The concept can be forged into a powerful two-pronged tool in your cholesterol tool kit. YOU CAN SIGNIFICANTLY LOWER YOUR CHOLESTEROL BY DECREASING THE AMOUNT OF BAD FAT IN YOUR DIET WHILE INCREASING THE AMOUNT OF GOOD FAT.

When nutritionists talk about good fat and bad fat they refer to the polyunsaturated/saturated fat or P/S ratio. The higher the P/S ratio, the greater the intake of good fat and the lower the intake of bad fat. A goal for healthy heart eating is a P/S ratio of about 1.0 which would indicate roughly equal consumption of polyunsaturates and saturates. The average P/S ratio for the British public is 0.24 which means that we are overconsuming saturated fat and underconsuming polyunsaturated fat.

As an overarching goal we should limit our consumption of all types of fat to 30−35 per cent of daily calories. This means that one should *not* attempt to raise the P/S ratio by simply boosting the intake of polyunsaturated fats. Polyunsaturated fats deserve their reputation as good fats since they can lower the blood cholesterol. But in excess any fat can be harmful. Measure for measure, fats have more

81

than twice the calories of carbohydrates and proteins so too much fat in the diet can contribute towards obesity, a cardiac risk factor in its own right. The eating plans in *Taking Charge of Cholesterol* encourage moderate decreases in saturated fat intake accompanied by moderate increases in polyunsaturated fat consumption.

OMEGA-3 FATTY ACIDS

Interest in the beneficial effects of fish and fish oils began to blossom when scientists proposed that the low incidence of atherosclerosis and coronary heart disease among Eskimos in Greenland was the result of their high intake of fish oils containing omega-3 fatty acids. This led other investigators to begin studies on the effects of omega-3 fatty acids on volunteers and patients with elevated cholesterols. In one study, volunteers with normal cholesterol and triglyceride levels were fed diets in which all the fat came from either salmon or corn oil. Cholesterol levels were lowered by 11 per cent by both diets whereas triglyceride levels fell only on the fish oil diet.

Another study on patients with elevated cholesterol and triglyceride levels showed that fish oils could lower cholesterol by up to 45 per cent and triglycerides by as much as 79 per cent. Vegetable oil and conventional low-fat diets were not as effective in these patients.

An epidemiologic study in the Netherlands focused on the dietary habits of 852 middle-aged men with coronary heart disease and followed the patients for twenty years. The Dutch researchers found that deaths from heart disease were over 50 per cent lower among men who ate more than 30 grams of fish per day compared to non-fish-eaters. These results are particularly impressive since protection was achieved by consuming only two or three fish dishes per week.

More recently, researchers in Wales conducted a large

study among 2,033 men recovering from heart attacks. They compared the long-term effects of three kinds of dietary advice: reduction in fat intake to 30 per cent with an increase in the P/S ration, and increase in fish intake (at least two weekly 200–400g portions of fatty fish.), and an increase in cereal fibre intake to 18 grams per day.

During the two-year study period advice on fat and fibre had little effect on the death rate. However, subjects who were advised to eat fatty fish had a 29 per cent reduction in mortality compared to men who were not encouraged to eat fish. The investigators, reporting in *The Lancet*, concluded that, 'a modest intake of fatty fish (two or three portions per week) may reduce mortality in men who have recovered from MI [heart attacks]'.

The information to date on fish polyunsaturates is fairly compelling and we have incorporated specific recommendations on fish consumption into our cholesterol-lowering eating plans.

THE MEDITERRANEAN DIET

People living in southern Italy, Greece and other parts of the Mediterranean basin have a surprisingly low incidence of coronary heart disease. Might high dietary factors have something to do with this phenomenon? The traditional Mediterranean diet relies heavily on the use of olive oil which is high in monounsaturated fatty acids. Fresh fruits and vegetables are also staples.

Early investigation by Keys and colleagues in America suggested that polyunsaturates were far more effective than monounsaturates in lowering cholesterol. However, more recently, additional studies have been performed by scientists interested in the possible virtues of the Mediterranean diet.

The latest study, done in the Netherlands and reported in *The New England Journal of Medicine* in 1989 is of particular interest since it involved men and women on realistic home diets rather than highly artificial hospital test diets. One group of people received a high-monounsaturate diet enriched with olive oil and another group received a high-polyunsaturate diet enriched with sunflower oil. After approximately five weeks, blood tests showed that LDL (bad cholesterol) levels fell even more on the monounsaturated diet than on the polyunsaturated diet (18 per cent versus 13 per cent). In men levels of HDL (good cholesterol) fell very slightly on both diets while in women HDL levels did not change.

This study and others suggest that diets rich in monounsaturated fats such as olive oil are at least as effective and possibly even more effective in lowering cholesterol levels than regular low-fat diets high in polyunsaturated fats. We think that a Mediterranean style of eating has much to offer a cholesterol-lowering programme and we have included recommendations on the use of olive oil and fresh fruits and vegetables in our plans.

TOOL 2:

RESTRICT THE AMOUNT OF CHOLESTEROL IN YOUR DIET

Cholesterol is present in all animal tissues and foods derived from animals such as milk, cream, cheese and eggs. Ounce for ounce, red meat contains more cholesterol than poultry or fish. Plants and plant products like vegetable oils and margarine are essentially cholesterol-free. Organ meats are extremely high in cholesterol. For example, four ounces of calves' liver contains 550 milligrams of cholesterol, compared to 100 milligrams contained in the same amount of trimmed beef.

Cholesterol is a vital building block for the cells and the body protects its interests by producing virtually all the cholesterol needed, in the liver. Strict vegetarians with zero cholesterol intake do not have problems with cholesterol deficiency.

The effect of dietary cholesterol on blood cholesterol levels has been debated for years. The early feeding experiments of Keys indicated that decreasing the cholesterol content in the diet decreased the cholesterol blood count, although decreasing saturated fat in the diet was far more effective. Over the ensuing decades, some investigators have reproduced Keys' results, others have refuted them, showing a negligible influence of dietary cholesterol on blood cholesterol levels.

It now seems clear that some individuals are very susceptible to the cholesterol-raising effects of dietary cholesterol and others are resistant. In other words, certain people can eat a high-cholesterol diet with minimal effect on their blood cholesterol while others are liable to have significant rises in their cholesterol counts on the same diet. There may also be interactions with other food items. For example, cholesterol feeding has a more pronounced effect on blood cholesterol when a diet is rich in saturated fats and low in polyunsaturated fats.

There is no simple way of determining whether you are someone whose blood cholesterol is significantly affected by the cholesterol in your diet. Indeed, you could already have a cholesterol count in the desirable range and you might well ask if it makes sense to watch your cholesterol intake at all. Some recent studies indicate that cholesterol restriction *may* be important for most people. More specifically, dietary cholesterol may have an independent effect on the risk of developing coronary heart disease over and above its effect on blood cholesterol.

Researchers from Houston and Chicago studied data from one of the best-known epidemiologic studies in America, the Western Electric study. Over 2,000 men aged 40–55 were selected in 1957 to undergo periodic assessments of their health and dietary habits. On the twenty-fifth anniversary of their first examination the health status of all participants was determined. In the intervening years over 600 men had died, many from coronary heart disease. An analysis of the relationship between dietary habits and cause of death revealed some striking findings. Those men who had relatively low intake of cholesterol (100 milligrams for every 1,000 calories eaten) had a 50 per cent reduction in their risk of fatal heart attack over men who were heavy consumers (300 milligrams of cholesterol per 1,000 calories).

These results could not be explained by differences in blood cholesterol levels. Instead, there appeared to be an independent effect of dietary cholesterol in promoting coronary heart disease. The mechanism of this effect is unknown but there is some evidence that dietary cholesterol may contribute to atherosclerosis by increasing the tendency of the blood to clot.

What conclusions about dietary cholesterol can be drawn in the light of available evidence? First, some, but not all, individuals will lower blood cholesterol by decreasing the cholesterol in their food. Second, even if dietary reduction fails to lower blood cholesterol there may still be considerable benefit in restricting cholesterol in your diet. In the UK, the average daily cholesterol intake is about 500 milligrams. We believe it is prudent to limit your cholesterol to 300 milligrams per day. This degree of reduction is not drastic and is easy to achieve.

Reducing dietary cholesterol and saturated fat go hand in hand since the two substances are usually present in the same foods. In *Taking Charge of Cholesterol* we focus on saturated fat reduction as the most important tool for lowering cholesterol. If you pay attention to saturated fats you will naturally lower your cholesterol intake at the same time. There are two notable food exceptions. Eggs and organ meats such as liver and kidneys are disproportionately high in cholesterol, possessing only moderate amounts of saturated fat. Cholesterol in eggs is carried in the yolk. Egg whites are virtually fat-free and are abundant sources of protein. A single egg yolk has 240 milligrams of cholesterol, almost our entire recommended daily amount. For this reason we advise limiting your egg intake to three per week and eating organ meat infrequently.

However, we want to make the following point very clearly: you do not have to deny yourself eggs, meat, dairy products or *any* food item to lower cholesterol and saturated fat intake to prudent levels. In the next chapter we will show you, step-by-step, how to lower your blood cholesterol without radically changing your eating habits.

TOOL 3:

INCREASE THE AMOUNT OF FIBRE IN YOUR DIET

We have already talked about the virtues of the Mediterranean diet. Another aspect of the Mediterranean style of eating that is beneficial in a cholesterol-lowering programme is a high consumption of fibre-rich foods − fresh fruits, vegetables, beans and whole grain products.

Evidence is available that certain high-fibre foods can reduce blood cholesterol. There are two broad categories of fibre, water-soluble and insoluble. Insoluble fibres like cellulose, commonly found in wheat bran, have not been shown to have much effect on blood cholesterol. The insoluble fibre in many wheat products helps prevent constipation and is believed to reduce the risk for developing colon cancer and other intestinal disorders. However, soluble fibres contained in foods like fruits, beans and oats seem to have a beneficial influence on cholesterol counts.

In recent years there has been a flood of publicity about the cholesterol-lowering properties of oat bran. Bran is the part of the cereal grain that is richest in fibre. Whole grain cereals contain the bran portion together with what is known as the germ, which provides vitamins and minerals. All-bran cereals have very high fibre concentrations but lack the nutrient-rich germ so manufacturers generally fortify the cereals with vitamins and minerals. Oat bran cereals and baked goods made from oat bran have become increasingly popular based on health claims as well as their pleasant taste and consistency.

How good is the evidence for the cholesterol-lowering properties of oat bran? Most of the studies conducted to date have been fairly small so the body of evidence is not overwhelming. However, most studies of oat bran (and other soluble fibres such as pectin and psyllium) have shown a cholesterol-lowering effect. The magnitude of the effect depends on the amount of oat bran consumed. In one study, the consumption of the equivalent of one bowl of oat bran cereal per day reduced cholesterol levels a further 3 per cent in volunteers who had already achieved reductions on a low-fat diet. Other studies of men who consumed the equivalent of three bowls of oat bran cereal per day show more impressive reductions in cholesterol counts, ranging on average from 13 to 19 per cent.

Three bowls of oat bran cereal a day is quite a load! While oat products are tasty and versatile it is just not practical to rely on them exclusively to boost your intake of soluble fibre. If you have a varied diet, containing a fair amount of fruits and vegetables, bran cereals and wholegrain products such as wholemeal pasta and brown rice you should have no trouble achieving a substantial increase in your daily consumption and with it a cholesterol-lowering effect.

In 1990 an interesting study was published in the *New England Journal of Medicine* which seriously questions the special rôle of oat bran in cholesterol reduction. Twenty healthy volunteers in Boston, Massachusetts ate diets supplemented with oat bran or with a refined low-fibre wheat cereal. Apart from the supplementation, the volunteers were allowed to eat any other foods they desired. As expected, the oat bran-enriched diet lowered blood cholesterol by an average of 7 per cent. But surprisingly, the low-fibre wheat-enriched diet lowered blood cholesterol by the same degree. The researchers further discovered that during the six weeks the volunteers spent on either of the two diets they ate less saturated fat and more polyunsaturated fat than usual. These changes in dietary fat consumption were enough to completely explain the amount of cholesterol reduction seen with the high-fibre and low-fibre diets.

If the conclusions of this study are correct, then oat bran does not have any specific cholesterol-lowering effect (such as decreasing the absorption of cholesterol from the intestine). Instead, filling complex carbohydrate foods simply decrease the desire for fatty foods that raise cholesterol.

In view of this new information, we think that it is unnecessary to focus exclusively on the cholesterol-lowering effect of oat bran and other soluble fibres. It is quite possible that any significant increase in non-fatty high-fibre or low-fibre foods will have an indirect beneficial effect on blood cholesterol by decreasing the appetite for fatty foods and snacks.

Nevertheless, we feel that it makes a great deal of sense to emphasize high-fibre foods in your efforts to reduce cholesterol, since fibre has a number of important health benefits. Foods high in soluble fibre like oat bran, beans and fruits are important since they are versatile, good-tasting and fit well into a cholesterol-lowering diet. But insoluble fibre wheat bran products such as wholemeal grains and cereals also have their place in a healthy diet.

How much fibre should you eat every day? Most worldwide nutritional authorities including the UK Health Education Authority recommend dietary fibre intakes of at least 30 grams per day. These recommendations have been largely based on the rôle of dietary fibre in the prevention of diseases of the large intestine. During the Second World War Britons consumed 32–40 grams of fibre per day. Since then, increased reliance on refined and processed convenience foods has driven the average fibre intake to well below 20 grams daily. To put this figure into perspective, many rural Africans eat over 100 grams of fibre daily and vegetarians in Western countries consume 40–50 grams. As a nation, we would do well to reverse the low-fibre trend and increase our intake of disease-preventing foods.

As part of our cholesterol-lowering plan we advocate the consumption of at least 30 grams per day of fibre. As a cholesterol-lowering tool, increasing fibre is not nearly as powerful as decreasing saturated fat. In some individuals it may be possible to achieve more substantial cholesterol reductions by using very large quantities of fibre but be advised that overconsumption of fibre can have unpleasant consequences. Apart from problems with palatability and monotony, an over-abundance of dietary fibre can cause intestinal cramping and even blockage from indigestible fibre plugs.

In Chapter 6 we describe a method for sensibly increasing fibre as part of our comprehensive cholesterol-lowering approach. If you follow a low-saturated fat, low-cholesterol plan *and* prudently increase your fibre intake you can expect to further lower your cholesterol count.

TOOL 4:

INCREASE YOUR LEVEL OF PHYSICAL ACTIVITY AND INCLUDE REGULAR AEROBIC EXERCISE IN YOUR WEEKLY ROUTINE

The idea that regular physical exercise is good for your heart is certainly a familiar concept. It is well accepted that people who exercise regularly have less coronary heart disease and live longer healthier lives. Unknown to many people, however, is the fact that many of the benefits of physical activity are derived from effects on blood cholesterol levels.

Exercise raises levels of HDL, or good cholesterol. As far as HDL cholesterol is concerned, the higher the better. LDL cholesterol levels are relatively unaffected by exercise. For exercise to have a positive influence on HDL cholesterol it must be aerobic. Aerobic exercises are continuous activities like brisk walking, cycling, jogging and swimming that get your heart beating faster than usual. Start-and-stop activities like sprinting and tennis are generally not aerobic.

By raising HDL cholesterol, aerobic exercise can significantly affect your blood cholesterol profile and lower your risk of heart disease. If you also lower your LDL cholesterol using the dietary tools we have discussed, your cholesterol ratio (see Chapter 4) will improve dramatically and your coronary heart disease risk will plummet.

It is worthwhile repeating a cautionary note we made earlier in the book. A total cholesterol blood test measures both LDL and HDL cholesterol. Some men will be able to achieve large increases in HDL levels after a few months on an aerobic programme. A total cholesterol blood test repeated well into the exercise programme might appear to show a minimal change *or even an increase* in the cholesterol count when, in reality, the cholesterol ratio has improved. Very real successes can be obscured by complete reliance on total cholesterol counts. The special HDL cholesterol blood test can easily clarify this kind of situation.

Aerobic exercise is effective in raising HDL cholesterol when it is moderately intensive. Extremely light and casual activities are ineffective. However, the exercise certainly does not have to be strenuous or exhausting. In fact there appears to be a plateau effect, where increasing the intensity or duration of an exercise session adds little or nothing to the benefits to be gained. A programme consisting of only twenty minutes of aerobic exercises three or four times a week is sufficient to achieve a substantial impact on HDLs. For example, it is possible to boost HDL cholesterol levels by 10 per cent or more by jogging three miles, three times a week. Men enjoy an advantage over women in this respect. Women have to exercise very much harder to achieve the same amount of HDL cholesterol elevation as men.

Another benefit of regular exercise is weight loss. Aerobic activities burn calories and help excess pounds melt away.

Furthermore, weight loss in and of itself leads to a reduction in LDL cholesterol levels.

In Chapter 9 we give you the information you need to embark safely on a sensible programme of regular aerobic exercise.

TOOL 5:

GET YOUR OTHER CORONARY HEART DISEASE RISK FACTORS UNDER CONTROL

Elevated cholesterol is one of the most important risk factors for coronary heart disease but it is not the only one. Other risk factors may be grouped into those that *cannot* be modified such as your age, sex and family history and those that *can* be modified. There is nothing you can do about the increased risk of being male or growing older or having unfavourable inherited tendencies towards heart disease. However, there is quite a lot you can do about cigarette smoking, being overweight, having high blood pressure or the type of diabetes associated with obesity. Controlling these so-called modifiable risk factors does not have a large direct impact on cholesterol counts but it does have a huge impact on your overall risk of developing coronary heart disease.

It is crucially important to recognize that the three major modifiable risk factors − blood cholesterol, cigarette smoking and high blood pressure have additive effects on the incidence of coronary heart disease. The presence of any one of these risk factors doubles your risk of coronary heart disease. If you have elevated cholesterol plus one of the other two factors your risk of developing heart disease quadruples. Finally, if you have high cholesterol, high blood pressure *and* you smoke your risk for coronary heart disease increase eightfold.

There is a clear message here: if you have a cholesterol problem and one or more other risk factors it makes a great deal of sense to tackle all of them. Consider a middle-aged man who has a moderate to severe cholesterol elevation, has poorly controlled high blood pressure and smokes twenty cigarettes per day. If that man eliminates each of these risk factors he could potentially reduce his chance of a fatal heart attack by 90 per cent and increase his life expectancy by twenty years. Think about it.

If you know or suspect you have other modifiable risk factors your overall strategy of taking charge of cholesterol should take them into account. If you are one of the twenty million men and women in Britain who smoke: STOP NOW. If you have not had your blood pressure checked lately, do so; if you have known high blood pressure that is not under good control work with your doctor to get it down. If diabetes runs in your family or if you have been feeling particularly thirsty, hungry, fatigued and perhaps bothered by excessive urination, see your doctor to have a simple diabetes test. If you are overweight, make a positive decision to restrict calories and increase physical activity. Fortunately, weight loss is comparatively easy on our cholesterol-lowering plans since high-fat, high-calorie foods are naturally limited.

TOOL 6:

IF YOUR CHOLESTEROL COUNT REMAINS TOO HIGH DESPITE THE USE OF OTHER TOOLS, FOLLOW YOUR DOCTOR'S ADVICE ON DRUG THERAPY

Some people will decrease their intake of saturated fat and cholesterol, increase fibre in their diet, take regular exercise and *still* have moderate to severe elevations in blood cholesterol. Individuals who start off with very high cholesterol counts, 270 (7.0) or greater, are the most likely to fall into this category. If you are such an individual your doctor may elect to place you on a cholesterol-lowering medication. Some of the newer medications are quite potent and can achieve up to 30 per cent reductions in cholesterol levels.

While these drugs are remarkably safe, the decision to use them should be carefully considered because doctor and patient are making a commitment to long-term, perhaps lifetime therapy. The drugs exert their effect only when they are taken. Discontinue them and the cholesterol count will creep up to the original level.

The best candidates for long-term drug treatment are people with two or more risk factors of coronary heart disease who have persistent cholesterol elevations despite adherence to our strict cholesterol-lowering plan. Drugs should *never* be used simply to avoid making necessary and prudent dietary and lifestyle changes.

MINOR TOOLS

In addition to the major tools at your disposal for lowering cholesterol and the risk of coronary heart disease, there are a few minor tools worthy of brief mention. We refer to them as minor tools since their effect is comparatively small and their benefit is far less established than the major tools discussed above.

Coffee

Coffee consumption *may* have a negative impact on blood cholesterol. The subject is controversial, since the evidence is often conflicting. The controversy began in 1983 with the publication of the Norwegian Tromso Heart Study. Researchers in Tromso found that coffee drinkers had significantly higher total cholesterol levels than non-drinkers. Coffee prepared by boiling seemed to be more of a problem than filter-made brews. In later work in Tromso it was noted that cholesterol count fell in those men and women who agreed to give up coffee for ten weeks.

Since these reports other researchers have had conflicting results. Some have failed to show any relationship between coffee consumption and cholesterol, others have agreed with the Norwegian findings. The most recent iron in the fire is a study from America that links consumption of decaffeinated coffee with elevations in LDL cholesterol but gives regular coffee a clean bill of health.

In the absence of clear data, we cannot give specific recommendations about coffee consumption. However, if you are a heavy coffee drinker, say six or more cups per day and your doctor is considering cholesterol-lowering drug therapy, it may be worthwhile to abstain from coffee for several weeks and having your cholesterol count retested.

Alcohol

The subject of alcohol and cholesterol is another controversial area. Over the past ten years several studies have suggested that moderate alcohol consumption, in the order of two drinks per day, protects against coronary heart disease by increasing levels of HDL, or good cholesterol. Any inclination to consider this information as a license to imbibe is foolish, since the risk of dying from all causes increases sharply beyond the two-drinks-per-day level. While the evidence is far from unanimous on this point. It does appear that moderate use of alcohol has a small beneficial effect on HDL cholesterol.

Our advice regarding alcohol and cholesterol is simple: if you are a non-drinker, don't start now! There are far healthier and more efficient ways to raise your HDL cholesterol, namely via exercise. If you are a heavy drinker, cut back. If you are a moderate drinker, enjoy your evening drink!

Garlic

Garlic has been used since ancient times as a medicinal plant.

Hippocrates extolled its virtues twenty-five centuries ago. Lately it has undergone a renaissance as serious scientists have explored its values in the treatment and prevention of heart disease.

A number of investigators have examined the properties of whole garlic, its powder and oil in normalizing blood cholesterol. Most of the studies have involved relatively few volunteers who have endured relatively large amounts of garlic so it is difficult to come to any firm conclusions or practical recommendations.

Nevertheless, results have been interesting, since garlic appears to consistently lower bad cholesterol and raise good cholesterol. Furthermore, epidemiologic studies indicate that countries and regions where garlic consumption is high, such as the Mediterranean basin, have low levels of coronary heart disease.

If you are a garlic lover, this is very good news.

6

TAKING CHARGE OF CHOLESTEROL

Up to this point we have discussed the subject of cholesterol control and why it is so important for you and your family. We have told you how to get a cholesterol test and how to interpret the result. We have also described the kinds of tools available to you in your battle against coronary heart disease. The foundations have been laid; now it is time to construct the building. This chapter presents a unique cholesterol-lowering plan you can start using today.

THE HEART OF A GOOD PLAN

In our experience, excellent nutritional plans are not easy to find. It is, of course, easy to dismiss fad diets that have no grounding in scientific fact. At best they may be nonsense, at worst, dangerous. Yet a nutritional plan may be firmly based on good science and still be 'bad'. What do we mean by this?

Unless a plan is practical and usable and ultimately leads to the desired nutritional effect then it is of little worth. Over the past ten years we have reviewed countless dietary plans and we have applied specific ones to our patients with disorders such as obesity, iron-deficiency anaemia, diabetes, gall stones, high blood pressure and elevated cholesterol. Our clinical experience instilled us with a healthy dose of frustration. Most of the plans at our disposal, created by experts with the very best intentions, were so difficult for our patients to follow that they failed to achieve their dietary goals.

A few years ago, we began creating our own dietary plans with an eye towards succeeding where others had failed. We have based our nutritional approach on the following bedrock principles: SIMPLICITY, EFFECTIVENESS and SAFETY. This approach led to a best-selling slimming book called *The Two-Day Diet* and it forms the basis of the cholesterol-lowering plan in this book.

In our opinion, all the cholesterol-reducing diets we have seen are either too general or too specific to be practical. On one extreme are the broad types of nutritional guidelines issued by public health authorities. We may be urged to decrease total fat and cholesterol consumption and increase polyunsaturates and fibre but how is one able to translate these general guidelines into a specific action plan? Very few people have enough knowledge of the nutritional content of foods to enact broad guidelines. Our cholesterol awareness survey (Chapter 1) demonstrates this point.

On the other extreme there are plans that do all the work for you and provide you with detailed daily diet menus. Almost everyone finds fixed meal plans completely impractical. It is impossible for most people to structure their lives around a diet that insists you have a particular set meal on a Tuesday evening!

In between these two extremes are diet plans that attempt to provide some blend of specificity and flexibility but come up with excessively complicated and fussy systems that require constant reference to thick lists of the cholesterol, fat and calorie content of foods.

Taking Charge of Cholesterol is a completely new and simple system for controlling cholesterol. Although it is incredibly easy to follow, it is a comprehensive, powerful approach to cholesterol control. The plan has these important features:

* It does not force you to radically change your present diet or to avoid *any* food you currently enjoy

* It is easy to understand and does not presume any knowledge about the nutritional content of foods

* It actually *teaches* you about healthy eating and cholesterol control. In a week or so, the plan becomes second nature and you will not have to rely on the book for guidance

* It is flexible enough to use at home, at work, at dinner parties and at restaurants

* It is suitable for entire families to use

As we noted in Chapter 5, the single most important tool for lowering cholesterol is reducing the amount of saturated fat in your diet. *Taking Charge of Cholesterol* focuses on this key cholesterol-reducing tool and makes it the cornerstone of the plan. We have devised an easy-to-use points system that lets you adjust your intake of saturated fat to the level that suits you the best. Coupled with a number of specific guidelines on the use of your other cholesterol-lowering tools, we believe we are providing you with the most comprehensive, user-friendly cholesterol control system ever developed.

BASIC FOR MOST, STRICT FOR SOME

We offer two plans, a Basic one that will be suitable for most people and a Strict one for those individuals who require extra control to reach their cholesterol-lowering goal.

We recommend that everyone start with the Basic plan. The principles that govern the Basic plan represent prevailing worldwide scientific opinion on effective ways of controlling cholesterol with diet. The nutritional goals of the Basic plan are slightly more aggressive that the latest UK official recommendations (contained in the 1984 COMA report) but they are in line with more recent official recommendations of the United States and Dutch governments and the European Atherosclerosis Society.

As we discussed in Chapter 3, it is not necessary to know your cholesterol count before you begin your healthy eating plan, but it is desirable. The Basic plan is a prudent, sensible approach to lifelong eating, irrespective of your cholesterol level. Nevertheless, knowledge of your cholesterol count places you at an advantage in your fight against heart disease.

If you are among the six out of ten people in the country who have higher than desirable blood cholesterol, awareness of your count and awareness of your goal give you a strong motivational focus for your efforts. In our experience, tangible goals are extremely important. Whether your goal is a particular body weight, a blood pressure reading or a certain cholesterol count, it is motivating to work towards that goal and it is satisfying to achieve it.

The other advantage in knowing your starting cholesterol count is that you can follow your progress and decide whether you need to move to the Strict plan or work with your doctor on non-dietary approaches such as prescription drug therapy.

HOW TO TRACK YOUR PROGRESS

In Chapter 3 we talked about establishing your personal action plan for cholesterol control. It is worth repeating the target goals for your blood cholesterol since they form the basis for the way in which you can track your progress.

First you must place yourself in one of two categories depending on your risk factors for coronary heart disease. Refer to the list of risk factors on page 68 for guidance. If these risk factors describe your personal situation you may consider yourself at higher risk of coronary heart disease.

If you do not meet these criteria you may consider yourself at lower risk for coronary heart disease.

Depending on your risk category, these are the blood cholesterol target goals you should aim to achieve:

CHOLESTEROL GOAL

HIGHER RISK INDIVIDUAL	LESS THAN 200 (5.2)
LOWER RISK INDIVIDUAL	LESS THAN 250 (6.5)

We recommend you track your progress using the scheme illustrated in our diagram.

Cholesterol counts do not fall immediately. After you begin a dietary plan it will take a couple of weeks to see a significant drop and several weeks to see the full effect. We recommend staying on the Basic plan at least eight weeks before rechecking your cholesterol level. Depending on your initial cholesterol count you may or may not achieve your goal in this time frame. If you have not reached your target it is advisable to spend another eight weeks on the diet plan since some people will have a more delayed response. Overall, you are likely to achieve a cholesterol reduction of 30−40 (.8−1) points on the Basic plan.

Most people will reach their cholesterol goal on the Basic plan. For these individuals, our advice for the future is clear and simple: make the Basic plan your healthy eating plan for the rest of your life. By this time you will fully appreciate that low-fat, low-cholesterol eating is delicious and fulfilling.

If your cholesterol count was already in the desirable range before you started the Basic plan and you keep up your healthy style of eating, you can wait as long as five years before rechecking your blood cholesterol.

If your cholesterol count was elevated initially and falls to your desired level, you too should make the Basic plan your everyday, lifelong eating style. Vigilance is helpful in maintaining your cholesterol count at or below its new level so you should recheck your blood test once or twice a year in the future.

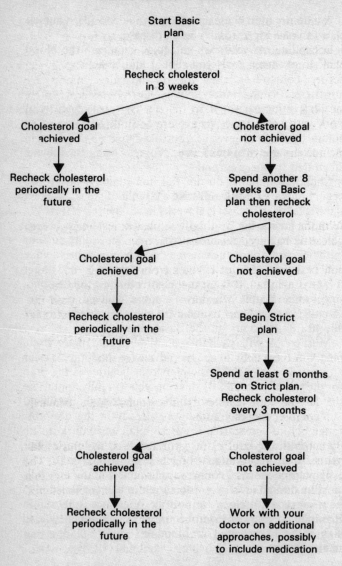

Start Basic plan
↓
Recheck cholesterol in 8 weeks

Cholesterol goal achieved → Recheck cholesterol periodically in the future

Cholesterol goal not achieved → Spend another 8 weeks on Basic plan then recheck cholesterol

Cholesterol goal achieved → Recheck cholesterol periodically in the future

Cholesterol goal not achieved → Begin Strict plan
↓
Spend at least 6 months on Strict plan. Recheck cholesterol every 3 months

Cholesterol goal achieved → Recheck cholesterol periodically in the future

Cholesterol goal not achieved → Work with your doctor on additional approaches, possibly to include medication

A minority of individuals will have to move onto the Strict plan to reach their goal. You can expect to further lower your cholesterol by another 15 (.4) points or so on the Strict plan. It is sensible to give the Strict plan a good long trial before concluding that dietary measures alone are insufficient to adequately reduce your cholesterol. In six months, if you are far short of your goal, we suggest you work with your doctor to explore additional measures to obtain the desired level of control. These measures may include the use of prescription drugs.

THE BASIC PLAN

With the Basic plan your daily meals will provide you with a healthy balanced diet consisting of:

* Less than 30% of calories from fat
  - Less than 10% of calories from saturated fat
  - Up to 10% of calories from polyunsaturated fat
  - Up to 10% of calories from monounsaturated fat

* Less than 300 milligrams per day of cholesterol

* Approximately 30 grams per day of fibre

* Up to 20% of calories from protein

* 50 – 60% of calories from carbohydrates, primarily complex carbohydrates

By emphasizing control of saturated fats, the Basic plan naturally accomplishes many of these nutritional goals. The explanation for this fortunate situation lies in the fact that most foods high in saturated fats are also high in cholesterol. As we shall see, there are important exceptions to this rule. However, all meat and full-fat dairy products are relatively high in both saturated fat *and* cholesterol. So limiting saturated fat intake also limits cholesterol intake. Also, nutritional authorities recommend that as we reduce the calories from fat we replace them with calories from complex carbohydrates such as pasta, breads, rice, beans and other vegetables rather than calories from protein. In Western societies we tend to eat more protein than is required. Meat and dairy products are rich protein sources and modest restrictions in their intake help to accomplish the protein and carbohydrate targets.

The Basic plan combines specific saturated fat recommendations with a number of more general dietary guidelines. This combination ensures a full effect by taking advantage of all the cholesterol-lowering tools at your disposal.

Saturated Fat Recommendations

If you are a typical woman who is not on a slimming diet you consume an average of 2,000 calories per day; a typical non-dieting man takes in an average of 2,400 calories daily. These calorie levels are based on the fairly sedentary activity levels common for most people. We are setting a target fewer than 10 per cent of calories from saturated. Therefore, an average woman should have no more than 200 calories a day from saturated fat and a man should have fewer than 240 calories. Fats, saturated and otherwise, contain 9 calories per gram (a gram is a unit of weight − 1,000 grams is a kilogram). A simple calculation yields the following saturated fat targets for average men and women:

MAXIMUM NUMBER OF
GRAMS OF SATURATED FAT
PERMITTED PER DAY

MEN	27
WOMEN	22

These saturated fat targets are appropriate for the great majority of adults. However, they would need to be adjusted in some cases to suit one's particular circumstances. For example, you may be on a slimming diet or a calorie-adjusted plan to maintain weight loss. Your daily calorie requirements would be lower and so would your saturated fat allowance. Or you may be a particularly vigorous person, a sportsman or a manual labourer, who has a higher daily calorie intake. In this case you would be allowed more saturated fat in your diet. For example, a competitive athlete may consume over 1,000 calories a day more than most people and would be permitted over 10 grams more saturated fat every day.

To individualize your saturated fat target simply use the worksheet.

SATURATED FAT WORKSHEET

Basic Plan

YOUR CALORIE
INTAKE EACH DAY

_____

MULTIPLIED BY
10% (.10)   =

_____

TOTAL GRAMS OF   DIVIDED BY 9 =
SATURATED FAT
PERMITTED DAILY   _____

To see how this works we have prepared a sample worksheet. Let's say that you are on a 1,200-calorie slimming diet. Multiply 1,200 by .10 to get 120. Then divide 120 by 9 to get 13.3. Round off this result to 13 and this would be your target number of saturated fat grams.

105

SAMPLE SATURATED FAT WORKSHEET

Basic Plan

YOUR CALORIE
INTAKE EACH DAY

___1,200___

MULTIPLIED BY
10% (.10)   =

___120___

TOTAL GRAMS OF   DIVIDED BY 9 =
SATURATED FAT
PERMITTED DAILY   ___13___

To carry on with this example, you may have lost some weight and found that 1,800 calories a day is your ideal level for weight maintenance. Your new saturated fat target would be 20 grams (1,800 multiplied by .10, divided by 9).

We would emphasize that for most people the recommended saturated fat target of *27* grams per day for men and *22* grams per day for women is appropriate.

Most foods contain mixtures of the three basic nutrients: protein, carbohydrate and fat. Very few foods are pure protein, pure carbohydrate or pure fat. Furthermore, high-fat foods usually contain mixtures of saturated fats, polyunsaturated fats and monounsaturated fats. For this reason, the saturated fat content of a particular food item is not obvious and very few people would have any idea how to determine it. Nutritional food labels (see Chapter 7) are often not very helpful since most do not provide a breakdown of the types of fat a food contains.

In *Taking Charge of Cholesterol* we have done all the work for you. At the end of this chapter you will find a table of the saturated fat content of virtually all common food items. The table is extremely easy to use. It is organized by food groups such as meat, poultry, pastries, fast foods etc. We have chosen standard portion sizes for snack foods, main courses and desserts (based mainly on Helen Crawley's *Food Portion Sizes*, HMSO, 1988). For each food item we note the number of grams of saturated fat each portion contains (rounded off to the nearest half gram). Those foods that have some saturated fat but not very much (less than .25 grams per portion) are designated as having 'trace' amounts. Many foods have no saturated fat at all or negligible amounts. Most fruits, vegetables, grain and non-dairy beverages are in this category. We have not included these foods in the table.

TO USE THE BASIC PLAN ALL YOU NEED TO DO IS COUNT SATURATED FAT POINTS.

Let's assume that you are a typical man whose saturated fat target is 27 grams a day. You can eat any combination of foods you desire up to a saturated fat point-count of 27. There is nothing magical or rigid in the count of 27. It is an approximate target. You can certainly eat less saturated fat than your target. In fact, if you eat less you can expect greater reductions in blood cholesterol. You can even exceed your target on any given day, even by a wide margin on a special-occasion binge when you just can't be bothered or it is inconvenient to keep a lid on high-fat foods. Your blood cholesterol level does not dramatically rise and fall with dietary changes. *The important factor is your average saturated fat intake over days and weeks*. Indulgences on one day can be compensated for on other days by a stricter approach. For instance, if there is a day in which you have a marvellous dinner with pâté, beef in a rich sauce, creamy chocolate mousse and a cheese board you may rack up over 40 points. Enjoy these occasions and don't worry about it. On the following two or three days simply trim your saturated fat target to under 20 points a day then resume your normal target of 27. You will get a fine cholesterol-lowering effect as long as your average saturated fat intake is below your target count.

You will surely recognize a key feature to our Basic plan: you do not have to deprive yourself at any special event or give up any food you enjoy to achieve your blood cholesterol goal. You don't have to forego your Sunday roast, your fish and chips or any traditional part of your regular diet completely. If you love fast-food quarter pound cheeseburgers (worth 13 points – half your daily allowance!) go ahead and have them as long as you are prepared to restrict other high-fat choices to keep within your target zone.

As you review the saturated fat table you may be struck by several items. First, some foods are incredibly high in saturated fat! A slice of cheesecake (20 points), a pork pie (15 points), a piece of quiche (15 points) all take a big bite out of your daily allowance. Also snack foods can add up quickly. One jam doughnut is 5 points, one filled chocolate bar is 5 points, one chocolate digestive biscuit is 2 points, one small bag of crisps is 3.5 points.

On the other hand, there are plenty of food choices that are relatively low in saturated fat, And you certainly don't have to be a strict vegetarian to keep to your target comfortably. A baked chicken leg quarter is 2 points, a thin slice of ham is.5 points, 3 ounces of lean roast beef is 3.5 points. We guarantee that you will not feel deprived with this healthy eating plan.

To launch you into the plan and to help you get the most out of saturated fat counting we offer this advice:

* It is useful to get a good idea of the amount of saturated fat you ordinarily eat. Write down everything you eat for two or three days and use the saturated fat table to determine your points score. Remember that the table does not contain every food item. Fruits, vegetables, cereal grains, non-dairy beverages, herbs and spices are omitted since they do not contain

significant amounts of saturated fat. If you cannot find a specific food item on your list pick a similar one for a points score. Once you have a notion about the greatest sources of saturated fat in your diet you can formulate a strategy for keeping within your saturated fat target zone.

* Skim through the saturated fat table at the end of the chapter and familiarize yourself with the point values of a variety of foods, particularly those you regularly include in your diet.

* For the first few days, people usually find it helpful to jot down their accumulated saturated fat points throughout the day. But we have found that in a very short time, usually a week or two, saturated fat awareness becomes second nature. So don't imagine that you will have to count points for the rest of your life! The points system is merely an educational tool to teach a vital component of lifelong cholesterol control. Incidently, you will no have to refer to any other food tables or charts to follow this plan. This is the easiest cholesterol control system we have ever seen – pure simplicity.

* You will often have the option of two versions of a similar food – high-fat and low-fat. Get in the habit of choosing the low-fat option. For example, pick semi-skimmed milk (1.5 points) or skimmed milk ('trace') instead of whole milk (3.5 points). Select reduced-fat cottage cheese (1 point) rather than ordinary cottage cheese (3 points). Choose lean beef cuts (3 points) instead of fatty cuts (7 points). Order grilled cod fillets ('trace') rather than cod in batter (4.5 points). Also, cut down on manufactured meat products – sausages, pies, pâtés – unless marked fat-reduced.

* Much of the saturated fat we eat is added to our food either in cooking (at home and in restaurants) or in

processing (in food production plants). Many convenience foods and accessible snack foods are packed with saturated fat. A fair amount of this fat can be avoided by following our food preparation tips (Chapter 8) and by examining nutrition labels when you shop and in general by being a careful consumer (Chapter 7).

* We have developed over one hundred low-fat recipes for you to use as you please. The recipes are there to enjoy, but also to teach about healthy cooking methods. We have placed an emphasis on light, tasty everyday dishes that will fit in seamlessly with your traditional family meals. Each recipe includes the number of grams of saturated fat per serving portion so you can fit them into your daily saturated fat target.

General Cholesterol-Lowering Guidelines

The following guidelines are intended to make full use of the cholesterol-lowering tools we described in Chapter 5. If you pay attention to the specific recommendations on saturated fat consumption and these general guidelines on other aspects of your diet you will be on your way towards cholesterol control

1. Your intake of dietary cholesterol will be substantially reduced simply by following our saturated fat points system. However, to ensure you take in under 300 milligrams of cholesterol per day it is also necessary to place some restrictions on those foods that are disproportionately high in cholesterol, namely eggs, shellfish (especially prawns) and organ meats – liver kidney and brains. One egg contains about 240 milligrams of cholesterol; 4 ounces of uncooked prawns contains 227 milligrams; 4 ounces of calves' liver has 420 milligrams; 4 ounces of lambs kidney contains 450 milligrams. Not too many people include

brains in their regular diet but 4 ounces of calves' brains contains a mind-boggling 2,500 milligrams of cholesterol – a whole week's worth! To place these values into perspective, 4 ounces of red meat contains about 100 milligrams of cholesterol.

To take account of these exceptional foods, we recommend limiting your intake of eggs (including eggs in baked dishes) to three per week. We also recommend limiting prawns, liver or kidney dishes to once per week.

2. One of the desirable goals of a healthy cholesterol-lowering diet is to increase the amount of polyunsaturated and monounsaturated fats in your diet as you lower your consumption of saturated fats. The easiest way to accomplish this goal is to shy away from butter, lard and certain vegetable oils such as coconut, palm and palm kernel oil and substitute healthier choices in your kitchen. The oils you substitute should be those with the most polyunsaturates relative to the amount of saturates (the highest P/S ratio – see Chapter 5).

For spreads, use a soft margarine labelled 'high in polyunsaturates' or a low-fat spread, preferably one high in polyunsaturates. Use sunflower, safflower, corn or soyabean oil for cooking and white fat labelled 'high in polyunsaturates' for pastry. Use these high-polyunsaturated fat products in moderation, however, since all fats are high in calories.

The best way to exploit the potential healthy benefits of monounsaturated fats is to use olive oil in the preparation of some of your dishes, especially those with a Mediterranean accent. We make good use of olive oil in many of our recipes.

3. To take full advantage of the healthy benefits of fish polyunsaturated fats (omega-3 fatty acids), we recommend you eat three or more portions of non-fried fish per week. Oily fish are best – pilchard, kipper, herring, sardines,

halibut, salmon, trout, bluefish and bass, but other fish are also beneficent.

4. Increase the amount of fibre in your diet. It is easy to reach a target of at least 30 grams of dietary fibre every day by including at least one portion of fibre-rich foods with each meal. You will have no trouble accomplishing this goal since so many common everyday foods are abundant sources of fibre. Wholegrain cereal products, fruits and vegetables are all loaded with fibre and as you cut back on fatty foods, these are the kind of foods you should use in replacement.

As a guide to the fibre content of various foods, refer to the table below. We have given the number of grams of fibre contained in one standard portion of each food (for example, one apple, one medium bowl of pasta). We have placed a star next to those items on the fibre table that are particularly high in soluble fibre. One of the most convenient and tasty ways to get a good daily supply of soluble fibre is to eat oat bran cereals and oat bran muffins. One large oat bran muffin contains 4.5 grams of dietary fibre, half of which is soluble fibre. We have included some delicious oat bran muffin recipes in the book.

5. Watch your overall calorie intake. If you are overweight this is a good time to tackle the problem with calorie restriction and increased physical activity. Obesity is a risk factor of coronary heart disease. One of the wonderful features of the Basic plan is that people naturally lose weight, sometimes a stone or more, just by restricting their consumption of foods high in saturated fat.

6. An exercise programme is an excellent accessory to the Basic plan. Exercise can boost your levels of good cholesterol. We strongly recommend following the exercise plan we offer in Chapter 9.

FIBRE CONTENT OF VARIOUS FOODS

Food	Grams of total fibre per standard portion
oat bran cereal	18.6*
wholemeal spaghetti	18.6
all-bran cereal	12.6
oatmeal	12.1*
baked beans	9.8*
blackberries	8.9
wholemeal pitta bread	8.5
dried apricots	7.2
peas	6.7*
leeks	6.2
sweet corn	5.8*
boiled spinach	5.7
muesli	5.2
broad beans	5.0*
macaroni	5.0
lentil soup	4.8
pear	4.8*
corn flakes	4.2*
bran flake cereal	4.3
apple	3.8*
figs	3.7
baked potato with skin	3.6
crusty brown roll	3.4
banana	3.4*
aubergines	3.2
rhubarb	3.0
runner beans	3.0*
carrots	2.6
brussel sprouts	2.6
orange with peel	2.5*
cabbage	2.5
strawberries	2.4
brown rice	2.2
prunes	2.2

* Particularly high in soluble fibre

THE STRICT PLAN

The Strict plan has a similar structure to the Basic plan. again the emphasis is on controlling consumption of saturated fat but your target will mean you to be more restrictive. Also your maximum allowable cholesterol intake will be lower. If you need to move from the Basic plan to the Strict plan, the transition should be quite manageable since you will already be well-versed in the principles of healthy eating.

Saturated Fat Recommendations

In the Basic plan, your goal was to restrict saturated fat calories to 10 per cent of your total calorie intake. In the Strict plan you will restrict them to 6 per cent of your total calories.

For a typical man who takes in 2,400 calories per day and a typical woman who eats 2,000 calories per day the Strict programme sets these targets for saturated fat consumption:

	MAXIMUM NUMBER OF GRAMS OF SATURATED FAT PERMITTED PER DAY
MEN	16
WOMEN	13

Your saturated fat target may be modified if your actual calorie intake is substantially different from the typical values given here. You may use this saturated fat worksheet to calculate your individualized target.

Your saturated fat targets will be lower but your overall approach to saturated fat control should be no different from the Basic plan. The same advice and recommendations offered in the Basic plan apply to the Strict plan. You will certainly notice that the Strict plan places greater limitations on your diet than the Basic plan but the same flexibility

114

SATURATED FAT WORKSHEET

Strict Plan

YOUR CALORIE
INTAKE EACH DAY

_____

MULTIPLIED BY
6% (.06)   =

_____

TOTAL GRAMS OF   DIVIDED BY 9 =
SATURATED FAT
PERMITTED EVERY DAY   _____

applies. You need not eliminate any favourite foods from your diet and on any given day you can exceed your saturated fat limit. Just make sure your average intake over several days is in line with your target.

General Cholesterol-Lowering Guidelines

The same six general cholesterol-lowering guidelines furnished for the Basic plan apply here. You should control your cholesterol intake, increase the amount of polyunsaturated and monounsaturated fat in your diet, eat fish often, increase dietary fibre, control your weight and use our exercise plan. However, there is one area where a stricter approach is prudent.

In your effort to control cholesterol, it is advisable to further lower your cholesterol intake to under 200 milligrams per day. The additional restrictions on saturated fat intake help accomplish this goal by further reducing your consumption of meat and full-fat dairy products. However, you should limit egg consumption to just one or two per week and eat organ meats and prawns only rarely.

If you fail to achieve your blood cholesterol goal with the Basic plan but are successful with the Strict plan you should have a great feeling of accomplishment. Through your own efforts you will have taken charge of cholesterol and avoided the need for prescription medication.

SATURATED FAT TABLE

for use with basic and strict plans

FOOD (g) = weight in grams	PORTION DESCRIPTION	SATURATED FAT POINTS (grams)
BREADS		
fried bread		
fried in bacon fat or lard (40g)	1 slice	6.0
puri (Indian) (40g)	1 puri	3.0
soda bread (130g)	1 farl	1.5
currant bread (30g)	1 average slice	Trace
wholemeal bread (35g)	1 slice	Trace
white bread (30g)	1 slice	Trace
rye bread (25g)	1 slice	Trace
granary bread (30g)	1 slice	Trace
crispbread (20g)	2 slices	Trace
pitta bread (35g)	1 mini picnic	Trace
garlic bread (30g)	1 average portion	5.0
(120g)	restaurant portion	20.0
rolls, white or wholemeal (35g)	1 roll	Trace
French bread (35g)	1 slice	Trace
crumpet (40g)	1 slice	Trace
buttered crumpet (45g)	1 slice	2.0
croissant (50g)	1 croissant	3.0
poppadom (13g)	1 poppadom	Trace
chapatti, with fat (60g)	1 chapatti	3.0
without fat	1 chapatti	Trace
malt loaf (35g)	1 slice	Trace

FOOD (g) = weight in grams	PORTION DESCRIPTION	SATURATED FAT POINTS (grams)
BREAKFAST CEREALS (without milk)		
all-bran cereals (50g)	medium bowl	Trace
cornflake cereals (40g)	medium bowl	Trace
puffed rice cereals (30g)	medium bowl	Trace
muesli (70g)	medium bowl	1.0
muesli, crunchy (80g)	medium bowl	2.0
porridge, made with water (180g)	medium bowl	Trace
oatmeal, raw (30g)	medium bowl	Trace
shredded wheat (22g)	1 biscuit	Trace
weetabix (20g)	1 biscuit	Trace
wheat or oat bran (28g)	1 oz	0.0
MILK, DAIRY AND EGGS		
Milk		
Channel Island/breakfast (146g)	5fl oz/¼ pint	5.0
whole milk (146g)	5fl oz/¼ pint	3.5
semi-skimmed (146g)	5fl oz/¼ pint	1.5
skimmed (146g)	5fl oz/¼ pint	Trace
buttermilk (146g)	5fl oz/¼ pint	0.5
condensed milk (15g)	1 tablespoon	1.0
evaporated milk (15g)	1 tablespoon	1.0
soya milk (146g)	5fl oz/¼ pint	0.0
coconut milk (146g)	5fl oz/¼ pint	31.0
goat's milk (146g)	5fl oz/¼ pint	3.5
sheep's milk (146g)	5fl oz/¼ pint	5.5
Milky Drinks		
cocoa, whole milk (250g)	1 mug	6.5
cocoa, semi-skimmed milk (250g)	1 mug	3.0

FOOD (g) = weight in grams	PORTION DESCRIPTION	SATURATED FAT POINTS (grams)
cocoa, skimmed milk (250g)	1 mug	1.0
drinking chocolate, whole milk (250g)	1 large glass	6.5
drinking chocolate, semi- skimmed milk (250g)	1 large glass	3.0
drinking chocolate, skimmed milk (250g)	1 large glass	1.0
milk shake, fast food chocolate (283g)	standard portion	7.0
other flavours (283g)	standard portion	5.0
Yoghurt		
thick Greek yoghurt with cream (150g)	5oz serving	8.0
whole milk, plain (150g)	5oz serving	2.5
whole milk, fruit (150g)	5oz serving	2.0
low-fat, plain (150g)	5oz/individual tub	1.0
low-fat, fruit or flavoured (150g)	5oz/individual tub	1.0
low-calorie, diet-type (150g)	5oz/individual tub	Trace
drinking yoghurt (200g)	7oz/individual carton	Trace
soya yoghurt (125g)	4oz serving	1.0
Cream		
fresh clotted cream (30g)	2 rounded teaspoons	12.0
double cream (30g)	1 tablespoon	9.0
single cream (20g)	1 tablespoon	2.5
whipping cream (30g)	2 tablespoons	11.0
whipped cream (30g)	1 rounded tablespoon	10.0
non-dairy double (30g)	1 tablespoon	9.0
non-dairy whipping (30g)	2 tablespoons	12.0

FOOD (g) = weight in grams	PORTION DESCRIPTION	SATURATED FAT POINTS (grams)
non-dairy single (20g)	1 tablespoon	2.5
half cream (30g)	2 tablespoons	2.5
aerosol cream (10g)	2 tablespoons	2.0
soured cream (30g)	1 tablespoon	3.5
whipped dessert topping (15g)	1 tablespoon	2.0
non-dairy powdered coffee cream (3g)	1 level teaspoon	1.0
ice cream, dairy (60g)	1 small scoop	4.0
ice cream, rich dairy (60g)	1 small scoop	6.0
ice cream, non-dairy (60g)	1 small scoop	2.5

Cheese

Cheddar (40g)	1½oz	8.5
Stilton (40g)	1½oz	9.0
Gouda (40g)	1½oz	8.0
Gruyère (40g)	1½oz	8.5
Emmental (40g)	1½oz	7.5
Danish blue (40g)	1½oz	7.5
Edam (40g)	1½oz	6.5
Brie (40g)	1½oz	6.5
Camembert (40g)	1½oz	6.0
Roquefort (40g)	1½oz	8.5
Lymeswold (40g)	1½oz	10.0
Mozzarella (30g)	1oz	4.0
reduced-fat Cheddar (40g)	1½oz	4.0
reduced-fat Edam (40g)	1½oz	2.5
feta (30g)	1oz	4.0
medium fat soft cheese (40g)	1½oz	3.5
goat's milk/chèvre (30g)	1oz	3.0
cottage cheese (125g)	4oz	3.0
reduced-fat (125g)	4oz	1.0

119

FOOD (g) = weight in grams	PORTION DESCRIPTION	SATURATED FAT POINTS (grams)
fromage frais (50g)	2oz	2.5
with fruit (50g)	2oz	2.0
fromage frais, very low-fat (50g)	2oz	Trace
ricotta (30g)	1oz	2.0
Parmesan (7g)	1/4oz	1.0
cream cheese, full-fat (30g)	1oz	9.0
cheese spread (30g)	1oz	4.0

Eggs

whole chicken egg (60g)	1 large egg	2.0
egg white (32g)	1	0.0
egg yolk (18g)	1	2.0
2 egg omelette, made with butter and milk (120g)	1 omelette	9.0
2 egg cheese omelette, made with butter and milk (150g)	1 omelette	18.5
whole duck egg (75g)	1 large egg	2.0

MEAT

Beef

beefburger, fried/grilled (60g)	1 standard burger	3.0
beef mince		
ordinary (150g)	average portion	12.5
lean (10% fat) (150g)	average portion	10.5
extra lean/steak (150g)	average portion	5.5
beef brisket, boiled lean and fat (200g)	average portion	20.0
roast beef		
forerib		
lean and fat (120g)	average portion	14.5

FOOD (g) = weight in grams	PORTION DESCRIPTION	SATURATED FAT POINTS (grams)
lean only (120g) topside	average portion	6.5
lean only (90g) sirloin	small average portion	1.5
lean only (90g) silverside of beef	small average portion	3.5
lean only (90g) stewing beef	small average portion	2.0
lean and fat (120g)	average portion	14.0
lean only (120g) steak	average portion	8.0
grilled rumpsteak		
lean and fat (120g)	small steak	6.0
lean only (120g) grilled T-bone	small steak	3.5
lean and fat (180g)	small steak	18.0
lean only (180g)	small steak	8.0
calves' liver, fried (70g)	average portion	3.0
ox liver (140g)	average portion	5.0
ox heart, stewed (85g)	average portion	2.5
Veal		
veal cutlet, fried (150g)	average portion	5.0
roast veal fillet (85g)	average portion	4.0
veal scallopine (85g)	average portion	2.0
Lamb		
grilled lamb chop		
with bone		
lean and fat (160g)	average chop	17.5
without bone		
lean only (90g)	average portion	5.5

121

FOOD (g) = weight in grams	PORTION DESCRIPTION	SATURATED FAT POINTS (grams)
roast lamb		
breast		
lean and fat (120g)	average portion	21.5
lean only (120g)	average portion	10.0
leg		
lean and fat (120g)	average portion	10.5
lean only (120g)	average portion	3.5
shoulder		
lean and fat (120g)	average portion	15.5
lean only (120g)	average portion	5.0
fried lamb's liver (70g)	average portion	3.5
fried lamb's kidney (90g)	1 whole kidney	2.0
Pork		
grilled pork chops		
with bone		
lean and fat (120g)	average chop	5.0
lean only (100g)	average chop	4.0
braised spare ribs (120g)	4 ribs	14.0
tenderloin, lean (85g)	small portion	1.0
roast leg of pork (90g)	average portion	2.5
Bacon		
boiled gammon joint		
lean and fat (170g)	average portion	13.0
lean only (170g)	average portion	4.0
gammon rashers		
lean and fat (170g)	1 average steak	8.5
lean only (170g)	1 average steak	3.5
fried streaky bacon (20g)	1 rasher	3.5
grilled streaky bacon (20g)	1 rasher	3.0
fried back bacon		
lean and fat (25g)	1 rasher	4.0
lean only (25g)	1 rasher	2.5

FOOD (g) = weight in grams	PORTION DESCRIPTION	SATURATED FAT POINTS (grams)
grilled back bacon		
lean and fat (25g)	1 rasher	3.5
lean only (25g)	1 rasher	2.0
Ham		
boiled ham (25g)	average slice	0.5
Prepared Meat Products		
salami (17g)	average slice	3.0
luncheon meat (14g)	average slice	1.5
liver sausage (40g)	average portion	3.5
corned beef (30g)	thin slice	1.5
pastrami (60g)	thick slice	6.0
sheep's tongue (25g)	average slice	2.0
meat paste (15g)	average portion	0.5
chopped ham and pork (45g)	average slice	3.5
pork sausage		
fried or grilled (35g)	1 thin sausage	3.5
fried or grilled (60g)	1 large sausage	6.0
frankfurter (hot dog) (35g)	1 average hot dog	5.0
beef sausage (35g)	1 thin sausage	2.5
beef sausage (60g)	1 large sausage	4.5
Meat Substitutes		
soy bean curd (tofu) (120g)	average block	1.0
textured vegetable protein – TVP (100g)	3½ ounces	1.0
vegetable burger – grilled or baked (60g)	1 burger	2.0
quorn (micro protein) (100g)	average serving	0.5

FOOD (g) = weight in grams	PORTION DESCRIPTION	SATURATED FAT POINTS (grams)

POULTRY

Chicken

roast chicken		
meat and skin (140g)	medium average portion	6.5
dark meat, no skin (140g)	medium average portion	3.0
light meat, no skin (140g)	½ breast/medium average portion	2.0
chicken portions (no skin) (190g)	1 leg quarter or 2 drumsticks	2.0
fried chicken liver (70g)	average portion	2.5

Turkey

roast turkey		
meat and skin (140g)	average portion	3.0
dark meat, no skin (140g)	average portion	2.0
light meat, no skin (140g)	average portion	1.0

Duck

roast duck (185g)	½ breast and wing	14.5

FISH AND SEAFOOD

plaice		
fried in breadcrumbs (90g)	medium fillet	4.5
fried in batter (150g)	medium fillet	10.0
steamed or poached (120g)	medium fillet	Trace
cod		
fried in batter (120g)	medium fillet	4.5
baked or steamed (120g)	medium fillet	Trace

cod roe, fried (120g)	average portion	5.0
haddock		
fried in batter (120g)	medium fillet	4.5
steamed or smoked (85g)	medium fillet	Trace
salmon		
steamed (100g)	1 average steak	2.5
tinned (100g)	½ can	2.0
smoked salmon (60g)	average portion	0.5
sole		
Dover sole (250g)	1 whole sole	Trace
lemon sole, fried (90g)	medium fillet	4.5
lemon sole, steamed (90g)	medium fillet	Trace
tuna		
tinned in oil (100g)	½ can	2.0
tinned in brine (100g)	½ can	Trace
sardines		
tinned in oil (100g)	½ can	2.5
in tomato sauce (100g)	½ can	Trace
pilchards (100g)	½ can	2.0
mackerel		
fried (200g)	1 large whole mackerel	12.0
grilled or poached (100g)	1 small whole mackerel	4.0
tinned (200g)	1 small can	8.0
herring		
fried (85g)	small fillet	3.0
grilled (85g)	small fillet	2.0
kipper, grilled (85g)	1 small kipper	2.0
whiting, fried with bones (120g)	small portion	4.0
Shellfish		
prawns, raw (60g)	average portion	Trace
shrimp, raw (80g)	average portion	Trace
oysters raw		
without shells (60g)	½ dozen oysters	Trace

125

FOOD (g) = weight in grams	PORTION DESCRIPTION	SATURATED FAT POINTS (grams)
mussels, shelled (40g)	average portion	Trace
crab (40g)	1 tablespoon crabmeat	Trace
lobster, boiled (85g)	2 tablespoons	0.5
lobster, boiled (250g)	½ dressed lobster	0.5

FATS AND OILS

Oils

coconut oil (13g)	1 tablespoon	11.0
palm oil (13g)	1 tablespoon	6.0
cottonseed oil (13g)	1 tablespoon	3.5
peanut oil (13g)	1 tablespoon	2.5
corn oil (13g)	1 tablespoon	2.0
soyabean oil (13g)	1 tablespoon	2.0
olive oil (13g)	1 tablespoon	2.0
sunflower oil (13g)	1 tablespoon	1.5
safflower oil (13g)	1 tablespoon	1.5
rapeseed oil (13g)	1 tablespoon	1.0
cod liver oil (5g)	1 teaspoon	0.0

Fats

butter (15g)	½ oz	8.0
butter (5g)	1 pat	3.0
lard (15g)	½ oz	6.0
beef dripping (15g)	½ oz	6.5
compound cooking fat (15g)	½ oz	6.0
ghee, butter (15g)	½ oz	9.0
ghee, palm (15g)	½ oz	6.5
margarine, hard from vegetable oils (15g)	½ oz	4.5
from animal and vegetable oils (15g)	½ oz	4.5

FOOD (g) = weight in grams	PORTION DESCRIPTION	SATURATED FAT POINTS (grams)
margarine, soft		
from vegetable oils		
(15g)	½ oz	3.5
from animal and		
vegetable oils (15g)	½ oz	3.5
margarine polyunsaturated		
sunflower (15g)	½ oz	2.0
dairy fat spread (15g)	½ oz	4.0
low-fat spread (15g)	½ oz	1.5
white vegetable		
shortening (15g)	½ oz	2.5

SOUPS, STARTERS AND SIDE DISHES

Soups

oxtail (220g)	medium bowl	Trace
lentil (220g)	medium bowl	1.0
cream of chicken		
condensed (220g)	medium bowl	1.0
made with milk		
(220g)	medium bowl	3.5
tomato, condensed		
(220g)	medium bowl	0.5
made with milk (220g)	medium bowl	3.0
mushroom		
condensed (220g)	medium bowl	1.5
made with milk		
(220g)	medium bowl	4.0
minestrone (220g)	medium bowl	Trace
vegetable (220g)	medium bowl	Trace
consommé (220g)	medium bowl	Trace
gazpacho (220g)	medium bowl	Trace
vichyssoise, with cream		
(220g)	medium bowl	5.0
beef and barley (220g)	medium bowl	2.0

FOOD (g) = weight in grams	PORTION DESCRIPTION	SATURATED FAT POINTS (grams)
chicken vegetable (220g)	medium bowl	1.0
cream of shrimp or lobster, with cream	medium bowl	6.0

Starters and Side Dishes

avocado pear (75g)	½ pear	2.0
with French dressing (90g)	½ pear	3.5
egg mayonnaise (90g)	1 serving	5.5
dhall (220g)	average portion	2.0
corn on the cob, buttered (146g)	1 medium ear	2.0
baked beans in tomato sauce (135g)	average portion	Trace
pâté de fois gras (30g)	average portion	4.0
dumplings, made with lard or suet (85g)	2 dumplings	6.0
potatoes		
chips (130g)	small portion	5.5
roast (50g)	1 small potato	1.0
mashed (60g)	1 scoop	0.5
instant mashed (60g)	1 scoop	Trace
boiled (40g)	1 small potato	Trace
potato salad (250g)	average portion	4.0

SAUCES AND GRAVY

bolognese sauce (220g)	average portion	7.5
cheese sauce		
whole milk (60g)	average portion	4.5
semi-skimmed milk (60g)	average portion	4.0
skimmed milk (60g)	average portion	3.0
white sauce (béchamel)		
whole milk (60g)	average portion	2.5

128

FOOD (g) = weight in grams	PORTION DESCRIPTION	SATURATED FAT POINTS (grams)
semi-skimmed milk (60g)	average portion	1.5
skimmed milk (60g)	average portion	1.0
tomato sauce (90g)	average portion	1.0
hollandaise sauce (25g)	1 tablespoon	5.0
béarnaise sauce (25g)	1 tablespoon	3.0
tartare sauce (30g)	2 tablespoons	4.0
barbecue sauce (60g)	average portion	Trace
prawn cocktail sauce (60g)	average portion	Trace
apple sauce (20g)	average portion	0.0
meat gravy dehydrated, made with water (70g)	average portion	Trace
with meat fat and juices (70g)	average portion	3.0

CONDIMENTS AND DRESSINGS

FOOD	PORTION	SAT FAT
mayonnaise (30g)	1 tablespoon	3.5
reduced calorie (30g)	1 tablespoon	1.0
salad cream (30g)	1 tablespoon	1.0
reduced calorie (30g)	1 tablespoon	0.5
ketchup (30g)	1 tablespoon	0.0
mint sauce (10g)	average portion	0.0
pickled cucumber (25g)	1 pickle	0.0
pickled onion (25g)	1 onion	0.0
salad dressing olive oil and vinegar (15g)	1 tablespoon	1.0
French (15g)	1 tablespoon	1.0
blue cheese (15g)	1 tablespoon	1.5
thousand island (15g)	1 tablespoon	1.0
diet (15g)	1 tablespoon	Trace
soy sauce (5g)	1 teaspoon	0.0

FOOD (g) = weight in grams	PORTION DESCRIPTION	SATURATED FAT POINTS (grams)
NUTS AND SEEDS		
peanuts		
roasted (25g)	small bag	2.5
peanut butter (12g)	thinly spread on bread	1.5
Brazil (10g)	3 whole nuts	1.5
walnuts (20g)	3 whole nuts	1.0
almonds (10g)	6 whole nuts	0.5
hazelnuts (20g)	10 whole nuts	0.5
chestnuts (50g)	5 whole nuts	0.5
cashew (25g)	small bag	3.0
pistachio nuts (14g)	20 kernels	1.0
macadamia (10g)	6 whole nuts	1.0
sesame tahini (20g)	1 rounded teaspoon	1.0
sesame seeds (8g)	1 tablespoon	1.0
sunflower seeds (14g)	1 tablespoon	1.0
coconut		
desiccated (28g)	1 oz	15.0
fresh (48g)	1 average piece	15.0

SAVOURY SNACKS AND BISCUITS		
cheese straws		
popcorn		
plain (6g)	1 cup	0.0
buttered (9g)	1 cup	1.0
popped in sunflower oil	1 cup	0.5
microwave with		
coconut oil	1 cup	4.5
with hydrogenated		
soybean oil	1 cup	1.0
crisps	small bag	3.5
twiglets (50g)	small bag	Trace

FOOD (g) = weight in grams	PORTION DESCRIPTION	SATURATED FAT POINTS (grams)
olives (36g)	10 pitted olives	0.5
sausage roll		
small (35g)	1 roll	5.0
large (85g)	1 roll	12.0
biscuits		
cream (20g)	4 crackers	0.5
water biscuits (15g)	5 biscuits	0.5
cheese crackers (20g)	6 round crackers	2.0
cheese sandwich (28g)	4 crackers	2.0
matzos (10g)	l large square	Trace
crispbread (15g)	2 pieces	0.5

BEVERAGES

Alcoholic Drinks

beer, ale, lager (574g)	1 pint	0.0
cider (574g)	1 pint	0.0
wine (125g)	1 glass	0.0
spirits (23g)	1 measure	0.0
Advocat (23g)	1 measure	0.5
pina colada cocktail (142g)	standard drink	9.5
creamed coconut mixer (19g)	1 tablespoon	3.0
liqueurs with cream (19g)	1 measure	5.0

Non alcoholic Drinks

milky drinks (see under dairy section)		
carbonated sodas (330g)	1 can	0.0
fruit juices, squash (220g)	large glass	0.0
coffee, tea, no milk (200g)	1 cup	0.0

FOOD (g) = weight in grams	PORTION DESCRIPTION	SATURATED FAT POINTS (grams)
MIXED DISHES		
quiche		
lorraine (120g)	1 average slice	15.0
cheese and egg (120g)	1 average slice	12.5
pizza		
cheese and tomato (280g)	1 average thin- crust slice	14.0
steak and kidney pie (200g)	1 individual pie	17.5
pork pie (140g)	1 individual pie	15.0
macaroni cheese		
with whole milk (300g)	average portion	17.0
moussaka (330g)	average portion	15.5
Cornish pasty (330g)	1 pasty	12.5
Irish Stew (330g)	average portion	11.5
Welsh rarebit (67g)	average portion	11.0
rabbit stew (170g)	average portion	2.5
fish fingers		
fried in oil (60g)	2 fish fingers	2.0
fish pie (250g)	average portion	5.5
fish kedgeree (300g)	average portion	7.0
chilli con carne (250g)	1 cup	7.5
Lancashire hot pot (330g)	average portion	6.0
shepherd's pie (300g)	average slice	7.5
cauliflower cheese (200g)	average portion	7.0
spaghetti		
bolognese (220g)	average portion	7.5
tomato sauce (125g)	average potion	Trace
chicken pie (230g)	1 average slice	11.0
chicken fricassee (230g)	average portion	7.0
scotch eggs (120g)	1 egg	5.0
cheese souflé (110g)	average portion	9.0

FOOD (g) = weight in grams	PORTION DESCRIPTION	SATURATED FAT POINTS (grams)
meat curry (200g)	average portion	8.0
chop suey, with pork (250g)	average portion	8.5
chicken chow mein (250g)	average portion	2.5
egg fried rice (300g)	average portion	4.5
egg fu yung (150g)	average portion	5.0
Stuffing		
sausagemeat stuffing (35g)	small portion	4.0
bread stuffing with butter & egg (35g)	small portion	3.0
bread stuffing with sunflower margarine only (35g)	small portion	0.5

SANDWICHES AND FAST FOODS

fast-food		
¼ pound hamburger in bun (160g)	1 burger	9.0
regular hamburger in bun (103g)	1 burger	5.0
¼ pound cheeseburger (180g)	1 burger	13.0
regular cheeseburger (120g)	1 burger	7.5
fried fish in bun with cheese and tartare sauce (143g)	1 sandwich	8.0
chicken nuggets (110g)	6 nuggets	7.0
fried chicken		
breast (100g)	1 portion	6.0
drumstick (60g)	1 portion	3.0

FOOD (g) = weight in grams	PORTION DESCRIPTION	SATURATED FAT POINTS (grams)
sausage in batter with chips (250g)	average portions	17.5
cod in batter with chips (250g)	average portions	10.0
tuna fish salad (110g)	1 sandwich	5.0
egg and cheese (110g)	1 sandwich	11.0
chicken (110g)	1 sandwich	5.0
bacon, lettuce and tomato (110g)	1 sandwich	7.0
ham and cheese (110g)	1 sandwich	8.5
roast beef (110g)	1 sandwich	6.0
cheese and pickle (110g)	1 sandwich	8.5
cheese and tomato roll (110g)	1 roll	8.5
ploughman's lunch (includes 100g of cheddar and 15g of butter)	1 portion	25.0

PUDDINGS AND PIES

suet pudding (150g)	average portion	15.0
sponge pudding (170g)	average portion	10.0
trifle		
fresh cream (170g)	average portion	9.0
whipped topping (170g)	average portion	4.0
bread and butter pudding (170g)	average portion	7.0
queen of puddings (150g)	average portion	6.0
rice pudding (200g)	average portion	3.0
Christmas pudding (100g)	average portion	5.5

FOOD (g) = weight in grams	PORTION DESCRIPTION	SATURATED FAT POINTS (grams)
milk pudding		
whole milk (200g)	average portion	5.5
semi-skimmed milk (200g)	average portion	2.0
skimmed milk (200g)	average portion	Trace
arctic roll (70g)	average slice	2.0
sweet pancakes (60g)	2 small pancakes	4.0
fruit pie		
1 crust (120g)	average slice	3.5
2 crust (120g)	average slice	7.0
fruit crumble (170g)	average portion	4.0
fruit pavlova (150g)	average slice	10.0
jelly (200g)	average portion	0.0
custard		
whole milk (150g)	average portion	4.0
semi-skimmed milk (150g)	average portion	2.0
skimmed milk (150g)	average portion	Trace
souflée, plain/lemon (110g)	average portion	5.5
Yorkshire pudding (90g)	average portion	4.0
creme caramel (90g)	average portion	2.0
lemon meringue pie (150g)	average slice	8.5
chocolate mousse, rich (60g)	average portion	13.5
frozen mousse, retail (60g)	average portion	2.0
chocolate ice (52g)	1 choc. ice	5.5
chocolate nut sundae (60g)	1 small tub	5.0
egg custard (140g)	average portion	4.5
blancmange (150g)	average portion	3.5
ice cream (see dairy section)		

FOOD (g) = weight in grams	PORTION DESCRIPTION	SATURATED FAT POINTS (grams)
CAKES AND PASTRIES		
chocolate éclairs, with fresh cream (90g)	1 éclair	11.0
mince pies (48g)	1 individual pie	4.0
jam tart (24g)	1 individual pie	1.5
doughnut		
fresh cream (75g)	1 doughnut	14.0
jam (75g)	1 doughnut	4.5
meringue		
with fresh cream (28g)	average portion	10.0
without cream (28g)	average portion	0.0
fruit cake, rich (90g)	average slice	5.0
rock cake (45g)	1 individual cake	3.0
gingerbread (50g)	average piece	2.5
cheese-cake		
homemade (110g)	average slice	20.5
frozen (110g)	average slice	6.0
chocolate cake, rich with filling (110g)	average slice	12.0
scones, plain (48g)	1 scone	2.5
Scotch pancakes (31g)	1 pancake	1.0
treacle tart (85g)	average slice	4.5
custard tart (113g)	1 large tart	8.0
currant buns (60g)	1 bun	2.0
apple Danish pastry (100g)	1 pastry	3.0
oatcakes, retail (13g)	average piece	5.0
BISCUITS		
butter biscuits (25g)	2 biscuits	2.0
chocolate biscuits,		
fully coated (24g)	2 biscuits	4.0
digestives (34g)	2 biscuits	4.0
chocolate chip (20g)	2 biscuits	2.0

FOOD (g) = weight in grams	PORTION DESCRIPTION	SATURATED FAT POINTS (grams)
fig rolls (28g)	2 biscuits	0.5
ginger nuts (14g)	2 biscuits	1.0
macaroons (38g)	2 biscuits	6.0
marshmallow biscuit		
coconut-covered (72g)	2 biscuits	3.0
chocolate-covered		
(52g)	2 biscuits	2.0
sandwich-type (25g)	2 biscuits	3.5
shortbread (15g)	2 biscuits	2.5
plain digestive (15g)	2 biscuits	0.5
sponge cake		
plain (53g)	average slice	5.0
cream filling (65g)	average slice	10.0
fancy iced cake (30g)	1 individual cake	3.0
Madeira cake (40g)	1 individual cake	4.0

SWEETS

chocolate		
milk chocolate (50g)	small choc. bar	9.0
plain (50g)	small choc. bar	8.5
filled bar (58g)	small choc. bar	5.0
fancy filled (32g)	4 pieces	5.0
fudge (11g)	1 square inch	0.5
toffees (8g)	1 piece	0.5
butterscotch (25g)	4 pieces	1.0
chocolate-covered raisins		
or peanuts (44g)	1 packet	4.5
chocolate-covered mint		
fondant (14g)	2 pieces	0.5
liquorice allsorts (115g)	small box	0.0
pastilles (40g)	1 tube	0.0
jelly babies (56g)	small bag	0.0
fruit gums (33g)	small tube	0.0
boiled sweets (2g)	1 piece	0.0

7

HOW TO BE A CHOLESTEROL-CONSCIOUS CONSUMER

Knowledge is power. The more you know about the nutritional content of the food you purchase and eat the greater your power to control cholesterol and improve the health prospects of yourself and your family. We want you to become wise, knowledgeable, cholesterol-conscious consumers.

As you are aware, the emphasis in *Taking Charge of Cholesterol* is on limiting the amount of saturated fat in your diet. That is because saturated fat, of all food constituents has the greatest impact on blood cholesterol levels. As you limit high-saturated fat food you inevitably lower your cholesterol intake at the same time. As far as we are concerned, being a smart cholesterol-conscious consumer means being as aware as possible about the fat content in foods.

Our Basic and Strict plans for cholesterol control, detailed in the previous chapter, focus on saturated fat and do all the work for you. It is possible to use the Saturated Fat Table as it is with great success. But we think it is even better to understand the basic nutritional principles that underlie the cholesterol-lowering plans. The purpose of this chapter is to reinforce your knowledge about the saturated fat content of foods and help you to read and understand nutritional food labels. If you use this information together with the Saturated Fat Table, in a short time you will be able to make wise choices on your own and healthy eating will become second nature to you.

In our opinion, the consumer is at a disadvantage when it comes to identifying the fat content of foods. Certainly, some fats are obvious — most people are well-aware that foods such as spreads, cooking oils and salad dressings are fats. Yet these foods account for only about a quarter of the fat we eat. The other three-quarters are 'hidden' fats, invisible to the eye. Foods with 'hidden' fats are meats, dairy products, processed, frozen and baked goods.

Currently, many food labels are inadequate, inconsistent and not specific enough to identify the type of fat present. You are not at fault if you are confused — and you are not alone! The name of the game and the challenge is spotting the 'hidden' fat.

THE COST OF EATING HEALTHILY

All good consumers worry about the cost of the goods they purchase. Health is important but so is value for money. People often use cost as a reason or excuse for not eating healthily. Does it have to cost a lot to have a healthier diet? This question is a major consideration for most people so we will address it first.

A few years ago, the London Food Commission studied this issue and concluded in a report call *Tightening Belts* that the cost of a healthy diet is 35 per cent more than the average amount spent on food by low-income households. The cost difference, say the authors, results in low-income families eating cheaper foods, higher in sugar and fat.

We're not sure we entirely agree with these conclusions. Without a doubt, some healthier food choices are expensive, especially fresh fish and lean cuts of meat. But eating healthily does not have to mean serving salmon instead of fried cod or sirloin steaks instead of sausages. Healthy eating *can* be inexpensive eating. You can replace foods high in saturated fats with vegetables, fruits and dried foods (beans, grains, pasta, rice) and actually save a bit on your food budget.

Convenience foods such as frozen meals, pies, cakes, are often full of saturated fat and rather expensive. Beef is usually more expensive (and more fatty) than turkey or chicken. Tinned fishes, like tuna and pilchards are not exorbitant and some fresh fishes can be quite reasonable. It is sensible to eat less meat, so the kind you buy can be leaner. A rice or pasta dish with small amounts of lean beef is far less expensive and much healthier than steaks, roasts, or chops. Also, fairly small amounts of meat in dishes like casseroles, curries and stews can be made to go a long way by using more beans, lentils and vegetables. Finally, low-fat milks are about the same price as whole milks and margarines are about half the price of butter.

We believe it is very possible to live within your food budget *and* provide yourself and your family with a healthier diet. We don't deny that it may take more care and planning for families on fixed tight food budgets to accomplish this goal. But considering the stakes, prevention of heart disease and long-term health and well-being, the effort is well worth it.

HEALTHY CHOICES

When you walk down the aisle of your supermarket or read through the menu at a restaurant or café you are bombarded with choices. Armed with knowledge about the fat content in food, you can consistently make sensible, nutritious choices.

Meats

If you scan the meat section of the Saturated Fat table (pages 120–123) one fact in particular leaps from the pages. While there are some differences among beef, veal, lamb and pork, the largest single factor determining the saturated fat content of a piece of meat is the cut. Some examples: an ordinary beef mince portion has 12.5 grams of saturated fat compared to 5.5 grams for extra-lean steak mince. Fatty roast leg of lamb has 10.5 grams of saturated fat while lean leg of lamb has 3.5 grams. A boiled gammon joint with lean and fat 13.0 grams, versus 4.0 grams for a joint which is lean only. There are enormous potential savings in saturated fat to be made by choosing leaner cuts of red meat. Furthermore, if you buy cuts of meat with visible fat, ask your butcher to trim away most of it or do it yourself at home before you cook it. If you are serious about sticking to a Basic plan target of, for example, no more than 27 grams of saturated fat per day, why not throw away 10 grams or so on a thick rind of fat on a piece of meat?

In general, beef and pork tend to be lower in saturated fat than lamb or veal. The choices absolutely lowest in saturated fat are lean topside or silverside of beef, lean T-bone steak, and pork tenderloin. All have 1 or less grams of saturated fat per serving and even people on the Strict plan can easily accommodate these items.

But we would also remind you of one of the flexible and fun aspects of our cholesterol-control plan. It's perfectly all right to indulge yourself in a higher-fat option on any day for any occasion and exceed your recommended saturated fat target. Just cut back on the next couple of days so your *average* intake does not exceed your target. So it's okay to have those spare ribs in the Chinese restaurant (14 grams saturated fat) without too much soul-searching.

As we have said before, organ meats such as liver and kidney are not terribly high in saturated fat but are extremely high in cholesterol so you should use them sparingly.

Don't overlook the potential of soy bean curd (tofu) and textured vegetable protein as meat substitutes. They are low in saturated fat, high in protein, relatively inexpensive and simulate the texture of meat. Some people are put off bean curd because they think of the taste and appearance of the raw product. Bean curd on its own is fairly unattractive and tasteless. However, when it is added to soups, stews, curried and oriental dishes and casseroles it picks up the flavour and colour of the sauce and beautifully compliments the dish.

Prepared Meat Products

Prepared meat products like sausages and frankfurters are quite high in saturated fat and are also extremely high in salt. You certainly don't have to avoid prepared meat products but we suggest you purchase them with care and try to orient your family towards healthier choices. For cold cuts and sandwiches, slices of chicken, turkey and ham make more sense than corned beef, luncheon meat and chopped ham and pork loaves.

We draw your attention to the astronomical saturated fat content of meat pasties and pies. They are usually made from cheap fatty cuts of meat and the pastry is prepared with lard and hard vegetable oils. The numbers speak for themselves: pork pie – 15.0 grams of saturated fat; steak and kidney pie – 17.5 grams; Cornish pasty – 12.5 grams; chicken pie – 11.0 grams. Let the buyer beware!

Poultry

Chicken is low in saturated fat but turkey is even lower and represents really outstanding nutritional and monetary value. Duck, on the other hand, is particularly high in saturated fat. Poultry light meat is lower in saturated fat than the dark meat. Light meat turkey has only 1.0 gram of saturated fat per serving. Poultry skin has very high amounts of saturated fat so it makes a lot of sense to skin the bird prior to cooking or serving. We cover this topic in detail in the next chapter.

Fish

You really can't go wrong when you buy fresh fish. Most fresh fish has only trace amounts of saturated fat and little cholesterol. The only time fresh fish becomes problem food is when it is prepared in a high-fat way, for example, grilled in butter or fried in batter. A portion of cod in batter has twice the amount of saturated fat that a lean piece of pork or beef has. See Chapter 8 for ideas on low-fat fish preparation techniques.

Frozen fillets of fish can be quite economical, but stick to plain unadulterated pieces rather than fillets and fish fingers done in batter. If your family likes fish fingers, choose breaded ones and grill them or fry with a small amount of sunflower oil.

Tinned fishes like tuna, pilchards and sardines are also good choices. It is better to buy these fishes packaged in brine or tomato sauce rather than oil. The saturated fat saving is impressive. Half a can of tuna in brine has only a trace of saturated fat while the same amount of tuna in oil has 2.5 grams of saturated fat. Many people, ourselves included, think tuna in brine tastes better too. If you have trouble finding tuna in brine, wash the tuna with water and drain off excess oil before serving.

Prepared Convenience Foods

Over the past few years our supermarket shelves have been filling up with increasing numbers and varieties of precooked frozen or tinned convenience foods. With the wide acceptance of microwave cookery, more and more people are turning to these foods – for the convenience. In earlier days, most convenience foods were extremely high in saturated fat and calories – breaded and fried chicken and fish, dishes in creamy sauces, burgers, chips. As the market for convenience foods has become more competitive, manufacturers have tried to keep pace with health trends and consumer desires. As a result there are now several reasonable choices for health-conscious shoppers.

Manufacturers of convenience food items that are truly healthy are not hesitant about voluntarily labelling the product with complete nutritional information, including the type and amount of fat it contains. (See the section on nutritional labelling in this chapter, p 148). We recommend you stay away from convenience foods that choose to omit the saturated fat content.

As you may have noticed, we have consciously avoided mentioning brand names in this book. However we are so encouraged by one recent product line developed by the convenience food industry in Britain that we are happy to name it. The Healthy Options line of savoury meals produced by Bird's Eye are very low in saturated fat. Many entrées contain less than 1 gram of saturated fat per meal and are clearly labelled as having such. They are also well-balanced in other nutrients and are relatively low in calories. We hope that other manufacturers follow suit and provide consumers with convenience food meals that are similarly low in saturated fat.

Milk and Dairy Foods

Whole milk is a high-fat food and many people do not fully appreciate this fact. Whole milk contains about 3.3 per cent fat which doesn't sound like a lot. But most of the weight of milk comes from water so this percentage is misleading. Fat accounts for about half the calories in a glass of whole milk and 5 fluid ounces (1/4 pint) contains 3.5 grams of saturated fat. Channel island (breakfast milk) has even more – 5.0 grams per glass.

We recommend you shift over to low-fat semi-skimmed milk for all members of your family over 5 years of age. Semi-skimmed milk is 2 per cent fat and the taste is pretty similar to whole milk. In fact, many prefer the taste of low-fat milk. Semi-skimmed milk also offers a substantial saving in saturated fat with only 1.5 grams per glass.

For those people who require the Strict plan for cholesterol control, skimmed milk is an option. Although it is fairly watery, it is virtually free of saturated fat and some people develop quite a taste for it.

It is important to stress that low-fat milk skimps on fat but it does not skimp on vitamins and calcium, a vital mineral for the formation of teeth and bones and the prevention of osteoporosis, the thinning of bones with aging.

Of course cream is high in saturated fat − very high. A tablespoon of single cream, only enough for one cup of fresh coffee has 2.5 grams of saturated fat! Now for a real shocker: the fresh clotted cream you would use on scones for a cream tea will cost you 12.0 grams of saturated fat! Soured cream also has loads of saturated fat. You really need to think twice (maybe three times) before you ladle cream onto your food.

The saturated fat content of yoghurts varies widely depending on the kind of milk used to make the products. At the high end are Greek yoghurts which are supplemented with cream and are up to 10 per cent fat. A 5 ounce carton of Greek yoghurt will deliver 8.0 grams of saturated fat. In contrast, a whole milk plain yoghurt has 2.5 grams. We recommend plain or fruit low-fat yoghurts made with semi-skimmed milk. They taste wonderful and they have only 1.0 gram of saturated fat per serving. Low-fat yoghurt also makes a good-tasting substitute for soured cream in recipes and dessert toppings and it has a fraction of the saturated fat.

The saturated fat content of cheeses also depends on the kind of milk used in production. Whole milk cheeses derive up to 90 per cent of their calories from fat, a half of which are from saturated fat. Most whole milk cheeses, including Cheddar, Brie, Gouda and many others contain 6−10 grams of saturated fat per 1½ ounce serving. Fortunately for cheese-lovers, there are lower-fat options. Reduced-fat Cheddar and Edam cheeses, for example, are widely available and contain about half the saturated fat of their full-fat relations. Reduced-fat cottage cheese has a third of the saturated fat of ordinary cottage cheese (1.0 versus 3.0 grams per serving). Another strategy for making the most of your cheese in cooking is to use smaller amounts of very sharp cheeses to impart plenty of flavour without adding too much fat.

Fats and Oils

There is no denying that butter tastes great but there is also no denying that it is remarkably high in saturated fat. A half ounce portion has 8.0 grams; a meagre pat of butter has 3.0 grams. You can use butter on a cholesterol-lowering plan but you must use it sparingly. It is far better to use alternative products for cooking and spreads.

Margarines vary in their ratio of polyunsaturated to saturated fat (the P/S ratio). The higher the ratio, the healthier the product. A ratio of 1.0 or greater is considered very good. Butter has a terribly low ratio: 0.05. Most soft or tub margarines have higher P/S ratios than hard margarines. We recommend you choose margarines made with sunflower oil. They have an excellent P/S ratio of about 3.0 and have a good buttery taste. It is worth noting, however, that even though sunflower margarines are healthier than butter, it is unwise to use margarine to excess. A half ounce of a margarine high in polyunsaturates also contains 2.0 grams of saturated fat.

There is an enormous range in the saturated fat content and P/S ratios of cooking oils and fats. In our opinion the oil with the best combination of a high P/S ratio (6.0), taste and general versatility is sunflower oil. We use sunflower oil in many of our recipes; a tablespoon contains 1.5 grams of saturated fat. Olive oil is another good choice. Although the P/S ratio of olive oil is only 0.7, it is very high in heart-healthy monunsaturated fat. With healthier options available, it simply makes very little sense to use butter, lard, dripping or ghee for cooking.

There are a variety of vegetable oils that are very high in saturated fats, low in polyunsaturated fats and should be avoided whenever possible. The problem for the consumer is that these oils are often hidden. The kind of oils we are referring to fall into two categories: hydrogenated vegetable oils and tropical oils. They are usually less expensive than sunflower, safflower, peanut, olive, rapeseed or maize oils

146

and they have different physical properties. They are solid at room temperature and have longer shelf-lives because they do not go rancid as quickly as more polyunsaturated oils. For all these reasons, they are widely used in commercially processed foods.

When vegetable oils are hydrogenated they solidify and are converted to cholesterol-raising saturated fats. Tropical oils are also rich in saturated fat. Coconut oil has 11.0 grams of saturated fat per tablespoon and an abysmal P/S ratio of 0.02! Palm oil and palm kernel oil are not much better. It is hard to find commercially-prepared peanut butter, for example, that is not loaded with palm oil to give the product texture and to prevent separation of oil and solid.

The best, and sometimes only, way to keep hydrogenated vegetable oils and tropical oils out of your diet is to read the nutritional labels on the foods you are thinking about purchasing. Pay special attention to the ingredients of baked goods. These oils often turn up in the most unexpected places. We recently bought some white and wholemeal bridge rolls. We didn't read the label before we brought them home and were surprised to find that each small roll contained 0.5 grams of saturated fat, unusual since most bread is virtually fat-free. The explanation was there on the nutritional label: 'contains hydrogenated vegetable oil'. If you see the words 'hydrogenated vegetable oil,' 'coconut oil,' 'palm oil', or 'palm kernel oil' on the food label you are better off buying an alternative product in our opinion.

Snack Foods and Desserts

The saturated fat in snack foods and desserts adds up quickly and before you know it you can use up most of your saturated fat allowance. Read through the Saturated Fat Table in the preceding chapter under the categories savoury snacks and crackers, nuts and seeds, pudding and pies, cakes and pastries, sweets and biscuits. Many snack food items are so small you hardly notice eating them, but if you are going to be a good cholesterol-conscious consumer it pays to give them more than passing attention.

A half a dozen walnuts will give you 2.0 grams of saturated fat, a small bag of peanuts, 2.5 grams, six cheese crackers, 2.0 grams, a couple of chocolate digestive biscuits, 4.0 grams, a small chocolate bar, 9.0 grams, a fresh cream doughnut, 14.0 grams. It makes good sense to turn away from these kinds of snack foods for everyday use. Apart from their fat content, their excessive calorie content is a large contributor to the obesity problem many people face.

The best snack foods to have around the house are fresh fruit and popcorn. Popcorn is low in calories, high in fibre and plain popcorn is fat-free. But popcorn can be made fatty and calorie-laden if it is coated in butter. Also, be aware that commercial popcorn, including microwave popcorn, is often prepared with hydrogenated vegetable or tropical oils. The best way to make popcorn is to pop it yourself in a covered saucepan with a tablespoon of sunflower oil.

Desserts can also have an enormous fat impact. A small chocolate mousse will deliver 13.5 grams of saturated fat, a slice of apple pie, 7.0 grams, a piece of homemade cheesecake, an artery-clogging 20.5 grams. As we have said, you don't have to give up any food entirely to stick to our healthy-eating, cholesterol-lowering plan but you have to use your head on occasion for the sake of your heart.

HOW TO READ FOOD LABELS

The law requires that most prepackaged foods have clearly visible labelling that reveals the nutritional content of the product. Specifically, the Food Labelling Regulations of 1984 (subsequently amended) force manufacturers to display the name of the food, a list of ingredients, an indication of minimal durability (sell-by or use-by information), storage conditions, instructions to aid in the appropriate preparation and consumption of the food and the manufacturers name and address.

With regard to the list of ingredients, the regulations state that the ingredients be listed in descending order of weight, determined at the time of their use in the preparation of the food. Since water is a substantial ingredient in most food production, it is often the first item on a nutritional label. Herbs, spices, preservative and colourings (when used) don't weigh very much so they are usually the last items. Apart from the ingredients list, the regulations also state that manufacturers must provide the number of calories the food item contains (expressed in kilojoules and kilocalories) and a breakdown of the carbohydrate, protein and fat content of the food per 100 grams of the item and per full pack serving.

On first glance that seems like quite a bit of information, but for the health-conscious consumer it is not enough. Where, for example, is information about the amount of salt in the food, added sugar, dietary fibre and, most importantly for cholesterol-control, the *type* of fats in the food?

It is likely that many of these holes in mandatory nutritional labelling will be filled by future government regulations. For the moment many responsible food manufacturers and supermarket chains have taken it upon themselves to voluntarily label their products with more complete nutritional information. But even among those who subscribe to voluntary disclosure, there is considerable variation in the format and content of the labelling, resulting, we are sure, in consumer confusion.

For the cholesterol-conscious consumer, the most critical piece of voluntary information on the product label is the number of grams of saturated fat per serving. When it appears on a label the information is usually present under the typical values for fat. The following nutritional information for a small can of beans and hamburger bits in tomato sauce is an example of a good-quality label that specifies the amount of saturated fat:

149

Typical values	Amount per 100 grams	Amount per serving (225 grams)
Energy	500kj/ 119kcal	1130kj/ 268kcal
Protein	7.3 g	16.4 g
Carbohydrate	15.4 g	34.7 g
(of which sugars)	(5.0 g)	(11.3 g)
Fat	3.5 g	7.9 g
(of which saturates)	(1.3 g)	(2.9 g)
Sodium	0.6 g	1.4 g
Dietary Fibre	7.3 g	16.4 g

This label tells the consumer exactly what he or she needs to know. The whole can of beans and burgers will deliver 2.9 grams of saturated fat which may or may not fit into their saturated fat budget for the day. It also informs him or her that the food is high in dietary fibre which is good, and high in sugar and salt, which is not so good. But at least you have been well-informed and the choice is yours.

You will note that the way saturated fat is expressed on voluntary food labels — number of grams per serving — is fully compatible with the format we have chosen for our Basic and Strict plans. This standard format should make it easy for you to supplement the information on our Saturated Fat Table with actual branded food items.

In time, we have no doubt that more complete food labelling for prepackaged goods will become compulsory. Until that happens, we suggest you view with suspicion those food items which do not voluntarily give you information on the saturated fat content. Do they have something to hide? Be especially wary of foods that fail to disclose saturated fat content but have on the list of ingredients hydrogenated vegetable oil, coconut oil, palm oil or palm kernel oil. You can be sure they are hiding the presence of considerable saturated fat.

The kinds of advertising claims made on food labels are also tightly regulated by the government but even so, there is plenty of opportunity for consumer confusion. For example, it is permissible to label a food as 'cholesterol-free' if it contains no more than 0.005 per cent cholesterol. Since cholesterol is contained only in animal products, a cynic would say that this claim is over-the-top for a vegetable product. Also, most consumers see 'cholesterol-free' and assume the product is healthy for the heart. This claim would be clearly misleading for products that may well be free of cholesterol but packed with high-saturated fat vegetable oils.

Other words to watch out for are 'light' 'lower-in-fat' and 'lean'. It is perfectly true items so labelled may be lower in fat than comparable products but they may still be very high in total fat and saturated fat. Some brands of cream cheese, for example are advertised as 'light'. While they may contain half the fat of regular cream cheese, an ounce of light cream cheese will still offer up 4.5 grams of saturated fat. Our advice: read the labels and make an informed decision.

HEALTHY EATING IN RESTAURANTS

When you enter a restaurant you don't have to hang up your brain when you hang up your coat. You can make the same kinds of wise cholesterol-conscious decisions in restaurants that you make in the supermarket. Remember these common-sense points: you are the one in control of your meal, not the waiter, not your fellow diners; the food choices are up to you. Don't be hesitant to ask how a dish is prepared or what ingredients are used. It's not rude, it's necessary. Assert yourself. Many good restaurants will be happy to prepare a dish the way you want it rather than the way it appears on the menu − fish grilled in lemon juice and a little oil rather than fried in butter, steak without the béarnaise sauce.

Generally orient yourself towards low-saturated fat

starters and main courses. Roasted poultry, fish grilled with oil, a small lean steak or pork tenderloin are all acceptable and widely available choices. Indian restaurants can be challenging since most main course and side dishes are swimming in high-saturated fat ghee. Tandoori-style dishes are reasonably low-fat choices. Vegetable purées often have added cream and butter and should be avoided. The same goes for creamed soups. Avoid dolloping soured cream on your baked potato. Order rice or other vegetables as side dishes rather than chips. In between courses, don't fill up on buttered bread. For desserts, choose fresh fruit salad rather than a rich pie, cake or pudding. If you do choose to indulge in a high-fat meal, remember to cut back on your saturated fat intake for the next few days to make up for it.

Fast food restaurants, cafés, bakeries and chip shops certainly offer convenience at moderate prices for working people, shoppers and teenagers. Unfortunately what they do not offer is much in the way of healthy choices. Fast food is big business in Britain. Last year consumers spent over four billion pounds on fast food, over 800 million pounds on fish and chips alone. Quite a bit of that money was spent on saturated fat. A quarter-pound cheeseburger has 13.0 grams of saturated fat. A chocolate milk shake has 7.5 grams. A fried chicken breast has 7.0 grams, a half dozen fried chicken nuggets, 6.0 grams. A standard portion of fish and chips has 10.0 grams. Sausage-in-batter and chips contains 17.5 grams.

The consumer in this country does not have enough healthy fast food options on the High Street. We would like to see more salad bars and more outlets that provide healthier low-fat choices. Until that happens the best fast food options are probably sandwiches and filled rolls from bakeries and other High Street food vendors – but many of these are unnecessarily high in saturated fat from the addition of butter, mayonnaise or salad cream. There is room for improvement in Britain's fast food scene.

8

FOOD PREPARATION TIPS

When asked to analyse the eating habits of people trying to lower their cholesterol we often discover more problems in the *way* people prepare their food than in the *kind* of food they eat. Healthy food choices can be turned into unhealthy choices simply by using cooking and food preparation methods that pile on loads of saturated fat. In the last chapter we told you how you could maker wiser choices when you purchase food in the supermarket and select meals in restaurants. The purpose of this chapter is to explore delicious low-fat ways to prepare food in your home.

HEALTHY COOKING

Most children learn to love high-fat cooking styles at home at the dining table. In time, children usually pass these preferences on to their offspring. Mothers may cook with love but they don't always cook with care. For the sake of you and your family it is time to break this cycle and change to a healthier style of cooking. Even if only one member of a family is actively trying to lower cholesterol it makes great sense for the entire family to eat well.

The single most important change you can make is to avoid frying. Fried food is problem food. When you fry in a saucepan or a deep-frier you add lots of calories, hide the natural flavour of the food and add unnecessary cholesterol-raising fat.

Let's take the example of fried fish. A 6-ounce serving of plaice contains virtually no saturated fat and is a very healthy food choice. That same piece of plaice, fried in batter will transform the fish into a rather unhealthy item that will deliver 10 grams of saturated fat. If your Basic plan saturated fat allowance is 22 grams, your decision to fry has used up almost half of your daily total. And there is the taste difference to consider. Poached plaice with fresh herbs tastes wonderful and leaves you satisfied without a heavy feeling. Fried plaice tastes more like fried breadcrumbs and leaves you with a brick in your stomach. Through force of habit you are likely to have chips with your fried food. a further load of high-calorie fat.

If you do wish occasionally to fry your food you can limit the fat and calories by these manoeuvres: use vegetable oils high in poly-or monounsaturated fat such as sunflower or olive oil rather than butter, lard, suet, white fat or drippings. Soak up excess fat by draining fried foods on absorbent kitchen paper before serving. Strain cooking oil after deep-frying and change to fresh oil when it has been used three or four times. When frying chips, remember that the shape of the chips can make a difference on their fat content. Cut the potato into thick slices to cut down on the surface area for absorbing fat and avoid crinkle-cut chips. Fry chips lightly – don't let them get dark brown. We include a delicious recipe for chips in this book which actually avoids frying altogether.

As a substitute for frying we suggest you get into the habit of using alternative approaches when preparing these staple foods:

Chicken

We don't have to tell you about the versatility of chicken as a main course. Entire cookery books have been devoted to chicken recipes. Chicken and other poultry can be very useful in a cholesterol-lowering programme. Chicken is naturally low in saturated fat, provided it is cooked in a low-fat manner and not drowned in a rich sauce.

It is a good idea to remove the skin of the chicken prior to cooking. Skinning saves nearly 200 calories per serving and lowers the saturated fat content by about three times (6.5 grams of saturated fat vs. 2 grams for a 5 oz chicken breast). The only drawback to skinning is that it can make the chicken dry. To get around this problem you can sear the skinned chicken first in a very hot nonstick saucepan with a little bit of vegetable oil. Searing will seal in the juices and flavour before the other ingredients are added. You can season the chicken before it is seared with a sprinkle of salt and pepper or other spices. When the chicken is golden-brown on both sides, add liquid and other ingredients as desired, reduce heat and simmer. Depending on the dish, chicken stock, wine, canned tomatoes or other vegetables can be added. A recipe that uses this cooking method is Honeyed Ginger Chicken, see page 216.

When you casserole chicken you should also remove the skin before cooking. For roasting it is better to remove the skin after cooking. Cook poultry (and meat) on a rack over a roasting tin so the fat drips underneath.

Another idea is to marinate your chicken before you grill it. Besides imparting flavour, marinating will also make your chicken fork-tender. It is also an excellent way to cook meat and fish. You may not realize it but marinating does not have to take many hours and lots of preplanning. You can get very nice results with one hour marinade. The basic marinade ingredients are sunflower oil, lemon juice, wine or wine vinegar, herbs and spices.

Another of our favourite ways to prepare chicken is stir-frying. Stir-frying is a classic Chinese cooking method that preserves the flavour and texture of food. It is a technique well-suited to low-fat cooking since only a small amount of oil is required. Chicken and Cashew Stir-Fry (page 216) is a delicious example of the kind of meal you can create. Of course, fish or meat can also be used in stir-frying, with the same excellent results.

Fish

Grilling, poaching, steaming and baking are the preferred techniques for tasty low-fat fish cooking.

Fish tends to become dry and tough without the benefit of butter or rich sauces. The secret of good low-fat low-calorie fish cooking is preventing the fish from drying out. You can keep fish moist and juicy by grilling with small amounts of vegetable oil and lemon juice. For naturally oily fish such as herring and mackerel, lemon juice is all you need. Grilling with lemon juice is also a fine way to cook shellfish. Always serve fish immediately after cooking.

You can also get excellent results baking fish in foil. Place the fish on lightly greased foil, add lemon juice and fresh herbs and wrap tightly with a big pocket of air. When you unwrap the dish at the dinner table, be prepared for wonderful aromas. Herrings Baked in Foil (page 231) is a nice example of the technique.

Poaching is an excellent way to keep fish moist and tender. Simmer fish fillets, steaks or whole fish in a covered pan. Vegetable stock, fish stock or water mixed with dry white wine all make wonderful poaching liquids. Try using different flavourings in the poaching liquid. Sprigs of thyme or rosemary, crushed cardamon pods, orange or lime slices add fabulous flavours to the fish and the strained liquid can be used to make sauces.

Fish cooks quickly in steam and comes out incredibly moist and tasty. Some people shy away from steaming because they think it is difficult. It's not, as long as you have a steaming rack. Simply place the fish on the rack lightly brushed with oil, put the rack in a saucepan, heat water to boil, cover tightly and cook for five to ten minutes, until the fish is flaky and tender.

Baking is the slowest of these cooking methods and thus the one most likely to need a sauce to keep the fish moist. You can bake fish brushed with vegetable oil or smother it in cooked onions and tomatoes, a sauce with no added fat. (See Fish Plaki, page 223.)

Meat

Meat is naturally high in saturated fat but with some care and attention it is certainly possible to use red meat in a cholesterol-lowering plan. Before you cook a piece of meat remove all visible fat with a sharp knife. Oven grilling is a good method for preparing low-calorie meat dishes. It works best with choicer cuts of meat. To oven grill, brush the meat pan with a little vegetable oil to prevent sticking.

Steak and chops should be at least 3/4 inch thick. Meat usually will not stick to a grill so additional oil is not needed for indoor and outdoor grilling. Pan grilling can be done with cuts of meat 1 inch thick or less. It is not always necessary to add oil especially if you use a non-stick frying pan since there is often plenty of fat in the meat. For a very lean quality of steak mince, for example, you may find it helpful to brush the pan with some vegetable oil to get the cooking started. Cook the meat slowly, uncovered, over a medium heat, turning occasionally to cook evenly. Pour off fat as it accumulates. If you are using a very lean cut and the meat is dry, add a little beef stock or red wine and cook to desired taste. Season as needed and serve immediately.

When you make a casserole or stew get in the habit of using less meat. Bulk up the quantity with extra vegetables, beans or dried fruits such as apricots or prunes. Since you are using less meat you can afford to buy better quality, leaner cuts. Casseroles and stews are best prepared the day before to allow flavours time to develop. This also gives you a chance to skim off excess fat from the surface before reheating. We have provided several meat casseroles and stews in the recipe section. Our favourite is Oriental Beef and Bean Stew (page 198).

Eggs

As part of the Basic plan you will limit egg consumption to three per week. However, when you do have eggs it makes sense to prepare them in a low-fat way. Of course, hard-boiled, soft-boiled and poached eggs need no butter or oil for cooking. But you should know that eggs can be scrambled or fried perfectly well in a good non-stick frying pan without butter or oil. In fact, the natural flavour of an egg comes through brilliantly without the grease.

Vegetables

If vegetables are properly cooked there will be no temptation to drench them in butter or a creamy sauce. The best way to prepare fresh vegetables is to steam them. Boiled vegetables lose valuable water-soluble vitamins. If over-cooked, vegetables become limp and lose colour. Taste, texture, colour and vitamin content are all maximized by cooking in steam. Steaming is done with a metal steaming basket, a Chinese bamboo steamer, or in a covered saucepan with a steaming tray. Steaming baskets are inexpensive and well worth the investment.

To steam, clean and cut vegetables and place in a steamer basket. Put 1 inch of water into a large saucepan and place the steamer basket inside. The basket should stand above the water line and none of the vegetables should be immersed. Cover the saucepan tightly and bring water to boil over high heat. Then reduce heat and simmer for a few minutes until vegetables are crisp-tender. Steaming times vary. For example, spinach leaves cook rapidly in two to three minutes while broccoli takes about eight to ten minutes. Frozen vegetables also cook nicely in a steamer.

They are usually partially cooked before freezing so steaming times are short.

If you do not have a steamer, you can boil vegetables in a small amount of water − just enough to prevent scorching − in a pot with a tightly fitting lid. Bring water to boil, then reduce heat and simmer until vegetables are crisp-tender. Your vegetable will be partly boiled and partly steamed. Serve vegetables immediately. Do not allow them to stand in water as flavours and nutrients will be lost.

It is worth remembering that a vegetarian diet does not necessarily mean a healthy diet. A dish may be meatless but if you sauté your vegetables in butter or oil then smother them in milk, eggs and cheese you might as well be eating a fry-up!

HEALTHY SUBSTITUTES

One important strategy for cutting down on saturated fat is substituting poultry and fish for red meat in your main courses. We encourage this strategy but there are other kinds of healthy substitutions to help you further reduce your intake of high-fat foods. For example, you can reduce your reliance on fatty main dishes by substituting filling and satisfying items like dried food and salads.

Dried foods can form the basis for an enormous variety of delicious, economical low-fat meals. We recommend you make liberal use of pasta, rice, dried peas, beans and lentils for main meals and side dishes. You can combine dried foods with vegetables and relatively small amounts of fish, poultry or meat, or use them to make meatless dishes. In our recipe section you will find numerous examples of how to use dried foods to your advantage. Here are a few general ideas:

Pasta dishes are very cheap and very filling. Spaghetti or macaroni can get boring after a while so look for types of pasta you haven't tried before like fresh tagliatelle or wholemeal pasta shells.

Keep a good supply of rice on hand. Brown rice has a wholesome nutty taste and is a good source of fibre. Brown rice takes longer to cook so it is sometimes considered inconvenient. You can cook it in advance and reheat it in about 20 minutes in a tightly covered greased pan in a moderate oven.

Stock up on dried peas, beans and lentils for soups, salads and savoury dishes. Beans are excellent foods in cholesterol-lowering diets. They are inexpensive, high in protein, cholesterol-free and virtually fat-free and they add a meaty texture to your dishes. And they are also very rich in soluble fibre. For convenience, soak and cook beans, peas and lentils in large batches. Freeze them in useful portions and add to soups and stews straight from the freezer.

In our recipe section we have included numerous dishes based on pasta, rice, beans, cereal grains and lentils.

If you are not accustomed to eating salads regularly because you find them dull and uninteresting we'd like you to think again. Side salads and main-course salads can be among the most satisfying and healthy foods you can eat and they don't have to taste like rabbit food. For example, we suggest you try Bean and Leaf Salad (page 261), Seafood Vinaigrette (page 256) and the other salads in our recipe section. But don't ruin your salads by covering them in fatty dressings and salad creams. We recommend lighter dressings such as the ones we describe in the book (page 264–267). There are also many commercial reduced-calorie brands available.

Other areas ripe for healthy substitutions are desserts and snacks. The best substitution for rich fatty puddings, cakes, pies, crisps, biscuits etc is fruit. Fresh and dried fruits are naturally sweet, naturally high in fibre and they are completely free of cholesterol and fat. If you get into the habit of reaching for a piece of fruit instead of your usual in-between meal snacks and afters your savings in saturated fat and calories will be enormous.

HEALTHY MODIFICATION

Many traditional recipes call for high-fat ingredients. It is natural to assume that modifying recipes by eliminating or changing ingredients will ruin the dish. That is not necessarily so. Many dishes can be made more healthy without changing the taste or texture. In fact, some 'lighter' dishes really taste better than the original. Consider both these quiche recipes:

Mushroom Quiche

Original Version	Lighter Version
Pastry:	
25g/1oz lard	25g/1oz white vegetable fat
25g/1oz block margarine	25g/1oz sunflower margarine
125g/4oz white flour	50g/2oz wholemeal flour
	50g/2oz white flour
Filling:	
300ml/½ pint single cream	300ml/½ pint semi-skimmed milk
3 eggs	2 eggs
4oz Swiss cheese	3 oz Edam cheese
250g/8oz mushrooms	250g/8oz mushrooms
25g/1oz butter (to sauté mushrooms	25g/1oz sunflower oil (to sauté mushrooms)

The original recipe has 17 grams of saturated fat and 300 calories per slice. The lighter version has only 6.5 grams of saturated fat and only 150 calories per slice. And we think the lighter version tastes better.

Some recipe modifications have virtually no effect on the taste and texture of a dish. When a recipe calls for butter, use margarine instead. Use low-fat yoghurt or buttermilk instead of soured cream, low-fat or skimmed milk instead

161

of whole milk. A good substitute for 1 tablespoon of chocolate in a recipe is one tablespoon of cocoa powder plus three tablespoons of margarine. When a recipe calls for three egg yolks, one egg yolk will do nicely. Instead of two whole eggs try one whole egg plus one egg white.

You can also make healthy modifications to sandwiches. You can 'ruin' a nice low-fat chicken or tuna sandwich with a thick layer of butter or mayonnaise. Use a little margarine instead, or a low-fat spread or reduced-calorie mayonnaise. And use plenty of fillers like crisp lettuce and tomato slices to give your sandwich bulk, rather than a mountain of fatty meat.

You can also modify an entire meal to good effect − even the traditional Sunday roast dinner. For example, you can significantly reduce saturated fat by using a lean joint of beef, serving new or jacket potatoes instead of roast potatoes and making Yorkshire pudding according to our recipe (page 200). Lean cuts of meat such as topside and sirloin can become dry so cooking the joint in red wine or stock can make the dish moist and succulent. For variety, have roast turkey instead of beef on occasion. Also, for pudding switch from apple pie with cream to fresh fruit salad or something more exotic like Gingered Apricot Compote (page 281) or Passion Fruit Pavlova (page 279).

If you pay attention to healthy cooking methods, healthy substitutions and healthy modifications you can dramatically lower your saturated fat consumption and achieve significant reductions in your cholesterol count.

9

EXERCISING YOUR RISK AWAY

Exercise is one of the major non-dietary tools at your disposal in your efforts to prevent coronary heart disease. Not only does exercise have a direct positive effect on the function of the heart muscle but it can boost the levels of HDL cholesterol, the type of blood cholesterol that exerts a protective effect against the development of atherosclerosis.

The 1980s have been the decade in which exercise has caught on in a big way in Britain. Health clubs, sports centres and home exercise gear have all proliferated and more people are participating in recreational exercise than ever before. Yet the vast majority of people who need it most are still sedentary.

Many people are interested in starting an exercise plan as part of an overall programme for healthy living but don't really know how to start and how to progress safely. Here, we offer a prudent, safe fitness programme that will make you feel healthier and more energetic within days and will help protect you against heart disease for years to come. We encourage you to get out and exercise as part of your strategy for taking charge of cholesterol.

EXERCISE WORKS: THE EVIDENCE

It is relatively easy to measure the effects of exercise on

blood cholesterol levels and we have described these beneficial effects in Chapter 5. However, we think you will be more persuaded by evidence that show that regular exercise actually affects the human life span and has a protective effect against heart disease.

The first important study of exercise and longevity was performed in London in the 1950s. Dr J.N. Morris and colleagues found that conductors on double-decker buses who walked up and down stairs all day had half the incidence of heart diseases that bus drivers who sat behind the wheel had. Another study of postmen by the same researchers had a similar result. Mail carriers had much less heart disease than their sedentary colleagues, post office clerks. In the 1970s Dr Morris and his colleagues also investigated the effects of leisure-time exercise on nearly 18,000 white-collar workers in England, observed for nine years. They discovered that men who played vigorous sports during their leisure time had less than half the incidence of heart attacks that their more sedentary peers had and this beneficial effect could not be explained by differences in other coronary risk factors.

During the past twenty years similar studies have been conducted in diverse population groups ranging from Finnish lumberjacks to Masai tribesmen in Africa, from Israeli kibbutz workers to longshoremen in San Francisco. All have had similar results: regular vigorous activity seems to be protective. One of the most instructive studies is a recent one involving 17,000 alumni of Harvard University who entered college between 1916 and 1950. A group of researchers headed by Dr R. Paffenbarger of Stanford University in California followed all the subjects until heart attack, death or conclusion of the study and recorded their level of physical activity throughout their lives.

The results of this study are highly relevant to people who wish to reduce their risk of coronary heart disease. Men who had a high physical activity level, namely participation in regular aerobic exercise, had a 26 per cent reduction in heart attack risk and this protection was valid for all age groups between 35 and 74. Importantly, the benefits of exercise applied only if one kept on exercising. Men who had been top athletes in their college years but who became sedentary in later life had the same heart attack risk as their classmates who had always been inactive. However, men who adopted an active lifestyle later in life still got the protective benefits.

The message from this research is highly optimistic for the sedentary millions who think they are over the hill. Even if you don't start an exercise programme until midlife you can still get considerable benefits. It's not too late to get fit.

WHAT IS FITNESS?

People have different conceptions of fitness. To some, it is represented by the thin body of a model. To others, it is reflected in the huge defined muscles of a body builder or in the lean frail appearance of a marathon runner. In fact, there is no precise definition of fitness. Perhaps it can best be described as a state of physical well-being derived from a balance between several well-developed body systems. Total fitness requires the following: 1) adequate muscle strength and endurance; 2) a favourable amount of body fat and muscle development; 3) reasonable joint flexibility; and 4) an efficient cardiovascular system.

Muscle strength is defined by the capacity to overcome maximum resistance in one repetition. Strength is specific to the muscle or muscle group involved. For example, an evaluation of your upper body strength would include a measurement of how much weight you could lift in one repetition of the bench press. Muscle endurance is the ability of a muscle or a muscle group to perform repeated contractions against resistance. Most of us have fairly good endurance of the arm and leg muscles just from everyday activities. Endurance of the abdominal muscles is a problem for most people, so sit-up type exercises often need to be included in a fitness programme.

There is an appropriate and desirable ratio of body fat and muscle to total body weight in men and women. For many people being overfat is obvious because the excess is stored visibly in the hips, abdomen and buttocks. Yet even people who appear thin can be overfat due to excess fat and too little muscle. Body composition is affected by diet and exercise. A programme of regular exercise coupled with a calorie-controlled diet will decrease fat weight and increase muscle mass. While these changes don't occur overnight, within a few weeks of starting a programme of healthy eating and increased physical activity you can expect to notice pleasant changes in your physical appearance.

Flexibility refers to the range of possible movement about a joint or group of joints. Most non-exercisers have poor flexibility especially in the lower back and hamstring muscles. In fact, the combination of poor lower back flexibility and weak abdominal muscles is the most common cause of low back pain, a problem that plagues millions of people.

Cardiovascular endurance is the ability to perform relatively vigorous exercise without undue fatigue and to recover rapidly once exercise has stopped. Cardiovascular endurance is the most essential component of total fitness because it relates positively to the efficiency of the heart, lungs and circulation. Also, as cardiovascular endurance improves, levels of good cholesterol rise.

Activities that are vigorous and continuous are called aerobic exercises. These include brisk walking, jogging, cycling, swimming, aerobic dancing and cross-country skiing. Stop-and-go kinds of exercise such as tennis, bowling, golf and cricket are not aerobic; they do not promote cardiovascular endurance.

HOW AEROBICALLY FIT ARE YOU?

Here is a quick test you can do at home to find out your

present level of cardiovascular endurance. This step test, developed by physiologist H.J. Montoye, measures aerobic fitness by determining how quickly your heart rate slows down after three minutes of exercise.

1. Find a bench eight inches in height, or use the bottom stair of a staircase if it is eight inches high.
2. Step on and off the bench or stair every five seconds. Keep this cadence up for exactly three minutes.
3. When your finish, rest for thirty seconds, then take your pulse for thirty seconds and note the number of beats you count. (You can easily find your pulse at the side of your neck behind the 'Adam's apple' or at the wrist on the thumb side. Use your fingers to count, not your thumb, since this has a pulse of its own.)
4. Compare your score with the step test classification in the table below. Anyone scoring below the 'good' category would benefit from starting an aerobic fitness programme.

HOW TO START AN AEROBIC FITNESS PROGRAMME

First of all, it is important to choose activities that are suitable for your interests and convenient for your schedule. You may love swimming but if it is difficult to make it to the pool you should not rely on this form of exercise. Activities should be self-paced. You should be able to start slowly and gradually work up to your target level. Many will choose to exercise on their own but group activities such as aerobic classes are fine. You can pace yourself rather than try to keep up with other class members. Here is a list of potential activities to choose from:

Brisk walking
Combination of walking and jogging

STEP TEST CLASSIFICATIONS. Based on 30-second recovery heart rate for men and women.*

Classification	Age			
	20–29	30–39	40–49	50 & Older
	Number of Beats			
Men				
Outstanding	34–36	35–38	37–39	37–40
Very Good	37–40	39–40	40–42	41–43
Good	41–42	42–43	43–44	44–45
Fair	43–47	44–47	45–49	46–49
Low	48–51	48–51	50–53	50–53
Poor	52–59	52–59	54–60	54–62
Women				
Outstanding	39–42	39–42	41–43	41–44
Very Good	43–44	43–45	44–45	45–47
Good	45–46	46–47	46–47	48–49
Fair	47–52	48–53	48–54	50–55
Low	53–56	54–56	55–57	56–58
Poor	57–66	57–66	58–67	59–66

* Thirty-second heart rate is counted beginning 30 seconds after exercise stops. Based on information in H.J. Montoye, *Physical Activity and Health: An Epidemiologic Study of an Entire Community* (Englewood Cliffs, N.J.: Prentice-Hall, 1975).

Jogging outdoors or on a treadmill
Cycling outdoors
Stationary cycling indoors
Aerobics class
Aerobics tape at home
Rowing machine
Swimming
Skipping
Jumping on a mini-trampoline
Racquet sport – where movement is continuous

You should pick the most pleasant environment possible to perform your activities. If you choose an outdoor activity find an attractive circuit around your neighbourhood or a local park. If it's indoor exercise, listen to music, watch your favourite TV show, or prop a book on the handlebars of a stationary bicycle. Keep exercise sessions varied to prevent monotony. Change walking routines, exercise indoors one day, outdoors another, mix different physical activities within the same session. Decide on the most convenient time of the day to exercise. There is no fixed rule, though we have found that keeping to a regular schedule tends to increase adherence to a programme.

Once you've picked the exercise that suits you, remember that developing and maintaining aerobic fitness requires the FIT principle – Frequency, Intensity and Time.

Frequency – You should exercise at least three times a week.

Intensity – During exercise, your heart rate should increase to a so-called target zone. The target zone is anywhere between 70 and 90 per cent of your age-predicted maximum heart rate. Refer to the chart below to help you find your target sone. For example, if you are 40 years old your target zone is 126–162 beats per minute.

Time – The exercise you perform must be continuous and last for at least twenty minutes.

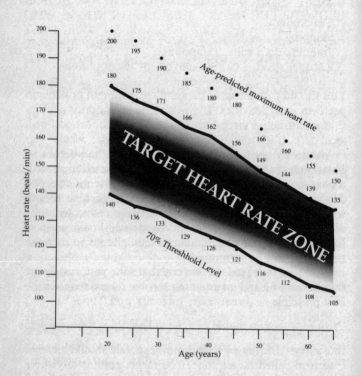

Guide to target heart rate

Before you begin, please pay attention to this medical note of caution:

INDIVIDUALS WITH KNOWN OR SUSPECTED HEART DISEASE SUCH AS THOSE WITH ANGINA (CHEST PAIN DUE TO LIMITATION OF BLOOD FLOW TO THE HEART MUSCLE) OR THOSE WHO HAVE HAD A HEART ATTACK IN THE PAST SHOULD EMBARK ON AN EXERCISE PROGRAMME ONLY AFTER CAREFUL CONSULTATION WITH THEIR DOCTOR.

IN ADDITION, ALL ADULTS OVER THE AGE OF FORTY CONTEMPLATING AN EXERCISE PRO-GRAMME SHOULD HAVE A COMPLETE SCREEN-ING MEDICAL EXAM.

We strongly believe that the best exercise for people who have been sedentary for a long time is brisk walking. It is a pastime that does not put great stress on your muscles, joints and heart but can offer substantial aerobic benefit to people who are starting off relatively unfit. Indeed a recent study conducted in Loughborough University in Leicestershire showed that middle-aged women who participated in a programme of brisk walking for about one hour per week for one year were able to significantly raise their levels of HDL, or good cholesterol, compared to their non-exercising counterparts.

When you have participated in an aerobic exercise programme for a while, you will experience something called 'the training effect'. Aerobic exercise places greater than normal demands on the cardiovascular system. In turn, the system adapts to these demands and becomes stronger and more efficient. The lungs are able to take in more air with each breath. The heart contracts more forcefully and efficiently and the heart rate at rest decreases. Muscles are able to extract more oxygen from the blood stream and blood vessels may decrease in diameter. You can measure the training effect by performing the three-minute step test at the beginning of your exercise programme and again every few weeks as you progress.

A TOTAL EXERCISE PROGRAMME

We recommend that you begin your exercise programme when you start the Basic dietary plan for cholesterol-lowering. That way you will be launching a two-pronged attack on cholesterol. Try to space your three weekly exercises sessions evenly. A Monday–Wednesday–Friday or Tuesday–Thursday–Saturday pattern suits most people.

Your total exercise programme will have the following structure:

ACTIVITY	DURATION
Warm-up	5 minutes
Aerobic Exercise Period	at least 20 minutes
Cool-down	5 minutes
Flexibility and Strengthening	5 minutes

The Warm-Up Phase

All sessions of aerobic exercise should start with an adequate warm-up. The warm-up should last about five minutes and will prepare your exercising muscles for the more vigorous activity to come. If done properly it will decrease the risk of muscle injury and post-exercise soreness.

During the warm-up you should gradually work up to your target heart-rate zone. Your goal should be to increase your heart rate slowly and steadily and progressively warm your muscles and joints. Most exercise sessions do not require any special kinds of warm-up activities. All you need to do is start your chosen exercise slowly and rhythmically. If you plan a brisk walk, start with a slow walk. If you are bicycling in the park, start slowly in low gear. Most good aerobic classes and videotapes have a warm-up phase included in the work-out. After five minutes increase your level of exertion until you have entered your target heart-rate zone. If you intend to exercise in cold weather, light stretching and limbering before you start is desirable to prevent muscle injury.

The Aerobic Exercise Period

The list of exercises we provided earlier is not all-inclusive. Any activity that continuously elevates your heart rate into the target zone qualifies as aerobic. If you have not exercised for a long time, even gentle exertion will get you into the target zone rapidly. Start your first few exercise sessions very slowly to avoid injury and excessive fatigue. In the early days of your exercise programme, aim to stay in the lower end of your target zone – the 70 per cent level. You should not be so breathless during exercise that you are unable to carry on a conversation. Later on, aim for the middle to high end of the target zone. Within a few days you will notice that it requires a quicker pace or greater intensity of effort to reach your target zone. This is an important and sure sign of the training effect. When it occurs you will know that your programme is achieving its goals – improved performance of the cardiovascular system and exercising muscles.

After a week or so you may feel so well that you are tempted to push yourself harder. Resist the temptation and keep yourself near the middle of your target zone. There is no reason to exercise to the point of exhaustion. With aerobic exercise you can get tremendous gain in the absence of pain. It is far better to extend your exercise period beyond twenty minutes than to subject your body to maximum exertion.

It is certainly permissible to mix two or more activities into the same exercise session. For example, spend ten minutes on a stationary bicycle followed by ten minutes working out with a videotape. Make sure that the transition from one activity to another is fairly rapid since your heart rate should remain continuously in the target zone for the entire exercise period.

If you miss a week or more of your programme; don't expect to perform at the same intensity as you left off. The training effect works both ways.

The Cool-Down

The cool-down is designed to return your body gradually and safely to resting conditions. It prevents post-exercise dizziness or light-headedness. Cool-down activities should last about five minutes. They are simply a slow, rhythmical extension of your aerobic exercise routine. If you've been swimming, walk back and forth in the shallow end of the pool. If you've been cycling, finish up a mile or so from home and pedal back slowly and easily. If you've been jogging, finish by walking for a quarter of a mile. Most aerobic videotapes and classes have a built-in cool-down. When you have completed the cool-down it is a good idea to perform the flexibility and strengthening exercises listed below.

Flexibility and Strengthening Exercises

If you are seriously interested in greatly improving your flexibility and muscle strength then you may wish to start a dedicated programme to do so. A description of such programmes is beyond the scope of this book but there are many excellent speciality books available and you can seek advice and guidance at a health club or sports centre.

Nevertheless, you can achieve noticeable improvement in your flexibility and strength by spending five minutes each exercise session on the following seven exercises. They work the problem areas for most people: the abdomen, lower back, upper arms, thighs and calves.

If you are overweight you will almost certainly lose weight with your cholesterol-control diet and aerobic exercise programme. Dieters are often disappointed that following weight loss their bodies seem to lack tone. Loose abdominal muscles and flabby upper arms certainly detract from physical appearance. It is desirable to work on these problem areas while dieting, not after. The goal is to take typically neglected muscle groups and make them supple and firm so you look your best when the diet is over.

Perform the flexibility and strengthening exercises in the following order:

Abdominal curl-up
Elbow–knee crunch
Lower back stretch
Push-ups
Upper back and side stretch
Hamstring stretch
Calf stretch

Abdominal Curl-up

Benefits. Tones and strengthens the upper abdominal area. Stronger abdominal muscles improve posture and appearance and protect the back from injury.

Starting Positions. Lie on your back with the knees bent and feet flat on floor. Cross arms in front of the chest placing hands near each shoulder.

Action. Keeping your chin close to your chest, curl up, bringing shoulders and upper back to about thirty degrees off the floor. Pause for one second then lower yourself back to the floor slowly. Keep your chin close to the chest at all times and do not let your head touch the floor between repetitions. The first few times you do this exercise try ten repetitions and see how it feels. Eventually aim to do twenty to thirty at a slow to medium speed.

Points. Do not try to curl up all the way. Curling up further may put strain on your lower back and will not further strengthen your abdominal muscles. When you have finished the abdominal curl-ups go straight into the elbow—knee crunches.

Elbow—Knee Crunch

Benefits. Tones and strengthens upper and lower abdominal muscles.

Starting Position. Lie on your back with knees bent and head flat on floor. Place hands behind head.

Action. Lift shoulders off the floor as in the curl-up and bring both feet off the floor at the same time. Move your elbows forward and touch the top of the knees. Lower shoulders and feet back to the floor as in the starting position.

Points. Concentrate on keeping the lower back on the floor at all times. Avoid pulling on your neck with your hands as you raise your upper body. Start with about ten elbow—knee crunches and work up to twenty to thirty slow repetitions per session.

Lower Back Stretch

Benefits. Stretches out the muscles of the lower back to prevent or relieve low back pain and improve posture.

Starting Position. Lie on your back on the floor.

Action. Place hands directly behind the right knee and bring it gently towards your chest until you feel a comfortable stretch. Hold this stretch for thirty seconds then repeat with the left leg. Stretch each leg twice.

Points. If you suffer from back stiffness it is a good idea to do the lower back stretch after rising in the morning and after a long period of sitting or standing.

Push-ups

Benefits. Tones and strengthens the upper body, particularly the chest and back of arms.

Starting Position. Lie down facing the floor. Place hands with fingers spread apart, parallel to each other a little more than shoulder width apart. Curl toes to maintain a good grip with the floor. Raise your body so you are in a straight line from head to toe.

Full push-ups are too difficult for many women. Start with a modified version. Assume the same starting position as above but keep your knees and lower legs flat on the floor at all times.

Action. Lower your body straight down until you almost touch your chest to the floor, then smoothly push yourself straight up again to the starting position. Keep your head, back, hips and legs in one line at all times.

Points. Try to do about ten push-ups with perfect form initially. Eventually work up into twenty to thirty per session. If you want particularly to work on chest muscles place your hands wider apart. To concentrate on the back of your upper arms, keep your hands shoulder-width apart with elbows tucked in next to the sides of your body.

Upper Back and Side Stretch

Benefits. Stretches out upper body muscles. Reduces stiffness and tension in the neck and shoulders. Particularly good for people who sit at a desk all day.

Starting Position. Stand with your feet shoulder-width apart and knees slightly bent. Extend arms over your head and grasp hands.

Action. Stretch arms upwards, squeeze shoulder blades together and hold stretch for fifteen seconds. Relax and assume the same starting position. Stretch the body over to

177

the right side as far as is comfortable and hold for fifteen seconds. Return to the starting position and repeat side stretch to the left side, holding for fifteen seconds. Repeat each sequence once.

Hamstring Stretch

Benefits. Improve flexibility of the low back and the backs of legs. Increased flexibility of these areas, helps prevent low back and upper leg injuries and aids good posture.

Starting Position. Sit on floor with legs together and straight.

Action. Keeping your back straight, bend forward and reach out with your arms. Hold a comfortable stretch for thirty seconds then relax. Repeat this stretch once.

Points. Flex your knees slightly to prevent ligament strain.

Calf Stretch

Benefits. Stretches out the back of the lower legs. Helps prevent muscle pulls and soreness.

Starting Position. Stand about arm's length from a wall. Step forward with your light leg and backward with your left leg. Toes should point straight ahead.

Action. Lean forward resting forearms and elbows against the wall. Move your hips forward until you feel a comfortable stretch in the back of your left leg. Concentrate on pressing your left heel 'into' the floor. Hold this stretch for thirty seconds. Relax, change the position of your legs then stretch your right leg for thirty seconds. Stretch each leg one more time.

Points. To prevent knee strains, do not bounce while stretching. Calf stretches are also useful before a long walk or jog, especially in cool weather.

Special Considerations for Women

Not too long ago it was considered neither safe − or ladylike for a woman to engage in vigorous exercise. Myths existed warning women of the potential for bodily harm.

Times have changed and the myths have been debunked. Women now participate freely in vigorous exercise and competitive athletics without deleterious effects. Many questions regarding women and exercise are nevertheless frequently asked. These questions concern reproduction, pregnancy and the risk of injury to reproductive organs.

Exercise does not appear to have a significant effect on reproductive function. Only when exercise is accompanied by a considerable reduction in the proportion of body fat to muscle (marathon runners or professional ballerinas, for example) is there a risk that a woman will stop her monthly cycle. This is not a serious problem but it may make the woman temporarily unable to conceive a child. Normal reproductive cycles invariably resume when the heavy activity is reduced or there is some weight gain. Pregnancy need not be a hindrance to an exercise programme. Women who have been exercising regularly before pregnancy can continue to do so while pregnant with the knowledge of their doctor. It is not wise, however, for an inactive woman to initiate a vigorous exercise programme at the onset of pregnancy or during pregnancy.

Jogging and other vigorous exercises do not promote injury to the breasts or internal reproductive organs. Full-figured women who wish to jog may purchase a special runner's bra for extra comfort and support. Jogging without a special bra will not cause the breasts to sag.

Finally, regular participation in strenuous exercise does not make a woman look masculine. Bulging muscles and huge shoulders will not develop because female hormones inhibit marked enlargement of muscle tissue. Exercise will, however, tone the muscles and accentuate the feminine figure.

10

RECIPES FOR A
LOW-FAT LIFESTYLE

Some people have the mistaken belief that low-fat cooking
produces listless, uninteresting, unappetizing dishes. It is
time to put that myth to rest. We firmly believe that low-
fat cooking methods can be used to create meals every bit
as satisfying as their high-fat counterparts and even more
tasty. Heavy use of fats and oils often masks the flavours
of foods whereas lighter cooking styles unleash the natural
wonders of the ingredients.

We present here numerous low-fat recipes from soups and
starters to desserts − and everything in between. We have
placed an emphasis on everyday, traditional kinds of dishes
rather than exotic, impractical items. We encourage you to
use these recipes in two ways. First, try them out on yourself
and your family to see how delicious low-fat cooking can
be. To help you incorporate these recipes into the Basic plan
for cholesterol reduction, the number of grams of saturated
fat per serving is given. Second, read through a number of
recipes, even if you don't prepare them, to get ideas how
to modify your own family recipes to make them lower in
fat and healthier.

SOUPS AND STARTERS

Carrot and Lentil Soup

6 whole green cardamoms
250g/8oz carrot, coarsely grated
125g/4oz onion, thinly sliced
50g/2oz sunflower margarine
50g/2oz split red lentils
1½ litres/ 2½ pints chicken stock
1 rasher lean back bacon
salt and freshly ground pepper to taste
carrots, lime or cucumber to garnish

1. Split the cardamoms, remove the seeds and finely crush
   with a rolling pin. Sauté together the carrot, cardamom
   and onion in the margarine for 4 to 5 minutes. Stir in
   the lentils and cook for a further 1 minute.
2. Add the stock and the bacon. Bring to the boil, cover
   and simmer gently for about 20 minutes or until the lentils
   are tender.
3. Remove the bacon and season with a little salt and pepper.
4. Garnish with small shapes of thinly sliced carrots and lime
   rind or cucumber skin.

Serves 6
GRAMS OF SATURATED FAT PER SERVING: 2.0

This cold, zesty soup makes an excellent starter during the
warmer months. Serve with crusty french bread or
homemade croutons.

Gazpacho

675g/1½ pounds ripe tomatoes, skinned, seeded and
chopped

2 stalks celery, finely chopped
½ red onion, finely chopped
2 spring onions, chopped
½ green pepper, chopped
4 inch piece of cucumber peeled and diced into ¼ inch cubes
2 cloves garlic, crushed
2 tablespoons chopped parsley leaves
2 tablespoons chopped fresh coriander
175ml/6fl oz tomato juice
1 tablespoon olive oil
1 tablespoon red wine vinegar
1 tablespoon fresh lime juice
salt and freshly ground pepper to taste
a few drops of tabasco sauce (optional)

1. Combine all ingredients in a mixing bowl. Taste to check the seasoning.
2. Cover the bowl with foil and chill thoroughly.

Serves 6
GRAMS OF SATURATED FAT PER SERVING: 0.5

This is a quick and delicious version of a famous, hearty soup from Italy.

Pasta Fagioli

2 rashers rindless, back bacon cut into small pieces
1 small onion, finely chopped
1 large clove of garlic, finely chopped
1 stalk of celery, chopped
1 tablespoon olive oil
1 400g/14oz-can chopped tomatoes
1 tablespoon tomato purée
1.1 litres/2 pints hot water
425g/15oz can kidney beans or chick peas, undrained

175g/6oz wholewheat macaroni or broken-up spaghetti
salt and freshly ground black pepper to taste
2 tablespoons Parmesan cheese

1. Sauté the bacon, onion, garlic and celery in the olive oil in a large saucepan or soup pot until golden.
2. Add the tomatoes, purée, hot water and beans or chick peas. Bring to the boil then add the macaroni.
3. Simmer uncovered for about 45 minutes, adding a little more water if necessary. When the soup is done crush some of the beans against the side of the pot with a wooden spoon.
4. Season with salt and pepper. Serve the soup with a sprinkling of Parmesan cheese.

Serves 6
GRAMS OF SATURATED FAT PER SERVING: 1.5

A tasty, filling soup that will make a satisfying lunch or supper dish. For a complete meal serve with warm bread rolls and a green salad.

Chicken and Barley Soup

2 chicken quarters, skinned, about 700g/1½lb total weight
salt and freshly ground black pepper to taste
slices of carrot, onion, 4 black peppercorns and 1 bay leaf for flavouring
1 litre/2 pints cold water
125g/4oz pearl barley
3 tablespoons chopped fresh parsley (or chopped, fresh coriander)
1 teaspoon chopped fresh thyme
3 tablespoons cornflour
pinch ground tumeric
150ml/¼ pint natural yoghurt

1. Place the chicken quarters in a large saucepan with a little salt and pepper, carrot, onion, peppercorns, bay leaf and water. Bring to the boil. Cover and simmer for about 40 minutes or until the chicken is cooked (test with skewer after 40 minutes). Remove the chicken and cool. Strain and reserve the chicken stock.
2. Cook the pearl barley in boiling water for about one hour, or until just tender. Drain well. Remove all the chicken flesh from the quarters and cut into bite-size pieces. Skim any fat from the surface of the reserved stock. Place in saucepan with reserved stock, the barley, parsley (or coriander) and thyme.
3. Mix the cornflour and the tumeric to a smooth paste with 6 tablespoons water. Stir into the chicken mixture. Bring to the boil and simmer for 10 minutes, stirring all the time. Remove from heat and whisk in yoghurt. Correct seasoning. Reheat gently without boiling. Garnish with extra chopped parsley.

Serves 4
GRAMS OF SATURATED FAT PER SERVING: 2.0

Although avocados are high in fat as far as fruits are concerned, you can turn them into fairly low-fat starters.

Avocado Cheese

1 very ripe avocado pear
1 tablespoon lemon juice
1 clove garlic, crushed
¼ onion grated
50g/2oz low-fat soft cheese or quark
salt and freshly ground pepper to taste
1 tomato, skinned, seeded and finely chopped

1. Peel the avocado, halve and remove the stone. Mash with

the lemon juice until smooth. Beat in the garlic, onion, cheese and a little salt and pepper. Cover and chill in refrigerator.

2. Sprinkle avocado cheese with chopped tomato and serve with wholemeal melba toast or fingers of warm pitta bread.

Serves 6
GRAMS OF SATURATED FAT PER SERVING: 1.0

Avocado with Grapes

2 heads chicory
3 bunches watercress, trimmed
175g/6oz bean sprouts
2 firm ripe avocados
½ cucumber, sliced
175g/6oz seedless green grapes, halved
Dressing
75ml/3fl oz sunflower oil
2 tablespoons white wine vinegar
1 clove garlic, crushed
2 tablespoons natural yoghurt
salt and freshly ground black pepper to taste

1. Tear the chicory into bite-size pieces. Wash, drain and pat dry on absorbent kitchen paper. Mix the chicory with the watercress and bean sprouts. Mix together and refrigerate in a large polythene bag.

2. To make the dressing, whisk together the oil, vinegar, garlic and yoghurt. Season with a little salt and pepper.

3. When ready to serve, peel, halve and stone the avocados and thickly slice into the dressing. Reserve a few slices for garnish.

4. Toss all remaining ingredients together and serve immediately, garnished with the reserved avocado.

Serves 6
GRAMS OF SATURATED FAT PER SERVING: 3.0

Smoked Mackerel Pâté

200g/7oz smoked mackerel, skinned, boned and flaked
125g/4oz low-fat soft cheese or quark
1 lemon
nutmeg
salt and freshly ground black pepper
parsley
cayenne pepper

1. Place fish, cheese and juice from half of the lemon in liquidizer or food processor. Blend until smooth. Transfer mixture to a bowl and season with a pinch of nutmeg, salt and freshly ground pepper.
2. Pack into a mould or serving bowl and chill for several hours before serving.
3. Sprinkle top of pâté with a little cayenne pepper and garnish with parsley and lemon wedges cut from remaining half.

Serves 8
GRAMS OF SATURATED FAT PER SERVING: 1.5

Hummus (dip or sandwich filling)

8oz dried chick peas, soaked and cooked, or
2 400g/14oz cans of cooked chick peas
2 tablespoons tahini (sesame paste)
2 cloves garlic, crushed
juice of 1 lemon
salt to taste
parsley, lemon wedges and paprika to garnish

1. Drain chick peas. Reserve liquid. In liquidizer or food processor, purée the chick peas with the tahini, garlic and lemon juice. Add enough of the chick pea liquid to the mixture to make a creamy consistency. Add salt to taste.
2. Divide mixture onto 4 serving plates and garnish with parsley, lemon wedges and paprika. If hummus is for sandwich filling, place in covered bowl and refrigerate until ready for use.

Serves 4
GRAMS OF SATURATED FAT PER SERVING: 1.0

Tapenade is an extremely robust tuna and olive dip or spread from the heart of Provence.

Tapenade

75g/3oz black olives
25g/1oz green olives
1-2 cloves garlic, crushed
1 tablespoon capers, drained
4 anchovy fillets
100g/3½oz tuna in brine, drained
1 bunch of fresh basil or parsley or both
juice of half a lemon
1 tablespoon olive oil

1. Combine all ingredients into liquidizer or food processor. Blend mixture until smooth.
2. Transfer mixture to a bowl. Cover and refrigerate until ready to use.
3. Serve the tapenade with fingers of wholemeal toast or thin it slightly and serve as a dip with a selection of fresh raw vegetables.

Serves 6
GRAMS OF SATURATED FAT PER SERVING: 1.0

This quick and easy dip is ideal for 'younger' taste-buds. Try it for children's parties.

Peanut Dip

125g/4oz fromage frais or low-fat soft cheese
2 tablespoons peanut butter, smooth or crunchy
1 clove garlic, crushed
freshly ground black pepper

1. Place the cheese in a bowl and mix in the peanut butter, garlic and pepper. Cover and refrigerate until ready to use.
2. Serve with a selection of fresh raw vegetables.

Optional Extras Try adding one of the following to the peanut—cheese mixture: 2 tablespoons mango chutney *or* 2 tablespoons chopped fresh chives and 1 tablespoon chopped cucumber

Serves 4
GRAMS OF SATURATED FAT PER SERVING: 2.5

Traditionally prepared garlic bread is incredibly high in saturated fat. This lighter version tastes just as good.

Hot Garlic-Cheese Bread

1 large white or wholemeal French loaf
3—4 garlic cloves, crushed
125g/4oz sunflower margarine
2 tablespoons grated Parmesan cheese

1. Preheat oven (200°C/400°F, Gas Mark 6)
2. Cut the French loaf into 8 slices without cutting all the

way through the bread. The bread should just hold together at the base.

3. Beat together the margarine, garlic and Parmesan cheese. Spread this mixture on both sides of the slices of bread.
4. Press bread back into its original loaf-shape. Wrap the loaf in foil and bake for 20 minutes.

Serves 8
GRAMS OF SATURATED FAT PER SERVING: 3.5

BREAKFAST DISHES

The traditional British breakfast is exceedingly high in fat and cholesterol. It is far better to start the day with a healthy, filling low-fat breakfast.

Breakfast is also a good time to get more fibre into your diet. These oat bran muffins also make terrific between-meal snacks instead of your usual doughnut, Danish pastry or chocolate bar.

Banana-Oat Bran Muffins

3 ripe bananas
75ml/3fl oz sunflower oil
2 eggs
2 tablespoons clear honey
175g/6oz plain flour
2 teaspoons baking powder
1 teaspoon ground cinnamon
175g/6oz oat bran

1. Preheat oven to 200°C/400°F/Gas Mark 6.
2. In large bowl, beat together bananas, oil, eggs and honey.
3. Sift flour, baking powder and cinnamon into the banana mixture. Add bran and fold in dry ingredients until just blended.
4. Put paper cases into patty tins. Spoon mixture into each case to at least two-thirds full.
4. Bake muffins just above the centre of oven for 15 to 20 minutes or until the muffins are golden and firm to the touch.

Makes 1 dozen
GRAMS OF SATURATED FAT PER MUFFIN: 1.0

Plain Oat Muffins

4 tablespoons sunflower oil
125g/4oz plain wholemeal flour
2 teaspoons baking powder
75g/3oz medium oatmeal
1 tablespoon wheatgerm
40g/1½oz soft brown sugar
1 egg
300ml/½ pint skimmed milk

1. Preheat oven to 200°C/400°F/Gas Mark 6.
2. Lightly brush 12 deep bun tins with a little of the oil.
3. Place all the dry ingredients in a bowl. Whisk together the egg, milk and remaining oil. Add to the dry ingredients until just blended – don't over beat.
4. Divide the mixture between the bun tins and bake for 25 to 30 minutes.

Makes 1 dozen
GRAMS OF SATURATED FAT PER MUFFIN: 0.5

4-Way American Pancakes

50g/2oz plain flour
50g/2oz whole wheat flour
2 teaspoons baking powder
pinch of salt
1 egg
150ml/¼ pint skimmed milk
2 tablespoons sunflower oil
4 teaspoons sunflower margarine
4 teaspoons honey or 4 tablespoons maple syrup

1. About 30 minutes before serving, sift flours, baking powder, and salt into mixing bowl. (Replace bran left in

sieve.) Make a well in the centre. Add the egg, milk and one tablespoon of the oil. Beat with a fork until pancake batter is smooth.

2. Heat a little of the remaining oil in frying pan on moderately high heat. When oil is very hot, drop about one tablespoon of batter on to pan to make one pancake. (Do three or four at a time.) Turn pancakes when bottoms are brown. Repeat using remaining batter and oil.
Note: add a little more milk if batter does not spread easily.

3. Serve hot with margarine and honey or maple syrup.

Variations

Banana Pancakes: just before cooking, mash one ripe banana into batter and blend well.

Cinnamon Raisin Pancakes: add 1 teaspoon cinnamon to dry ingredients and stir in 25g/1oz raisins into the finished batter.

Oat Bran Pancakes: substitute 50g/2oz oat bran for the wholemeal flour. Add 75ml/3fl oz more milk.

Serves 4 (Makes about 12 pancakes)
GRAMS OF SATURATED FAT PER SERVING: 3.0

Cinnamon French Toast

2 egg whites
2 tablespoons skimmed milk
2–3 drops vanilla essence
½ teaspoon cinnamon
4 one-inch slices day-old French bread or wholewheat bread
2 teaspoons margarine

1. Mix egg whites in shallow dish with milk, vanilla and cinnamon.
2. Soak both sides of the bread in mixture.
3. Heat margarine in large frying pan. Add soaked bread slices and cook until golden on both sides.

Serves 4
GRAMS OF SATURATED FAT PER SERVING: 0.5

As an alternative to butter or syrup, serve this light fluffy spread with muffins, pancakes and French toast.

Citrus Spread

125g/4oz sunflower margarine
125g/4oz low-fat soft cheese or quark
grated rind of 1 lemon
grated rind of 1 orange or grapefruit
pinch soft brown sugar

1. Beat together all the ingredients until very smooth.
2. Spoon into a small serving dish. Cover and chill well.

Serves 8
GRAMS OF SATURATED FAT PER SERVING: 3.5

Fruit Muesli

250g/8oz rolled oats
75g/3oz wholewheat flakes or barley flakes
25g/1oz whole bran-type cereal
2 tablespoons oat bran
25g/1oz toasted hazelnuts or almonds, skinned and chopped
75g/3oz sunflower seeds
300g/10oz mixed dried fruit (e.g. sultanas, chopped dried apricots, chopped dried apple rings)

1. Mix together all the ingredients and store in an airtight container. The mixture can remain fresh for up to six weeks. Serve with skimmed milk or natural yoghurt.

Serves 8
GRAMS OF SATURATED FAT PER SERVING: Trace

Mushroom Kedgeree

125g/4oz long-grain brown rice
250g/8oz smoked haddock fillet, skinned
25g/1oz sunflower margarine
50g/2oz button mushrooms, thinly sliced
1 egg, hard-boiled and chopped or 2 chopped egg whites
freshly ground black pepper
parsley and lemon to garnish

1. Cook the rice in plenty of boiling water for about 35 minutes or until just tender. Drain well.
2. Place haddock fillet in a saucepan. Cover with cold water. Bring to the boil and simmer for 10 to 15 minutes. Drain, reserving ¼ pint of the fish liquid. Skin and flake the fish.
3. Melt the margarine in a large frying pan. Add the mushrooms and sauté for about 5 minutes. Stir in the rice and the reserved fish liquid. Cook, stirring for a further 3 to 4 minutes. Stir in the chopped egg or egg whites and season with black pepper.
4. Garnish with fresh parsley and lemon wedges.

Serves 4
GRAMS OF SATURATED FAT PER SERVING: 2.0

You can drink this delicious, high-fibre breakfast. It is guaranteed to sustain you all morning so it is good for dieters and those in a hurry.

Banana Oat Bran Shake

2 tablespoons oatbran
1 banana
225ml/8fl oz skimmed milk
1–2 teaspoons honey (optional)

Put all the ingredients into a blender or food processor with
2 to 3 ice cubes. Blend for 10 to 15 seconds.

Serves 1
GRAMS OF SATURATED FAT PER SERVING: Trace

MEAT, POULTRY AND GAME

You can make this hearty, substantial dish in advance and freeze it for future use. Any kind of canned or dried beans can be substituted for butter beans.

Beef and Bean Bake

50g/2oz sunflower margarine
1 onion, chopped
250g/8oz extra lean minced beef
65g/2½oz flour
200ml/7fl oz beef stock
freshly ground black pepper
250g/8oz tomatoes, skinned and chopped
400g/14oz-can butter beans or 125g/4oz dried beans soaked and cooked
1 tablespoon tomato purée
¼ teaspoon oregano
¼ teaspoon dried basil
pinch of English mustard powder
300ml/½ pint skimmed milk
50g/2oz Mozzarella cheese, grated

1. Preheat oven to 200°C/400°F/Gas Mark 6.
2. Melt 25g/1oz margarine in a medium saucepan. Stir in the onion and sauté for 3 or 4 minutes until golden. Add the minced beef and cook, stirring over a high heat for 3 or 4 minutes. Pour off any excess fat. Stir in 40g/1½oz flour, the stock and pepper. Bring to the boil and cook, uncovered, for 2 or 3 minutes. Place in a 1.7-litre/3-pint ovenproof dish.
3. Add the tomatoes, drained beans, tomato purée and herbs to the saucepan. Simmer uncovered, for 2 or 3 minutes or until quite thick. Spoon over the meat mixture.
4. Melt the remaining margarine in a saucepan. Stir in the

remaining flour and mustard powder. Cook stirring for 1 or 2 minutes, then gradually add the milk. Bring to the boil and simmer until thickened. Remove from heat, beat in half the cheese and pour over the bean mixture.
5. Sprinkle with the remaining cheese and bake in oven for about 25 or 30 minutes until golden brown.

Serves 4
GRAMS OF SATURATED FAT PER SERVING: 5.0

Winter beef casserole tastes particularly good if made the day before. Serve with boiled parsleyed potatoes.

Winter Beef Casserole

1 tablespoon sunflower oil
2 leeks, sliced
4 carrots, sliced
1 peeled and chopped 350g/12oz turnip
125g/4oz button mushrooms, sliced
500g/1lb lean braising steak, trimmed and cut into strips
125g/4oz pearl barley
600ml/1 pint beef stock
300ml/½ pint stout or light ale
3 tablespoons chopped fresh parsley or watercress
salt and freshly ground black pepper to taste

1. Heat the oil in a large frying pan. Add the leeks, carrots, turnip and mushrooms. Cook for 2 to 3 minutes, stirring. Place the vegetables in a casserole with a slotted spoon.
2. Add the meat to the frying pan; fry quickly to brown evenly. Stir in the barley, stock, stout or light ale, parsley or watercress and a little salt and pepper. Bring to the boil.
3. Pour the meat mixture into the casserole and stir well.

Cover and cook in oven for 1½ to 2 hours or until the meat is tender. Serve garnished with watercress sprigs.

Serves 4
GRAMS OF SATURATED FAT PER SERVING: 3.5

This a special spicy version of ordinary beef stew. It has a golden colour and a mild curry-flavour. Serve with rice and mango chutney.

Oriental Beef and Bean Stew

2 teaspoons fresh ginger root, grated, or 1 teaspoon ground ginger
1 teaspoon tumeric
1 teaspoon cumin
a little salt and freshly ground black pepper
350g/12oz lean chuck or braising steak cut into ½-inch cubes
1 tablespoon sunflower oil
1 onion, chopped
1 clove garlic, finely chopped
4 carrots, diced
4 stalks celery, diced
300ml/½ pint beef stock
400g/14oz-tin chopped tomatoes
175g/6oz mung or aduki beans, soaked and cooked

1. Combine ginger, tumeric, cumin, salt and pepper. Dredge the meat cubes in mixture.
2. Heat oil in large saucepan or flame-proof casserole and add the meat. Fry gently until light brown.
3. Add the onion, garlic, carrots and celery and cook for 5 minutes. Add stock, tomatoes and beans. Simmer covered for 1½ hours or until meat is tender.

Serves 4
GRAMS OF SATURATED FAT PER SERVING: 2.0

This authentic-tasting chilli should be made with the leanest mince. Serve with brown rice, French bread, green salad, raw chopped onion and natural yoghurt.

Chilli con Carne

1 tablespoon corn or sunflower oil
1 large onion, chopped
2 cloves garlic, finely chopped
1 green pepper, diced
350g/12oz lean mince
½ teaspoon salt
1 teaspoon oregano
2 teaspoons cumin
½ to 1 teaspoon chilli powder, depending on desired hotness
½ teaspoon freshly ground black pepper
2 teaspoons prepared mild or Dijon mustard
2 tablespoons tomato purée
400g/14oz-tin chopped tomatoes
400g/14oz cooked red kidney beans, drained

1. Heat oil in large frying pan or saucepan. Add onion, garlic and green pepper. Sauté for 5 minutes. Add the meat and lightly brown on high heat, stirring frequently.
2. Turn down the heat and stir in the seasonings, mustard and tomato purée.
3. Add the tomatoes, and kidney beans and simmer, uncovered, for 25 minutes until sauce is rich and thick. Taste and correct seasoning if necessary.

Serves 4
GRAMS OF SATURATED FAT PER SERVING 2.0

The cut of beef and cooking method can greatly influence the amount of saturated fat present in the meat. This recipe succeeds in producing a succulent, tasty roast, substantially lower in saturated fat (and calories). Serve with parsleyed potatoes and a selection of vegetables.

Roast Beef in Red Wine with Yorkshire Pudding

1½kg/3lb piece of rolled topside
1 clove garlic, halved
1 tablespoon flour
1 teaspoon English mustard powder
200ml/⅓ pint red wine
celery leaves to garnish

1. Preheat the oven to 220°C/425°F/Gas Mark 7.
2. Wipe the meat. Trim off any excess fat, leaving only a thin covering. Rub the joint with garlic. Mix together the mustard and flour and rub over beef. Set the joint on a rack over a roasting tin.
3. Place meat in oven for 15 minutes. Lower the heat to 190°C/375°F/Gas Mark 5 and roast for 1 hour for rare, 1¼ hours for well done. Halfway through the cooking time pour all the fat from the pan and pour the wine over the meat. Baste occasionally.
4. At the end of the cooking time, strain the pan juices to make the gravy. Garnish the beef with celery leaves.

Serves 6
GRAMS OF SATURATED FAT PER SERVING: 4.0

Yorkshire Pudding

125g/4oz plain or wholemeal flour, or half of each
a little salt
2 eggs

200ml/⅓ pint skimmed milk
75ml/3fl oz water
3 tablespoons sunflower oil

1. Place the flour and salt in a bowl. Make a well in the centre and add the eggs and half the liquid. Gradually whisk together to form a smooth batter. Stir in the remaining liquid.
2. Forty minutes before the meat is cooked raise the oven temperature to 220°C/425°F/Gas Mark 7. Place the joint lower in the oven. Put the oil in an oven proof dish, and heat on the top shelf for about 5 to 7 minutes until smoking hot. Quickly pour in the batter. Replace in the oven and cook for about 40 minutes or until risen and crisp.

Serves 6
GRAMS OF SATURATED FAT PER SERVING: 1.5

The simple pepper, treated with a little imagination, can be transformed into a delicious supper dish. These peppers are also good with other herbs such as parsley and coriander.

Eastern Peppers

4 mixed peppers (yellow, red, green)
2 tablespoons sunflower oil
1 large onion, chopped
1 clove garlic, crushed
1 tablespoon fresh mint
½ teaspoon cinnamon
½ teaspoon paprika
325g/12oz steak mince or leg of lamb, minced
175g/6oz tomatoes, skinned and chopped
175g/6oz long-grain white rice
125g/4oz raisins

6 tablespoons beef stock
50g/2oz walnut pieces chopped
600ml/1 pint water

1. Preheat oven to 190°C/375°F/Gas Mark 5.
2. Cut a thin slice from the stalk end of each pepper and reserve. Remove the seeds. Place side by side in a shallow, ovenproof dish.
3. Heat the oil in a saucepan and sauté the onion with the garlic, mint, cinnamon and paprika for 3 to 4 minutes. Add the minced beef or lamb and cook, stirring over a high heat until lightly browned. Carefully pour off the excess fat. Stir in the remaining ingredients, bring to the boil and simmer for 10 minutes until the rice is half-cooked and the liquids almost absorbed.
4. Fill the peppers with meat and rice mixture. Replace the reserved tops. Cover the dish loosely with the foil.
5. Bake in the oven for about 40 minutes. Serve immediately.

Serves 4
GRAMS OF SATURATED FAT PER SERVING: 3.0

Bulgar wheat is one of the quickest-cooking grains and makes a refreshing change from rice in this elegant, light marinated pork dish.

Pilaff of Pork

Marinade:
4 tablespoons natural yoghurt
2 teaspoons clear honey
grated rind and juice of 1 lime
2 fresh bay leaves

Pilaff:
350g/12oz pork tenderloin, trimmed and sliced

175g/6oz bulgar wheat
1 tablespoon sunflower oil
3 spring onions, chopped
125g/4oz mushrooms, sliced
1 yellow pepper, seeded and chopped
600ml/1 pint chicken stock
125g/4oz cooked broad beans
125g/4oz cooked green beans or peas
a little salt and freshly ground black pepper
fresh bay leaves to garnish

1. Mix together in a bowl, the yoghurt, honey, lime rind and juice and bay leaves. Add the pork and stir to coat evenly. Cover the bowl with cling film and leave overnight in a cool place.
2. Place the bulgar wheat on a piece of foil in a grill pan and toast under a moderate heat until golden brown.
3. Heat the oil in a saucepan, add the onion and mushrooms and pepper and cook for 2 to 3 minutes until tender. Stir in the wheat and stock, bring to the boil, cover and cook very gently for about 10 minutes until all the stock has been absorbed. Keep warm.
4. Add the broad beans and green beans or peas to the bulgar wheat mixture stirring well until evenly mixed. Season with a little salt and pepper.
5. Place the pork in the grill pan and cook under a moderate heat for 6 to 8 minutes, turning once.
6. Arrange the bulgar wheat pilaff on a warmed serving dish with the pork and garnish with fresh bay leaves.

Serves 4
GRAMS OF SATURATED FAT PER SERVING: 2.0

West Country Cobbler

1 tablespoon sunflower oil
500g/1lb lean pork tenderloin, thinly sliced

1 onion, sliced
1 cooking apple, peeled, cored and chopped
4 tomatoes, skinned and chopped
150ml/¼ pint pure unsweetened apple juice
a little salt and freshly ground pepper
Topping:
250g/8oz self-raising wholemeal flour
50g/2oz sunflower margarine
½ teaspoon dried sage
150ml/¼ pint natural yoghurt

1. Preheat the oven to 200°C/400°F/Gas Mark 6.
2. Heat the oil in a frying pan, add the pork and fry quickly until evenly coloured. Using a slotted spoon place the pork in a shallow ovenproof dish.
3. Add the onions and apple to the frying pan and cook for 2 minutes, then stir in the tomatoes, apple juice and a little salt and pepper. Bring to the boil and pour evenly over the pork.
4. Sieve the flour into a bowl, add the margarine and rub in finely until the mixture resembles breadcrumbs. Stir in the sage and yoghurt with a fork and mix lightly until the mixture forms a soft dough. Turn out on a floured surface and knead very lightly.
5. Roll out the dough to 1cm/½inch thickness and cut out into 15 5cm/2-inch rounds with a plain cutter. Arrange the scone rounds in an even overlapping circle around the edge of the dish. Bake in oven for 20 minutes or until the scones are well risen, golden brown and just firm to the touch.

Serves 4
GRAMS OF SATURATED FAT PER SERVING: 4.0

Creole sauce from Louisiana, USA, is a zesty, vegetable-laden concoction suitable for meat, fish and poultry. Serve with rice and a green salad.

Pork Chops in Creole Sauce

4 large loin chops, about 225g/8oz each
salt and freshly ground black pepper
1 tablespoon olive oil
1 onion, chopped
1 clove garlic, finely chopped
2 stalks celery, chopped
4 spring onions, chopped
1 red or green pepper, diced
400g/14oz-tin chopped tomatoes
1 dried bay leaf
a few red pepper flakes
2 tablespoons fresh parsley, chopped

1. Trim away as much fat as you can from pork chops. Sprinkle with a little salt and freshly ground black pepper.
2. Heat olive oil in large frying pan. Add the onion, garlic, celery, spring onions and the red or green pepper. Sauté for 5 minutes, stirring vegetables frequently.
3. Add tomatoes, by leaf and red pepper flakes. Cover and cook on low heat for 45 minutes or until the pork chops are fork-tender. Just before serving add the chopped parsley.

Serves 4
GRAMS OF SATURATED FAT PER SERVING: 4.5

This moussaka recipe has substantially less fat and calories than its traditional counterpart.

Moussaka

3 aubergines, peeled and cut into ¼ inch thick slices
1 tablespoon sunflower oil
1 large onion, chopped or sliced

500g/1lb lean lamb, minced
2 tomatoes, skinned and chopped
1 tablespoon tomato purée
150ml/¼ pint brown stock
½ teaspoon cinnamon
salt and freshly ground black pepper
300ml/½ pint skimmed milk
25g/1oz flour or cornflour
25g/1oz sunflower margarine
pinch of nutmeg

1. Steam the aubergines for 20 minutes until tender.
2. Heat oil in frying pan. Add the onions and sauté until they soften. Add the meat and stir until it becomes brown. Drain fat from the pan. Add the tomatoes, purée, stock and cinnamon and seasonings and simmer, uncovered, until most of the liquid is gone.
3. Preheat oven to 190°C/375°F/Gas Mark 5.
4. Put alternate layers of aubergine slices and the lamb mixture in a baking dish (preferably a transparent one). Finish with a layer of aubergines.
5. To make sauce, put milk, flour or cornflour into a saucepan. Whisk continuously over a moderate heat. Bring to the boil and cook for 2 to 3 minutes until thickened and smooth. Pour the sauce over the top layer of aubergines and bake in oven for 45 minutes until the top is golden.

Serves 4
GRAMS OF SATURATED FAT PER SERVING: 6.5

Savoury Lamb Crumble

1 teaspoon sunflower margarine
1 onion, finely chopped
1 tablespoon flour

206

500g/1lb cooked minced lamb
1 tablespoon light soy sauce
150ml/¼ pint beef stock
1 tablespoon tomato purée
a little salt and freshly ground black pepper
Topping:
125g/4oz wholemeal flour
50g/2oz jumbo oats
1 tablespoon sesame seeds

1. Preheat the oven to 190°C/375°F/Gas Mark 5.
2. Heat the margarine in a saucepan, add the onion and cook for 2 minutes until tender. Stir in the flour, lamb, soy sauce, stock, tomato purée and a little salt and pepper. Bring to the boil, stirring, and cook for one minute. Pour the lamb mixture into a shallow ovenproof dish.
3. Place the flour in a bowl, add the margarine and rub in finely until the mixture resembles breadcrumbs. Stir in the oats and sesame seeds until well mixed.
4. Spread the crumble topping evenly over the meat to cover completely.
5. Place in oven for 25 to 30 minutes until the topping is golden brown.

Serves 4
GRAMS OF SATURATED FAT PER SERVING: 5.5

Gratin of Veal

2 tablespoons olive oil
1 small onion, chopped
6 black olives, pitted and chopped
198g/7oz tuna fish in brine, drained
50g/2oz fresh wholemeal breadcrumbs
2 tablespoons wine vinegar

salt and freshly ground black pepper
6 veal escalopes
50g/2oz sunflower margarine
4 tablespoons plain flour
black olives and watercress to garnish
600ml/1 pint skimmed milk
175g/6oz low-fat soft cheese
1 tablespoon grated Parmesan cheese

1. Preheat the oven to 180°C/350°F/Gas Mark 4.
2. Heat 1 tablespoon of the oil in a sauté pan. Sauté the onion and olives for 1 to 2 minutes. Stir in the tuna fish and breadcrumbs. Remove pan from the heat and add the vinegar and a little salt and pepper. Cool.
3. Place the veal escalopes between two layers of cling film and beat out very thinly (or get the butcher to do it for you). Divide the fish mixture between the escalopes and fold and roll to form neat parcels. Tie securely with fine string.
4. Brown the veal parcels well in the remaining oil. Remove the string and place the parcels, seam side down, in a shallow casserole.
5. Melt the margarine in a saucepan. Stir in the flour and cook for 1 minute. Stir in the milk. Bring to the boil. Simmer for 1 minute. Remove pan from the heat, beat in the soft cheese and Parmesan with a little salt and pepper.
6. Pour the sauce over the veal. Cover and cook in oven for 45 minutes. Garnish with black olives and watercress. Serve on a bed of tagliatelle.

Serves 6
GRAMS OF SATURATED FAT PER SERVING: 5.0

Veal Escalopes with Lemon

8 thin escalopes of veal
salt and freshly ground black pepper

1 tablespoon olive oil
25g/1oz sunflower margarine
2 tablespoons dry white wine
150ml/¼ pint chicken stock
the juice of 1 lemon
1 tablespoon finely chopped fresh parsley leaves

1. Place the veal escalopes between two layers of cling film and beat out very thinly. Sprinkle both sides of veal with a little salt and pepper.
2. Heat oil in a frying pan. Add veal (2 to 3 pieces at a time). Sauté at high heat for 1 minute on each side. Transfer the cooked pieces to a warm plate.
3. Melt margarine in frying pan. Return the veal to the pan with its juices. Add the wine, stock, lemon and parsley. Cook the veal for 3 minutes turning it once. Serve immediately.

Servers 4
GRAMS OF SATURATED FAT PER SERVING: 4.0

Drunken pheasant is suitable for your most elegant dinner party but it is remarkably simple to prepare.

Drunken Pheasant

50g/2oz sunflower margarine
3 small pheasants
salt and freshly ground black pepper
8 juniper berries, crushed
3 rashers of lean back bacon, rinded
600ml/1 pint dry cider
300ml/½ pint chicken stock
2 tablespoons flour
3 tablespoons gin
grated rind and juice of 1 orange

1 tablespoon redcurrant or cranberry jelly
watercress and orange to garnish

1. Preheat the oven to 200°C/400°F/Gas Mark 6.
2. Spread the margarine over the pheasants. Place in a large
   casserole and season with a little salt and pepper. Sprinkle
   with the juniper berries. Stretch the bacon with the back
   of a knife and place one rasher over each bird. Pour over
   the cider and bake for 50 to 60 minutes, or until the
   pheasants are tender and cooked through.
3. Remove the birds to a warmed serving dish and keep
   warm. Skim off any fat from the casserole liquid then
   whisk in the flour. Continue whisking and add the stock,
   gin, orange rind, 3 tablespoons orange juice and the
   redcurrant or cranberry jelly. Bring to the boil and
   simmer for 2–3 minutes.
4. Carve or simply halve the pheasants. Garnish with
   watercress sprigs and twists of orange. Strain the gravy
   into a warmed sauce boat and serve.

Serves 6
GRAMS OF SATURATED FAT PER SERVING: 2.5

Like poultry, rabbit is much lower in saturated fat than beef,
pork and lamb. Rabbit can be bland so it requires distinctive
spices and flavourings to bring it alive. The following two
recipes do the trick.

Rabbit Bean Pot

75g/3oz dried red kidney beans, soaked overnight
75g/3oz dried cannellini beans, soaked overnight
1 tablespoon sunflower oil
2 leeks, sliced
4 carrots, sliced
4 rabbit joints, skinned

600ml/1 pint chicken stock
salt and freshly ground black pepper
1 tablespoon cornflour
1 tablespoon cold water
2 tablespoons chopped fresh parsley or coriander

1. Preheat the oven to 160°C/325°F/Gas Mark 3.
2. Rinse the beans in fresh water, place in a saucepan and cover with cold water. Bring to the boil and cook rapidly for 10 minutes, then drain.
3. Heat the oil in a large frying pan add the leeks and the carrots and cook for 2 to 3 minutes. Using a slotted spoon, place the vegetables in a flameproof casserole.
4. Add the rabbit joints to the frying pan, bring to the boil and cook quickly to brown on all sides. Drain on absorbent kitchen paper. Arrange the rabbit on top of the vegetables.
5. Pour the stock into the frying pan, add the beans, bring to the boil and add a little salt and pepper. Transfer the stock and beans to the casserole, cover and cook in oven for 2 hours or until the rabbit and beans are tender.
6. Blend the cornflour and water together to a smooth paste, then stir into the casserole. Bring to the boil. Simmer until thickened. Sprinkle with chopped parsley or coriander and serve hot.

Serves 4
GRAMS OF SATURATED FAT PER SERVING: 3.0

Rabbit in Mustard Sauce

2 tablespoons sunflower oil
1 rabbit, cut into serving pieces and skinned
salt and freshly ground black pepper
Dijon mustard
1 clove garlic, finely chopped

1 large onion, coarsely chopped
250g/8oz button mushrooms, sliced
1 bay leaf
½ teaspoon dried thyme
150ml/¼ pint chicken stock
150ml/¼ pint dry white wine
2 tablespoons chopped fresh parsley to garnish

1. Heat oil in large frying pan. Sprinkle rabbit with a little salt and pepper. Lightly brown rabbit on all sides. Remove from heat.
2. Using a pastry brush or finger-tips, coat all the pieces of rabbit with the mustard. Use more or less according to taste.
3. Add the garlic, onion, mushrooms, bay leaf and thyme and cook for 5 minutes. Add the chicken stock and wine and simmer, covered for 40 minutes or until the rabbit is tender.
4. Remove rabbit pieces and stir the gravy over high heat until thick. Garnish with chopped parsley and serve.

Serves 4
GRAMS OF SATURATED FAT PER SERVING: 3.5

It shouldn't surprise you to find plenty of chicken dishes here. Chicken and low-fat cooking go hand-in-hand and pound for pound you can't get a better buy for your family. The distinctive tang of orange and lime, combined with subtle spices, turns this chicken dish into a very special main course.

Spicy Citrus Chicken

1 tablespoon flour
½ teaspoon each ground tumeric, ground coriander, ground cumin
freshly ground black pepper

4 chicken breast fillets or chicken thighs, skinned
1 tablespoon sunflower oil
grated rind and juice of 1 orange
grated rind and juice of 1 lime
2 teaspoons clear honey
1 onion, finely chopped
250g/8oz split red lentils
600ml/1 pint chicken stock
coriander, orange and lime to garnish

1. Place the flour, tumeric, coriander, cumin and pepper in a polythene bag. Add the chicken and shake well to coat evenly.
2. Heat the oil in a frying pan, add the chicken and cook gently for 4 minutes, turning once. Stir in any remaining spice mixture, grated orange and lime rinds and juice and the honey. Bring to the boil, cover and simmer for 15 minutes, or until tender. Test with a skewer. The juices should run clear.
3. Meanwhile place the onion, lentils and stock in a saucepan, bring to the boil, cover and cook very gently for about 25 minutes until all the stock has been absorbed.
4. Arrange the lentils around the edge of a warmed serving dish. Place the chicken in the centre and pour over the sauce. Garnish with coriander leaves, orange and lime twists.

Serves 4
GRAMS OF SATURATED FAT PER SERVING: 3.0

It is important to use good, red Burgundy wine in this classic dish.

Coq au Vin

2 tablespoons olive oil
1.5kg/3lbs chicken pieces, skinned

1 clove garlic, chopped
1 large onion, chopped
2 carrots, coarsely chopped
250g/8oz small button mushrooms
300ml/½ pint red burgundy
150ml/¼ pint chicken stock
1 bay leaf
Salt and freshly ground black pepper
1 tablespoon flour
freshly chopped parsley to garnish

1. Heat oil in a large saucepan or flameproof casserole. Add chicken and brown on all sides. Remove chicken and set aside.
2. Add garlic and onion to the pan. Sauté onions until they are transparent. Add carrots, mushrooms, wine, stock bay leaf, a little salt and freshly ground black pepper. Cook stirring, until the stew comes to a boil.
3. Reduce heat, cover and simmer for 35 minutes or until the chicken is tender. Remove from heat.
4. Mix flour with a little cold water and add to the casserole. Stir and cook for another 3 minutes.
5. Discard bay leaf and sprinkle with fresh parsley.

Serves 4
GRAMS OF SATURATED FAT PER SERVING: 4.0

Chicken prepared teriyaki-style is tender, succulent and brimming with flavour. For an even more economical dish use skinned chicken joints and marinate for several hours before baking. Serve with stir-fried vegetables and rice.

Chicken Teriyaki

675g/1½lbs skinless, boneless chicken breast fillets
2 tablespoons teriyaki or light soy sauce

1 tablespoon sunflower oil
1 tablespoon wine or rice vinegar
2 tablespoons of finely shredded or rindless marmalade
1 large garlic clove, crushed
2 teaspoons fresh ginger root, minced
freshly ground black pepper
orange to garnish

1. Cut chicken breasts into serving pieces.
2. Mix remaining ingredients in a bowl and pour into a shallow dish or roasting tin. Add chicken and coat each piece well. Cover with cling film and refrigerate for 1 hour.
3. Preheat the oven to 200°C/400°F/Gas Mark 6. Bake chicken uncovered for 15 to 20 minutes until chicken is fork-tender. It is important not to over-cook. Baste the chicken with marinade a few times during the cooking.
4. Serve chicken immediately, garnished with twists of orange.

Serves 4
GRAMS OF SATURATED FAT PER SERVING: 3.0

Chicken with Lemon and Herbs

4 chicken portions, skinned
2 tablespoons fresh or 2 teaspoons dried chopped herbs —
sage, marjoram, chives
150ml/¼ pint chicken stock
grated rind and juice of 1 lemon
salt and freshly ground black pepper
parsley to garnish, optional

1. Preheat the oven to 180°C/350°F/Gas Mark 4.
2. Score the chicken, place in ovenproof dish, sprinkle over herbs and salt and pepper, pour over stock. lemon juice

215

and rind. Cover with foil or a lid. Bake for 1 hour until cooked, basting 2 or 3 times. Serve garnished with parsley.

Serves 4
GRAMS OF SATURATED FAT PER SERVING: 2.0

Honeyed Ginger Chicken

25g/1oz sunflower margarine
675g/1½lbs skinless, boneless chicken breast fillets
1 teaspoon soy sauce
3 tablespoons clear honey
½ teaspoon ground ginger
150ml/¼ pint dry white wine

1. Melt the margarine in a large frying pan, add the chicken breasts and sauté on both sides until lightly golden.
2. Add the soy sauce, honey and ginger to the pan. Bring to the boil and simmer for 15 to 20 minutes until tender, turning them during cooking. Lift the chicken out of the pan onto heated serving plates and keep warm while finishing the sauce.
3. Pour the wine into the pan, stir into the honey sauce and bring to the boil. Continue to boil for 3 to 5 minutes until the sauce reduces and becomes slightly syrupy. Pour over the chicken breasts and serve immediately.

Serves 4
GRAMS OF SATURATED FAT PER SERVING: 3.0

Chicken and Cashew Stir-Fry

2 oranges
2 tablespoons sunflower oil

50g/2oz cashew nuts
350g/12oz chicken breast, skinned and cut into strips
1 leek, sliced
3 sticks celery, sliced
½ red pepper, sliced

1. Peel one of the oranges, removing all the pith and cut into segments. Squeeze the juice from the other orange and reserve.
2. Heat the oil in a large frying pan or wok. Add the cashew nuts and fry just long enough to lightly brown them. Remove with a slotted spoon and drain on kitchen paper.
3. Add the chicken to the pan and stir-fry until lightly brown. Add leek, celery and pepper and cook for 4 minutes, until just tender (the vegetables should be 'al dente'). Stir the orange juice into the pan and bring to the boil. Add orange segments and cashew nuts and stir carefully until heated through. Serve immediately. ·

Serves 4
GRAMS OF SATURATED FAT PER SERVING: 2.5

Left-over cooked chicken or turkey can be used to make this delicious, low-fat chilli.

Chicken Chilli

1 tablespoon sunflower or corn oil
1 medium onion, chopped
1 clove garlic, finely chopped
150g/5oz-can tomato purée
1 teaspoon dry mustard
1 tablespoon Worcestershire sauce
350g/12oz cooked chicken or turkey, cubed
450g/15oz-can baked beans
200g/7oz-can sweetcorn kernels, drained
½ teaspoon chilli powder

1. Heat oil in a large saucepan. Add onion and garlic and sauté for 3 to 4 minutes.
2. Add the remainder of the ingredients and simmer, uncovered, for 25 minutes.

Serves 4
GRAMS OF SATURATED FAT PER SERVING: 2.0

This barbecued chicken recipe is ideal for informal supper parties. It is also delicious eaten cold. In the summer, prepare the chicken in the same way, then cook it on an outside grill or barbecue.

Barbecued Chicken

8 chicken drumsticks (or other chicken joints), skinned
4 tablespoons tomato ketchup
1 tablespoon wine vinegar
1 tablespoon sunflower oil
1 tablespoon clear honey or brown sugar
2 tablespoons light soy sauce

1. Preheat the oven to 200°C/400°F/Gas Mark 6.
2. Make 2 to 3 slits with a sharp knife in chicken flesh to allow the sauce to penetrate.
3. Mix remainder of ingredients in bowl or shallow dish.
4. Add chicken to the sauce. Make sure each piece is well coated.
5. Place chicken on a lightly-oiled or non-stick roasting tin. Bake for 25 to 30 minutes, removing once to baste chicken with left over sauce.

Serves 4
GRAMS OF SATURATED FAT PER SERVING: 2.5

Sesame Chicken

8 chicken drumsticks, skinned
2 teaspoons sunflower oil
2 teaspoons mild curry powder
salt and freshly ground black pepper
1 tablespoon sesame seeds
lemon and parsley to garnish

1. Preheat oven to 200°C/400°F/Gas Mark 6.
2. Brush chicken with oil and set aside.
3. Mix together the remainder of the ingredients and spread on plate. Roll each drumstick in the mixture making sure each one is well coated.
4. Cook the chicken in the oven for 30 to 35 minutes.
5. Serve hot or cold, garnished with lemon wedges and parsley.

Serves 4
GRAMS OF SATURATED FAT PER SERVING: 2.5

Spicy Drumsticks

8 chicken drumsticks, skinned
3 tablespoons natural yoghurt
1 teaspoon each coriander, paprika and ginger
½ teaspoon cumin
1 clove garlic, crushed
2 tablespoons sunflower oil

1. Make 2 deep cuts with a sharp knife into the flesh of each drumstick.
2. Mix the yoghurt with the spices, garlic and oil and use to coat the drumsticks. Place in shallow heatproof dish. Cover and leave to marinate in the refrigerator for 2 hours.

3. Grill the drumsticks, basting with the marinade, for about 8 to 10 minutes on each side until cooked. Test with a skewer. The juices should run clear. Serve hot or cold.

Serves 4
GRAMS OF SATURATED FAT PER SERVING: 3.0

Indian Chicken Kebabs

500g/1lb skinless, boneless chicken breasts, cubed
1 tablespoon wine vinegar
175g/6oz natural yoghurt
salt and freshly ground black pepper
1 clove garlic, crushed
½ teaspoon ginger
½ teaspoon cumin
½ teaspoon coriander
½ teaspoon tumeric
½ chilli powder, (optional)

1. Place all the ingredients in a bowl, mix well and marinate for one hour in the refrigerator.
2. Thread chicken on to skewers.
3. Grill under a hot grill for 10 to 15 minutes, turning frequently. Serve immediately.

Serves 4
GRAMS OF SATURATED FAT PER SERVING: 2.0

Serve these devilled turkey fillets in warm pitta bread with a salad of shredded lettuce, thinly sliced onion and cucumber to make a light but satisfying meal.

Devilled Turkey Fillets

4 turkey breast fillets, skinned or 4 chicken thighs, skinned and boned
3 tablespoons natural yoghurt
2 tablespoons paprika
2 teaspoons mild chilli seasoning
1 tablespoon sunflower oil
1 clove garlic, crushed
salt and freshly ground black pepper
grated rind and juice of 1 lemon

1. With a sharp knife, make a lattice of cuts across the surface of each turkey fillet. Beat together the yoghurt, paprika, chilli seasoning, oil, garlic and a little salt and pepper. Stir in the lemon rind and 3 tablespoons of juice.
2. Place the turkey in a shallow flameproof dish. Spoon over the yoghurt mixture. Cover and refrigerate for at least one hour or preferably overnight.
3. Cook the turkey under a preheated grill for about 5 minutes each side, basting with the marinade as it cooks. (allow 7 to 8 minutes if using chicken thighs.)

Serves 4
GRAMS OF SATURATED FAT PER SERVING: 1.0

This attractive turkey loaf is created from a mixture of fresh and dried fruit, tender turkey and crisp pastry.

Turkey Loaf

Pastry:
125g/4oz wholemeal flour
50g/2oz white vegetable fat
1–2 tablespoons water

Filling:
three 250g/8oz turkey fillets, skinned
Stuffing:
1 small onion, finely chopped
2 tablespoons finely chopped cooking apple
75g/3oz dried apricots, chopped
2 teaspoons sunflower margarine
25g/1oz fresh wholemeal breadcrumbs
2 teaspoons chopped fresh thyme
freshly ground black pepper
beaten egg to glaze
apricot, apple and parsley to garnish

1. Make pastry. Place the white vegetable fat in a bowl with the water and 1 tablespoon of the flour. Cream together with a fork until well mixed. Add remaining flour and continue mixing with fork to form a firm dough. Refrigerate until ready to use.
2. Preheat the oven to 190°C/375°F/Gas Mark 5.
3. Place the turkey fillets between two pieces of cling film and beat to flatten with a rolling pin.
4. Sauté the onion, apple and apricots in the margarine. Stir in the breadcrumbs, thyme and pepper.
5. Brush the base of a roasting tin with a little oil and lay one turkey fillet on it. Spread the fillet with half of the stuffing, then place another turkey fillet on top. Cover with the remaining stuffing and turkey fillet.
6. Roll the pastry out thinly on a lightly floured surface and cut out narrow strips. Arrange the strips in a lattice over the turkey and trim to fit it. Brush with beaten egg to glaze.
7. Bake in oven for 45 minutes or until golden. Garnish with apricot, apple slices and parsley.

Serves 6
GRAMS OF SATURATED FAT PER SERVING: 2.5

FISH AND SEAFOOD

Fried fish is fine once in a while, but there are so many more interesting and healthy ways to cook fish. Here are several alternative ideas for fish preparation. For example, this Greek recipe makes plain white fish positively exciting.

Fish Plaki

675g/1½lbs fish fillets (e.g cod or haddock)
juice of 1 lemon
salt and freshly ground black pepper
1 tablespoon olive oil
1 onion, finely chopped
2 cloves garlic, finely chopped
1 green pepper, diced
4 ripe tomatoes, skinned and chopped
1 teaspoon oregano
2 tablespoons chopped fresh parsley leaves

1. Preheat the oven to 180°C/350°F/Gas Mark 4.
2. Cut fish into serving pieces. Place in shallow baking dish or roasting tin and sprinkle with a little salt, pepper and lemon juice.
3. Heat oil in frying pan. Sauté onions, garlic and green pepper for 5 minutes. Add tomatoes and herbs and simmer covered, on low heat for 10 minutes.
4. Pour sauce over fish and bake for 20 to 25 minutes or until fish flakes when tested with a knife.

Serves 4
GRAMS OF SATURATED FAT PER SERVING: 0.5

Fisherman's Pie

500g/1lb haddock fillet, skinned
300ml/½ pint skimmed milk

25g/1oz sunflower margarine
125g/4oz celery, thinly sliced
25g/1oz flour
2 hard-boiled egg whites, chopped
1 tablespoon chopped celery tops
salt and freshly ground black pepper
Topping:
500g/1lb potatoes, peeled and roughly diced
1 teaspoon sunflower margarine
50g/2oz Edam or low-fat Cheddar-type cheese, grated
lemon twists and celery tops to garnish

1. Cut the fish into 4 pieces and place in a saucepan with the milk. Bring to the boil and cook gently for 3 to 4 minutes until the fish flakes easily. Remove using a slotted spoon and flake with a fork. Reserve the milk.
2. Heat the margarine in a saucepan. Stir in the celery, cook for 3 to 4 minutes. Stir in the flour, add the milk and slowly bring to the boil. Cook sauce for 2 minutes then stir in the egg whites, celery tops, fish, a little salt and pepper until well mixed. Pour into four individual ovenproof dishes.
3. Cook the potatoes in boiling, lightly salted water for 2 to 3 minutes until almost tender. Drain well then toss in the margarine.
4. Pile the potatoes on top of the fish mixture and sprinkle with grated cheese. Garnish with lemon twists and celery tops.

Serves 4
GRAMS OF SATURATED FAT PER SERVING 4.0

Gingered Lime Trout

4 250g/8oz rainbow trout cleaned
1 tablespoon peeled and grated ginger root

grated rind and juice of 1 lime
1 teaspoon clear honey
1 tablespoon chopped fresh dill
25g/1oz pine kernels or flaked almonds
salt and freshly ground black pepper
sprigs of dill and lime twists to garnish

1. Preheat oven to 190°C/375°F/Gas Mark 5.
2. Remove the heads and fins from the trout if wished.
   Wash well on absorbent kitchen paper. Arrange the trout
   in a shallow ovenproof dish.
3. Mix together in a bowl the ginger, lime rind and juice,
   honey, dill, half of the pine kernels or almonds and a
   little salt and pepper. Spoon some of the ginger mixture
   into the cavity of each fish and pour the remainder
   around the trout. Cover with foil.
4. Place the trout in oven for about 20 minutes or until the
   fish flakes easily with a knife.
5. Toast the remaining pine kernels or almonds under a
   moderate grill until golden brown. Arrange the trout on
   a warmed serving dish, garnish with the toasted pine
   kernels or almonds, sprigs of dill and lime twists.

Serves 4
GRAMS OF SATURATED FAT PER SERVING: 2.0

Mackerel, red mullet or trout can also be used instead of
bass in this stir-fry recipe.

Seabass with Stir-Fry Vegetables

1kg/2lb sea bass, cleaned
1 shallot, finely chopped
1 tablespoon chopped fresh parsley
150ml/¼ pint dry white wine or cider
freshly ground black pepper

1 tablespoon sunflower oil
2 carrots, cut into strips
2 courgettes, cut into strips
1 small fennel bulb, cut into strips
125g/4oz button mushrooms, thinly sliced
1 teaspoon cornflour
½ teaspoon clear honey
fennel tops and lemon wedges to garnish

1. Preheat the oven to 190°C/375°F/Gas Mark 5.
2. To serve the fish whole, remove the backbone from the fish, keeping the head and tail intact. Alternatively, remove the head and tail and cut into eight steaks.
3. Place the shallot, parsley, wine or cider in a shallow ovenproof dish and lay the fish on top. Cover with foil and place in oven for 30 to 40 minutes for whole fish and 15 to 20 minutes for steaks. Place the fish on a warmed serving dish. Cover and keep fish warm in a low oven. Reserve fish liquid.
4. Heat the oil in a large frying pan or wok. Add the carrots, courgettes, fennel and mushrooms. Cook for 2 to 3 minutes, stirring well until the vegetables are almost tender. Arrange around the fish and keep warm.
5. Pour the reserved fish liquid into the pan and bring to the boil. Blend the cornflour with a little cold water and stir into the fish liquor with the honey. Cook for one minute. Pour the sauce over the fish and garnish with the feathery fennel tops and lemon wedges.

Serves 4
GRAMS OF SATURATED FAT PER SERVING: 2.5

These splendid seafood kebabs are excellent served straight from the grill and wrapped in hot, split pitta bread with shredded green salad.

226

Saffron Seafood Kebabs

500g/1lb monkfish or cod fillet skinned
125g/4oz cucumber
1 red pepper
1 lemon, thinly sliced
8 large cooked, shelled Pacific prawns
4 bay leaves
75ml/3fl oz dry white wine
few strands saffron
pinch ground nutmeg
salt and freshly ground black pepper
lemon, cucumber and bay leaves to garnish

1. Cut the monkfish or cod into 2.5cm/1 inch pieces. Halve the cucumber lengthways and thickly slice. Chop the pepper into 2.5cm/1 inch pieces.
2. Wrap a lemon slice around each prawn. Thread on to 4 large skewers alternately with the fish, cucumber and pepper. Finish with a bay leaf. Place in a shallow flameproof dish.
3. Whisk together the remaining ingredients and pour over the kebabs. Cover and marinate in the refrigerator for one hour.
4. Cook under a preheated grill for about 5 minutes each side. Serve immediately, garnished with lemon and cucumber slices and bay leaves.

Serves 4
GRAMS OF SATURATED FAT PER SERVING: 0.5

This is a very economical fish dish, well-suited for any white fish fillets. You can use frozen fish fillets without thawing first.

Fish Crumble

575g/1¼lb white fish fillets
300ml/½ pint skimmed milk
1 bay leaf
1 small onion, peeled and chopped
25g/1oz sunflower margarine
25g/1oz flour
2 tablespoons chopped parsley
50g/2oz mushrooms, sliced
Topping:
40g/1½oz porridge oats
50g/2oz wholemeal flour
50g/2oz sunflower margarine
50g/2oz matured English Cheddar cheese, grated

1. Preheat the oven to 180°C/350°F/Gas Mark 4.
2. Poach the fish in milk with bay leaf and onion for 15 to 20 minutes. Strain the milk into a jug and make up to 300ml/½ pint if necessary.
3. Place margarine, flour and milk in a saucepan and bring to the boil, whisking continuously. Cook 2 to 3 minutes. Add flaked fish and remaining filling ingredients and stir gently. Place in an ovenproof dish.
4. For the topping, place oats, flour and margarine in a bowl and, using a fork, mix the margarine into the dry ingredients. Stir in the cheese and spoon the crumble mixture over the fish. Bake for 30 to 40 minutes and serve immediately.

Serves 4
GRAMS OF SATURATED FAT PER SERVING: 6.5

This dish takes just minutes to prepare from start to finish and is low in fat and calories. If you prefer, use fresh chives instead of dill and omit the mustard.

Fish in Yoghurt-Dill Sauce

575g/1¼lbs white fish or salmon fillet
175g/6oz natural yoghurt
2 teaspoons Dijon mustard
4 spring onions, thinly sliced
1 tablespoon finely chopped fresh dill
freshly ground black pepper to taste
fresh dill and lemon to garnish

1. Preheat the oven to 180°C/350°F/Gas Mark 4.
2. Place fish fillets in shallow, ovenproof dish.
3. Mix yoghurt, mustard, spring onions, dill and black pepper. Spread over fish.
4. Bake in oven for about 20 minutes depending on thickness of fish. Fish is ready when it flakes easily with a knife.
5. Garnish with sprigs of fresh dill and lemon wedges.

Serves 4
GRAMS OF SATURATED FAT PER SERVING: 0.5

Here is our version of the famous fish dish from Louisiana, USA. This is a dish for those who love spicy-hot food. It is a healthy and exciting alternative to steak au poivre.

Cajun Peppered Plaice

25g/1oz sunflower margarine
575g/1¼lbs plaice fillets, skinned
Seasoning mix:
1 teaspoon sweet paprika pepper
½ teaspoon white pepper
½ teaspoon black pepper
¼ teaspoon cayenne pepper
½ teaspoon garlic granules
½ teaspoon onion granules
½ teaspoon dried thyme

½ teaspoon dried oregano
a little salt
1 tablespoon olive oil
lemon to garnish

1. Melt margarine in small saucepan then remove from heat.
2. Cut the fillets cross-wise into wide serving-size pieces.
   Coat both sides of each piece of fish with the melted
   margarine.
3. Combine the dry seasoning mix ingredients in a small
   bowl and sprinkle seasoning evenly on both sides of the
   fish, patting it in by hand.
4. Heat a heavy frying pan over high heat until it is very
   hot. Add the olive oil and wait until it starts to smoke.
   Add the fish fillets as many pieces at a time as possible.
   Cook for one and a half minutes each side turning the
   fish carefully with a spatula. Repeat using remaining
   fillets. Serve piping hot garnished with lemon wedges.

Serves 4
GRAMS OF SATURATED FAT PER SERVING: 2.0

For those who love the taste of butter, a little bit can go
a long way and provide a delightful, crunchy, butter almond
topping to fresh white fish fillets.

Baked Fish with Buttery Almonds

500g/1lb thin white fish fillets such as sole or plaice
salt and freshly ground black pepper
juice of ½ lemon
15g/½oz butter
2 tablespoons almond flakes
lemon and parsley to garnish

1. Preheat the oven to 200°C/400°F/Gas Mark 6.

2. Sprinkle the fish with a little salt and pepper and the lemon juice and place on foil on roasting tin.
3. Melt the butter in a small saucepan and stir in the almonds. Remove from heat.
4. Arrange the buttered almonds evenly over the fish. Bake for 8 to 10 minutes. Garnish with lemon wedges and parsley.

Serves 4
GRAMS OF SATURATED FAT PER SERVING: 2.5

Fish retains its moisture and natural flavour especially well when baked in foil.

Herrings Baked in Foil

4 herring fillets, cleaned
25g/1oz sunflower margarine
juice of 1 lime
salt and freshly ground black pepper
1 medium onion, peeled and thinly sliced
1 teaspoon capers

1. Preheat oven to 200°C/400°F/Gas Mark 6.
2. Cut 4 rectangles of tin foil which are big enough to wrap the fish fillets loosely. Spread each piece of foil with some of the margarine. Place a fish fillet on each piece of prepared foil.
3. Sprinkle lime juice and a little salt and pepper over the fillets. Cover the fillets completely with a thin layer of onion slices and a few capers.
4. Seal each foil packet well but do not cover the fish tightly. Set them on a baking sheet and bake for 10 minutes. Slit the packets open at the table for full appreciation of the trapped aroma.

Serves 4
GRAMS OF SATURATED FAT PER SERVING: 3.5

MEATLESS MAIN COURSES

Vegetable Curry

750ml/1¼ pints light stock
125g/4oz carrots, chopped
125g/4oz turnips, chopped
125g/4oz Jerusalem artichokes, chopped (optional)
125g/4oz potatoes, chopped
125g/4oz cauliflower florets
4 sticks celery, sliced
2 onions, sliced
1 tablespoon flora oil
2 tablespoons plain flour
2 tablespoons garam masala
6 green cardamom pods
1 tablespoon peeled and grated fresh ginger root
grated rind and juice of 1 lemon
400g/14oz-can chick peas, drained or 125g/4oz dried chick peas, soaked and cooked

1. Place the stock in a large saucepan, bring to the boil and add the carrots, turnips, artichokes (if using), potatoes, cauliflower, celery and onions. Cook gently for 2 to 3 minutes until almost tender. Strain, reserving the stock.
2. Make the sauce. Heat the oil in a saucepan. Stir in all the remaining ingredients except the chick peas. Cook, stirring, for 1 to 2 minutes before adding the reserved stock. Bring to the boil, cover and cook gently for 30 minutes.
3. Add all the vegetables and chick peas and stir over a moderate heat until the vegetables are hot, about 3 to 4 minutes. Serve the vegetable curry with the cooked rice and raita (natural yoghurt and diced cucumber).

Serves 4
GRAMS OF SATURATED FAT PER SERVING: 0.5

Vegetarian Moussaka

675g/1½lb aubergine
2 tablespoons olive oil
250g/8oz onion, chopped
125g/4oz mushrooms, sliced
1 clove garlic, finely chopped
1 tablespoon chopped fresh parsley
675g/1½lbs tomatoes, chopped
1 tablespoon peanut butter
freshly ground black pepper
50g/2oz fresh wholemeal breadcrumbs
Sauce:
25g/1oz sunflower margarine
25g/1oz plain flour
300ml/½ pint skimmed milk
50g/2oz Brie, chopped
1 egg, separated

1. Preheat the oven to 180°C/350°F/Gas Mark 4.
2. Slice the aubergine. Blanch in boiling water for 4 minutes. Drain. Brown under a hot grill.
3. Heat the oil and sauté the onion, mushrooms and garlic for 2 to 3 minutes. Stir in the parsley, tomatoes, peanut butter and pepper.
4. Arrange layers of aubergine, tomato mixture and breadcrumbs in an ovenproof casserole, finishing with a layer of aubergines.
5. Melt the margarine. Stir in the flour. Cook, stirring for 1 to 2 minutes before adding the milk. Bring to the boil, simmer for 2 to 3 minutes. Beat in the Brie and egg yolk. Stiffly whisk the egg white and fold into the sauce. Spoon evenly over the aubergine. Bake for 45 minutes.

Serves 4
GRAMS OF SATURATED FAT PER SERVING: 5.5

Steaming aubergine instead of cooking in oil saves hundreds of calories. This wonderful Italian dish can be served with pasta or as it is with crusty French bread and a green salad.

Aubergine Parmesan

2 medium aubergines, unpeeled
1 tablespoon olive oil
1 clove of garlic, finely chopped
1 onion, chopped
400g/14oz-can chopped tomatoes
1 teaspoon dried basil
salt and freshly ground black pepper
40g/1½oz grated Parmesan cheese
125g/4oz grated Mozzarella cheese

1. Preheat the oven to 180°C/350°F/Gas Mark 4.
2. Slice the aubergines into pieces about 1 cm/½ inch thick. Cook in steamer for 20 minutes until soft. Drain and pat dry with kitchen paper.
3. Heat large frying pan with oil. Add garlic and onion. Cook until onion is transparent. Add tomatoes, basil a little salt and pepper. Simmer over low heat for 10 minutes until sauce is rich and thick.
4. Arrange half the aubergines on bottom of shallow baking dish. Spread with half of the tomato sauce and half of the grated cheeses. Repeat using the remainder of the aubergines, tomato sauce and cheese. The top layer should be cheese. Bake for 35.minutes.

Serves 4
GRAMS OF SATURATED FAT PER SERVING: 6.5

Cheese and Leek Jacket Potatoes

4 medium-sized baking potatoes
1 tablespoon sunflower oil

2 medium leeks, cleaned and chopped
250g/8oz low-fat soft cheese or quark
salt and freshly ground black pepper
chopped chives or parsley to garnish

1. Preheat the oven to 200°C/400°F/Gas Mark 6.
2. Scrub the potatoes and prick several times with a fork. Bake in oven for about 1 hour or until soft cooked.
3. Heat oil in frying pan. Add the leeks and cook slowly for 10 minutes.
4. Cut the cooked potatoes in half. Carefully scoop out the centres. Blend with the leeks and cheese in a bowl until smooth. Season with a little salt and pepper. Spoon potato mixture back into shells. Garnish with chopped chives or parsley.

Serves 4
GRAMS OF SATURATED FAT PER SERVING: 3.0

This one-crust spinach pie is delicious hot or cold.

Spinach Pie

Pastry:
25g/1oz sunflower margarine
50g/2oz white vegetable fat
2–3 tablespoons cold water
75g/3oz white flour
75g/3oz wholemeal flour
Filling:
500g/1lb fresh spinach, washed, sorted and chopped (or 10oz frozen, thawed)
350g/12oz low-fat cottage cheese
1 large egg, beaten
½ teaspoon nutmeg
40g/1½oz grated Parmesan cheese

25g/1oz plain wholemeal or white flour
salt and freshly ground black pepper

1. Make pastry. Mix margarine and white fat, water and
   2 tablespoons of the wholemeal flour in a bowl. Stir in
   the remaining flour and mix to a firm dough. Turn out
   onto a lightly-floured surface and knead gently until
   smooth. Roll out the pastry to fit a 20cm/8 inch flan dish.
   Line the dish and prick the base with a fork. Refrigerate
   until ready to use.
2. Preheat oven to 180°C/350°F/Gas Mark 4.
3. Barely cook the spinach in a minimum of water. (If using
   frozen spinach, squeeze out excess moisture.)
4. Put cottage cheese, spinach, egg, nutmeg, Parmesan
   cheese, flour, a little salt and pepper in a bowl. Stir until
   well blended. Pour filling into the prepared pastry-shell.
   Bake for 35 to 40 minutes until pastry is light brown and
   filling is puffed and toasty.

Serves 6
GRAMS OF SATURATED FAT PER SERVING: 4.0

This tempting vegetable and nut quiche has a fraction of
the saturated fat of traditional quiche recipes.

Broccoli and Walnut Quiche

1 20cm/8 inch wholemeal pastry case (see previous recipe
for method)
Filling:
15g/½oz sunflower margarine
1 small onion, peeled and finely chopped
1 clove garlic, finely chopped
125g/4oz broccoli florets, blanched in boiling water for 2
minutes
75g/3oz walnuts, chopped

50g/2oz strong-flavoured Cheddar cheese, grated
2 eggs
150g/5oz carton low-fat natural yoghurt

1. Preheat the oven 190°C/375°F/Gas Mark 5.
2. To make filling, melt margarine and sauté onion and garlic until soft. Place in the prepared pastry case with the broccoli, walnuts, and grated cheese.
3. Whisk together the eggs and yoghurt. Pour over the filling. Bake in the oven for 30 to 40 minutes. Garnish with salad.

Serves 6
GRAMS OF SATURATED FAT PER SERVING: 3.0

Bean Goulash

4 tablespoons sunflower oil
2 cloves garlic, finely chopped
500g/1lb onions, peeled and sliced
2 large green peppers, sliced
350g/12oz courgettes, sliced
400g/14oz-can kidney, baked or other beans
800g/1lb 12oz-canned tomatoes in juice
3 tablespoons tomato purée
175g/6oz-can sweetcorn, drained
1 tablespoon paprika
½ teaspoon sugar
salt and freshly ground black pepper

1. Heat oil in large saucepan and cook garlic and onion until softened. Add green pepper and cook for 2 minutes. Stir in the courgettes and cook for a further 2 minutes.
2. Drain and rinse beans, stir in with remaining ingredients. Correct seasoning. Simmer mixture, uncovered, for about

15 minutes until vegetables are soft. Serve piping hot with low-fat plain yoghurt if liked.

Serves 4
GRAMS OF SATURATED FAT PER SERVING: 1.5

An old favourite adapted to provide more fibre and much less fat.

Quick Pizza

Scone base:
25g/1oz sunflower margarine
125g/4oz wholemeal self-raising flour
½ teaspoon baking powder
½ teaspoon mixed herbs
1 egg, beaten
1 tablespoon skimmed milk
Topping:
1 tablespoon olive oil
1 small onion, chopped
125g/4oz mushrooms, chopped
1 tablespoon tomato purée
salt and freshly ground black pepper
1 teaspoon oregano, or mixed herbs
3 tomatoes, sliced
75g/3oz Edam or low-fat Cheddar-type cheese, grated
Optional topping:
4 anchovies, drained and halved
25g/1oz black olives, halved and stoned

1. Preheat the oven to 200°C/400°F/Gas Mark 6.
2. Place all scone ingredients together in a mixing bowl. Mix with a wooden spoon to form a soft dough. Knead lightly on a floured board, place on a baking sheet and form into a 25cm/10-inch round.

3. Heat oil in pan. Cook onion lightly, add mushrooms and cook for 3 minutes. Stir in the tomato purée, seasoning and oregano or mixed herbs. Arrange slices of tomato over scone base and spread mixture on top. Sprinkle with cheese and decorate with anchovies and olives if desired. Bake for 25 to 30 minutes.

Serves 4
GRAMS OF SATURATED FAT PER SERVING: 5.0

This tasty bean casserole has a rich home-made barbecue sauce flavour and goes particularly well with food cooked on an outside grill.

Three-Bean Casserole

1 tablespoon sunflower oil
1 large onion, finely chopped
400g/14oz-can baked beans
400g/14oz-can butter beans, drained
400g/14oz-can kidney beans, drained
2 tablespoons tomato ketchup
2 tablespoons brown sugar
1 tablespoon Worcestershire sauce
50g/2oz Edam cheese, grated

1. Preheat the oven to 180°C/350°F/Gas Mark 4.
2. Heat sunflower oil in frying pan. Add onion and cook over medium heat for 2 to 3 minutes.
3. Mix the beans, ketchup, sugar and Worcestershire sauce in a bowl. Add the sautéed onion to the mixture. Stir well and transfer mixture to an ovenproof dish. Cover with grated cheese. Bake, uncovered, for 30 minutes.

Serves 4
GRAMS OF SATURATED FAT PER SERVING: 2.5

This recipe is another variation on a well-known theme. It contains far less saturated fat than the original version and shows how a traditional recipe can be made more healthy.

Cauliflower and Mushroom Cheese

1 medium cauliflower in florets
500g/1lb courgettes, sliced or green beans, cooked
25g/1oz sunflower margarine
125g/4oz mushrooms, sliced
25g/1oz plain flour or cornflour
300ml/½ pint skimmed milk
salt and freshly ground black pepper
125g/4oz Edam or low-fat Cheddar-type cheese, grated
2 tablespoons wholemeal breadcrumbs
tomato and parsley to garnish

1. Cook cauliflower in lightly salted boiling water for 10 to 15 minutes until just tender, adding courgettes or green beans for the last 3 minutes. Drain.
2. Melt margarine in a saucepan and cook mushrooms lightly for 3 to 4 minutes. Place flour or cornflour and milk in the same pan and whisk continuously over medium heat. When sauce comes to the boil cook for 2 to 3 minutes. Season to taste then add half the cheese and stir until melted.
3. Place the cauliflower, courgettes or beans in an ovenproof dish and pour the cheese sauce over the top.
4. Mix remaining cheese with breadcrumbs and sprinkle over the top of sauce and vegetables. Place under a moderate grill and grill until browned. Garnish with sliced tomato and parsley.

Serves 4
GRAMS OF SATURATED FAT PER SERVING: 6.0

PASTA AND RICE DISHES

Pasta salads are colourful one-dish meals that are suitable to serve all year round. This is a spicy, piquant sauce for pasta that embodies some of the healthy features of the Mediterranean diet − olive oil and plenty of vegetables.

Tomato and Artichoke Pasta Sauce

1 large onion, chopped
2 cloves garlic, finely chopped
1 tablespoon olive oil
1 tablespoon dried basil
2 tablespoons chopped fresh parsley
2 400g/14oz-cans chopped Italian tomatoes
400g/14oz-can artichoke hearts, drained and quartered
salt and freshly ground black pepper
2 tablespoons grated Parmesan cheese

1. Sauté the onion and garlic in olive oil in large saucepan until onion has softened. Add the basil, parsley, and continue to sauté for another 5 minutes.
2. Add the tomatoes, a little salt and plenty of black pepper. Simmer uncovered for 1 hour.
3. Add the artichokes and simmer until the sauce becomes rich and thick.
4. Stir in the Parmesan cheese and serve on your favourite pasta.

Serves 4
GRAMS OF SATURATED FAT PER SERVING: 1.5

Salmon goes particularly well with pasta. In this recipe, one of our favourites, salmon is steamed on a bed of Julienne vegetables in wine and fresh dill. Finally all the ingredients are tossed together to form a most colourful and succulent dish.

Pasta with Salmon and Julienne Vegetables

2 shallots, chopped
1 clove garlic, finely chopped
50g/2oz sunflower margarine
1 courgette
2 carrots, peeled
2 stalks celery
1 red pepper
300ml/¼ pint dry white wine or vegetable stock
2 tablespoons freshly chopped dill or 1 teaspoon dried dill
250g/8oz pasta such as fettucine
1 tablespoon lemon juice
350g/12oz salmon fillet, skinned
salt and freshly ground black pepper to taste

1. In large frying pan, sauté the shallots and garlic in 25g/1oz of the margarine until softened. Set aside.
2. Cut the courgette, carrots, celery and red pepper into thin matchstick-size slices — 'julienne'. Add vegetables to the pan with the wine or stock and dill. Return to heat and simmer, covered for 2 minutes. Set aside.
3. Cook the pasta in plenty of boiling water until firm but tender. Meanwhile cut salmon into small, thin slices and sprinkle with the lemon, salt and pepper. Place the salmon on top of the vegetables in pan. Cover and steam salmon on low heat for 6 to 8 minutes or until salmon is just done.
4. Drain pasta and toss with remaining 25g/1oz margarine. Add the salmon-vegetable mixture to the pasta. Toss lightly in a warm serving dish. Serve immediately.

Serves 4
GRAMS OF SATURATED FAT PER SERVING: 5.0

Serve this dish as a starter or as a light main course with rolls and a tomato salad.

Linguine with Pesto

50g/2oz fresh basil leaves
2 medium cloves
25g/1oz pine kernels
40g/1½oz grated Parmesan cheese
4 tablespoons olive oil
salt and freshly ground black pepper to taste
250g/8oz linguine pasta

1. Put all ingredients (except pasta!) in blender or food processor. Process until mixture becomes smooth. Alternatively, the ingredients may be chopped then ground with a mortar and pestle. Taste and correct seasoning.
2. Cook linguine in plenty of boiling water. Drain and toss with the pesto and serve immediately.

Serves 4
GRAMS OF SATURATED FAT PER SERVING: 4.0

Wholewheat Pasta and Vegetable Bake

225g/8oz wholewheat pasta shapes
600ml/½ pint skimmed milk
25g/1oz flour of cornflour
½ teaspoon prepared English mustard
salt and freshly ground black pepper to taste
75g/3oz matured English cheddar, grated
25g/1oz sunflower margarine
1 small onion, chopped
50g/2oz frozen or cooked peas
50g/2oz frozen or cooked sweetcorn

1. Preheat oven to 180°C/350°F/Gas Mark 4.
2. Cook pasta in plenty of boiling water until tender but firm.
3. Place milk, flour, salt and pepper and mustard in saucepan. Whisk continuously over moderate heat. Bring to the boil and cook for 2 to 3 minutes until thickened and smooth. Stir in 50g/2oz of the grated cheese. Set aside.
4. Melt margarine in pan. Add onion and pepper and sauté for 2 to 3 minutes. Add the peas and corn. Continue to cook until just heated through.
5. Add the vegetables and drained pasta to the sauce. Mix well and place in baking dish. Sprinkle with remaining grated cheese.
6. Bake in oven for 25 to 30 minutes.

Serves 4
GRAMS OF SATURATED FAT PER SERVING: 5.0

Tagliatelle with Courgette and Tomato Sauce

1 tablespoon sunflower oil
1 small onion, chopped
1 clove garlic, finely chopped
2 courgettes, diced
2 tomatoes, skinned and chopped
½ teaspoon dried basil
25g/1oz sunflower margarine
25g/1oz flour
300ml/½ pint vegetable stock
50g/2oz cooked peas
250g/8oz tagliatelle or wholewheat spaghetti

1. Heat oil in pan and sauté onion and garlic until softened. Add courgette and sauté for a further 5 minutes. Add tomatoes and basil and cook for 1 to 2 minutes

2. Melt margarine in pan, stir in flour, then, gradually add stock. Bring to the boil whisking continuously. Cook for 2 to 3 minutes until thickened and smooth.
3. Add the courgette mixture and peas and simmer for about 5 minutes, stirring.
4. Cook pasta in plenty of boiling water until just tender. Place pasta in serving dish. Pour over the sauce and serve immediately.

Serves 4
GRAMS OF SATURATED FAT PER SERVING: 1.5

Red lentils in this bolognese sauce allow you to use less meat without compromising taste or texture.

Spaghetti Lentil Bolognese

125g/4oz split red lentils
300ml/½ pint water
1 bay leaf
2 carrots, diced
2 stalks celery, chopped
1 tablespoon dried basil
400g/14oz-can chopped tomatoes
1 tablespoon olive oil
1 onion, peeled and chopped
1 large garlic clove, finely chopped
250g/8oz extra lean minced beef
3 tablespoons red wine
2 tablespoons tomato purée
salt and freshly ground black pepper
350g/12oz spaghetti
2 tablespoons grated Parmesan cheese

1. Place lentils, water, bay leaf, carrot, celery, basil and tomatoes in a saucepan. Bring to the boil and simmer,

covered, for about 25 minutes, until the lentils are tender. Set aside.

2. Heat olive oil in large saucepan. Add the onion and garlic and simmer until tender. Stir in the mince, and brown it quickly. Add the lentil-tomato mixture, wine and tomato purée. Simmer, covered for 25 to 30 minutes until sauce is rich and thick. Correct seasoning.

3. Cook the pasta in plenty of boiling water. Drain well then pile the spaghetti into a warm serving dish. Pour the lentil bolognese on top. Sprinkle on the Parmesan cheese.

Serves 4
GRAMS OF SATURATED FAT PER SERVING: 4.0

Tuna fish is very versatile, meaty fish. Keep a few cans of tuna in brine on hand for quick, low-fat meals.

Tuna Pasta Provençal

1 tablespoon olive oil
1 onion chopped
2 cloves garlic, finely chopped
1 green pepper, diced
400g/14oz-can tomatoes
200g/7oz-can tuna in brine, drained
1 tablespoon capers
4 drained anchovy fillets, chopped
½ teaspoon dried oregano
salt and freshly ground pepper to taste
350g/12oz penne or fusili pasta

1. Heat the olive oil in a frying pan. Add the onion, garlic, green pepper and sauté until vegetables have softened.

2. Add the tomatoes and simmer for 20 minutes.

3. Flake the tuna fish with a fork, stir it gently into the

tomatoes with the capers, anchovies and oregano. Add a little salt (if necessary) and pepper.
4. Simmer on low heat for 10 minutes.
5. Cook pasta in plenty of boiling water until firm but tender. Drain and turn into a warm serving dish. Pour the sauce on top and serve immediately.

Serves 4
GRAMS OF SATURATED FAT PER SERVING: 1.0

This is a delicious way of using up left-over turkey. We have it every Boxing Day.

Turkey Tettrazini

25g/1oz sunflower margarine
1 onion, chopped
125g/2oz button mushrooms, sliced
300ml/½ pint skimmed milk
150ml/¼ pint turkey or chicken stock
40g/1½oz flour
50g/2oz matured Cheddar cheese, grated
1 tablespoon sherry, optional
pinch of nutmeg
salt and freshly ground black pepper to taste
350g/12oz cooked turkey, diced
1 tablespoon finely chopped fresh parsley
350g/12oz linguine pasta

1. Heat the margarine in a saucepan. Add the onion and mushrooms and sauté for about 5 minutes.
2. To the same pan add the milk, stock and flour and bring to the boil, whisking continuously. Reduce heat and simmer for 2 to 3 minutes until sauce is thick and smooth. Stir in the cheese, sherry (if used) and season with nutmeg and a little salt and pepper.

3. Add the turkey to the sauce and, finally, the fresh parsley. Keep warm over a very low heat.
4. Cook the linguine in plenty of boiling water until firm but tender. Drain well. Turn into a warm serving dish and pour the sauce over the top.

Serves 4
GRAMS OF SATURATED FAT PER SERVING: 5.0

Marinated Chicken with Pasta Shells and Broccoli

Marinade:
2 tablespoons tomato purée
4 tablespoons red wine
1 tablespoon dried basil
1 clove garlic, crushed
1 teaspoon sugar
Other ingredients:
500g/1lb boneless, skinless, chicken breast cut into bite-sized pieces
500g/1lb broccoli
350g/12oz pasta shells
1 tablespoon olive oil
2 tablespoons grated Parmesan cheese

1. Blend the marinade ingredients together in a shallow dish.
2. Add chicken pieces to marinade. Toss well and ensure each piece is well-coated with the marinade. Refrigerate for 30 minutes.
3. While chicken is marinating cut broccoli into florets and chop tender part of stems into bite-size pieces. Cook broccoli until tender. Drain and set aside.
4. Cook pasta in plenty of boiling water until just tender. Drain well.
5. Heat olive oil in large frying pan. Cook chicken over

medium heat for 8 to 10 minutes until chicken is done. Remove from heat.
6. Place pasta in a warm serving dish add broccoli and chicken and toss until they are well mixed. Sprinkle with grated Parmesan cheese.

Serves 4
GRAMS OF SATURATED FAT PER SERVING: 4.0

Rice and beans are a staple dish in South America. The combination is complete in protein, low in fat and high in fibre. There are myriad variations of the dish using different kinds of beans, spices and other vegetables. Take this basic recipe and use your imagination.

Rice and Beans

175g/6oz long grain brown rice
1 tablespoon olive oil
1 medium onion, chopped
1 garlic clove, finely chopped
1 green pepper, chopped
2 teaspoons ground coriander
¼ – ½ teaspoon chilli powder or cayenne
salt and freshly ground black pepper
400g/14oz-can red kidney beans, drained
4 tablespoons dry red wine or stock

1. Cook the rice in plenty of boiling water for about 35 minutes or until just tender.
2. While rice is cooking, heat oil in frying pan. Add onion and cook until softened. Add the garlic and green pepper and cook for another minute or two. Add the coriander, chilli or cayenne and a little salt and pepper. Add the wine or stock and cook for a further 10 minutes.

3. Stir in the beans and the cooked rice and spoon onto a warmed serving dish.

Serves 4
GRAMS OF SATURATED FAT PER SERVING: 0.5

This is our healthy version of a hearty rice stew from New Orleans, USA.

Jambalaya

2 tablespoons sunflower oil
125g/4oz smoked ham, cubed
350g/12oz boneless, skinless chicken cut into bite-size pieces
1 large onion, chopped
4 stalks celery, chopped
1 small bunch of spring onions, chopped
1 green pepper, chopped
1–2 cloves garlic, finely chopped
400g/14oz-can tomatoes, drained, reserving juice
2 tablespoons tomato purée
1 teaspoon thyme
1 teaspoon black pepper
½ teaspoon cayenne
2 bay leaves
salt to taste
175g/6oz rice
450ml/¾ pint chicken stock
1 tablespoon Worcestershire sauce

1. Heat oil in large saucepan. Lightly brown the ham and chicken. Remove and set aside.
2. In the same pan sauté the onion, celery, spring onions, green pepper and garlic until tender. Add tomatoes, tomato purée, thyme, pepper, cayenne and bay leaves. Cook for 5 minutes then stir in the rice.

3. Mix together the juice from tomatoes, stock and Worcestershire sauce to make 600ml/1 pint. Add to rice, bring to the boil and reduce to a simmer.
4. Add the reserved chicken and ham and cook uncovered on fairly low heat for about 30 minutes or until rice is just tender. Remove bay leaves and spoon onto a warmed serving dish.

Serves 4
GRAMS OF SATURATED FAT PER SERVING: 3.0

Instead of plain boiled rice try a tasty pilaff. It makes an excellent accompaniment to fish, meat and poultry dishes.

Rice Pilaff

175g/6oz long-grain brown rice
25g/1oz sunflower margarine
1 medium onion, finely chopped
600ml/1 pint hot well-flavoured stock
salt and freshly ground black pepper

1. Melt the margarine in a saucepan. Sauté the onions until a light golden colour.
2. Add the rice and continue to cook stirring for one minute.
3. Add the hot stock, a little salt and freshly ground black pepper. Bring the liquid to the boil. Lower the heat and cover the saucepan and simmer rice mixture until all the liquid is absorbed. Serve immediately.

Variations

Armenian Pilaff: Add 50g/2oz pine nuts and 50g/2oz currants to the rice mixture before adding the stock.

Tomato pilaff: Stir 2 tablespoons of tomato purée into the stock before adding to the rice mixture.

Serves 4
GRAMS OF SATURATED FAT PER SERVING: 1.0
  Armenian Pilaff: 1.5
  Tomato Pilaff: 1.0

Rice, Spinach and Cheese Casserole

175g/6oz brown rice
600ml/1 pint chicken or vegetable stock
2 tablespoons olive oil
500g/1lb fresh spinach, washed, sorted and chopped
½ teaspoon nutmeg
1 large egg
175g/6oz fromage frais or quark
250g/8oz low-fat cottage cheese
1 tablespoon of finely chopped fresh parsley
40g/1½oz grated Parmesan cheese

1. Preheat the oven to 200°C/400°F/Gas Mark 6.
2. Bring the rice to a boil in the stock then lower the heat. Cover and simmer until rice is tender and liquid is absorbed.
3. Heat the olive oil in a large saucepan. Add spinach leaves. Toss over medium heat until spinach has softened and appears very glossy. Remove from heat. Add the cooked rice and the rest of the ingredients.
4. Turn the mixture into an ovenproof casserole dish and bake for 30 minutes until golden on top.

Serves 4
GRAMS OF SATURATED FAT PER SERVING: 5.0

Chicken and Lemon Risotto

175g/6oz chicken breast fillets, skinned
75g/3oz onion, sliced

252

1 clove garlic, crushed
grated rind of 1 lemon
1 litre/1¾ pints chicken stock
250g/8oz long-grain brown rice
50g/2oz button mushrooms
½ teaspoon tumeric or paprika
salt and freshly ground black pepper
125g/4oz cooked mussels or peeled, cooked prawns
50g/2oz frozen peas
prawns and lemon to garnish

1. Cut the chicken into bite-sized pieces. Place all the ingredients except the mussels (or prawns) and peas in a large saucepan. Bring to a boil, then simmer, uncovered, for 35 to 40 minutes, stirring occasionally.
2 Stir in the mussels (or prawns) and peas. Continue stirring over a high heat for 4 to 5 minutes until most of the liquid has been absorbed.
3. Spoon onto a warm serving dish and garnish with whole prawns and lemon wedges.

Serves 4
GRAMS OF SATURATED FAT PER SERVING 1.0

SALADS AND VEGETABLES

Main Meal Salads

Saffron Chicken Salad

1 small onion, finely chopped
1 tablespoon sunflower oil
few strands of saffron
2 teaspoons mild curry powder
juice and grated rind of 1 orange
2 teaspoons tomato purée
1 tablespoon sieved apricot jam
175g/6oz low-fat natural yoghurt
2 tablespoons mayonnaise
salt and freshly ground black pepper
1½kg/3lb oven ready chicken
slices of lemon and onion and 1 bay leaf for flavouring
50g/2oz walnuts
500g/1lb french beans, cooked
watercress and orange to garnish

1. Sauté the onion in oil for 3 to 4 minutes until soft. Stir in the saffron and curry powder. Cook, stirring, for 1 minute before adding the orange juice and the rind, and tomato purée. Simmer, uncovered, and cook on high heat for 1 minute to reduce slightly. Strain and cool.
2. In a small bowl, stir the apricot jam into the cooled curry mixture. Whisk in the yoghurt and gradually fold in to the mayonnaise. Season with a little salt and pepper. Cover and refrigerate.
3. Poach the chicken in water with the flavouring ingredients. Allow 20 minutes per 500g/1lb plus 15 minutes. Remove from the liquid and leave to cool. Skin and remove the flesh. Cut into large strips and place in a bowl with the walnuts. Pour in the mayonnaise-curry

mixture and stir until well blended. Cover and refrigerate for a maximum of 3 hours.

4. Arrange the chicken salad on a bed of French beans. Garnish with watercress sprigs and orange twists.

Serves 4
GRAMS OF SATURATED FAT PER SERVING: 5.0

Italian Pasta Salad

50g/2oz wholewheat or egg pasta shells
50g/2oz spinach pasta shells
1 red pepper, chopped
1 yellow pepper, chopped
198g/7oz-can tuna in brine, drained
12 black olives, stoned
75g/3oz French beans
125g/4oz cauliflower florets
75g/3oz mangetouts
2 hardboiled eggs, shelled and quartered
Dressing:
3 tablespoons natural yoghurt
grated rind and juice of 1 orange
1 teaspoon dried basil

1. Cook the pasta shells in plenty of boiling water until just tender. Drain and rinse under cold water.
2. Place the pasta, peppers, tuna and olives in a bowl and mix gently together.
3. Cook the beans and cauliflower in a pan of boiling salted water for 3 minutes. Add the mangetouts and cook for 3 more minutes. Drain and plunge the vegetables immediately into a bowl of cold water to maintain their crispness. Drain well and set vegetables aside.
4. Place the pasta shells in a serving dish with the vegetables and eggs.
5. Mix together the yoghurt, orange rind and 3 tablespoons

orange juice. Pour the dressing over the salad and toss gently to coat evenly.

Serves 4
GRAMS OF SATURATED FAT PER SERVING: 1.5

Smoked Haddock and Broccoli Pasta Salad

225g/8oz pasta spirals
500g/1lb smoked haddock fillet, skinned
500g/1lb broccoli
4 spring onions, sliced
1 red pepper, sliced
1 tablespoon finely chopped fresh parsley
salt and pepper to taste

1. Cook pasta in boiling water until firm but tender. Drain and rinse in cold water.
2. Place fish in frying pan. Cover with boiling water and poach for 10 minutes. Remove fish and when cool enough break fish up into large flakes removing any skin or bones.
3. Cut broccoli into florets with short stems (use tender part of stem for soups or stews). Place floret in boiling, slightly salted water for 3 minutes. Drain and cool.
4. Combined pasta, fish, broccoli and other ingredients in a glass serving bowl and chill well in refrigerator. Toss with 150ml/¼ pint French dressing (recipe p. 264).

Serves 4
GRAMS OF SATURATED FAT PER SERVING (with dressing)*: 1.0*

Seafood Vinaigrette

250g/8oz couscous
675g/1½lbs monkfish or cod fillet, skinned

1 bay leaf
250g/8oz long grain brown rice
500g/1lb red peppers, seeded and chopped
350g/12oz spring onions, finely chopped
350g/12oz peeled cooked prawns
8 tablespoons chopped fresh coriander or parsley
salt and freshly ground black pepper
Vinaigrette:
150ml/¼ pint olive oil
50ml/2fl oz white wine vinegar
salt and freshly ground black pepper
pinch of caster sugar
4 tablespoons chopped fresh chives

1. Place the couscous in a large mixing bowl. Cover with cold water to come about 5cm/2 inch above the level of the grains. Leave to soak overnight. Drain well if necessary. The couscous should have absorbed most of the liquid.
2. Cut the monkfish or cod into bite-size pieces. Place in a saucepan with the bay leaf, cover with cold water and simmer for 12 to 15 minutes, or until just cooked. Drain well and cool.
3. Cook the rice in plenty of boiling water for about 35 minutes until just cooked. Drain and stir into the couscous.
4. Carefully stir the peppers, monkfish, spring onions, prawns and coriander or parsley into the rice and couscous. Season with a little salt and pepper.
5. To make the vinaigrette, whisk together the ingredients. Stir in to the salad mixture. Cover and refrigerate until required.

Serves 6
GRAMS OF SATURATED FAT PER SERVING: 4.0

Sesame Cheese Roll on a Bed of Rice Salad

250g/8oz low-fat soft cheese
2 tablespoons finely chopped parsley
1 tablespoon sesame seeds
Salad Dressing:
3 tablespoons low-fat natural yoghurt
1 tablespoon red wine vinegar
1 teaspoon clear honey
Salad:
125g/4oz long-grain white rice
a little salt
2 red-skinned apples, cored and chopped
4 sticks celery, chopped
10cm/4 inch piece cucumber, chopped
8 radishes, thinly sliced

1. Form the cheese into a short roll about 4cm/1½ inches
   across. Mix together on a plate the parsley and sesame
   seeds until evenly blended. Turn the cheese roll in the
   parsley mixture until evenly coated. Place on a plate and
   chill.
2. Place the yoghurt, vinegar and honey in a bowl and stir
   until well blended.
3. Cook the rice in boiling, lightly salted water for 12 to
   15 minutes until the grains are tender. Drain and rinse
   under cold water.
4. Add the rice, apples, celery, cucumber and radish slices
   to the salad dressing and stir gently to coat evenly.
5. Spread the rice salad evenly over a serving plate. Place
   the cheese roll on the salad and cut into thick slices.

Serves 4
GRAMS OF SATURATED FAT PER SERVING: 3.0

Accompaniment Salads

Fresh mint, parsley and lemon juice impart a distinctive, aromatic flavour to this hearty grain salad. Serve with Fish Plaki or Sesame Chicken and warm pitta bread.

Mideastern Bulgar Salad (Tabbouleh)

125g/4oz bulgar wheat
1 small onion, finely chopped
2 spring onions, finely sliced
2 tablespoons finely chopped mint leaves
salt and freshly ground black pepper
2 tablespoons olive oil
4 tablespoons finely chopped parsley
2 tablespoons lemon juice
2 tomatoes cut into wedges
lettuce leaves

1. Soak bulgar in water for 30 minutes. Drain on a cloth and squeeze out as much moisture as possible. The bulgar should be dry before adding to the other ingredients.
2. Toss the remainder of ingredients except lettuce with the bulgar. Taste and adjust the amount of lemon juice, salt and pepper if desired.
3. Serve the bulgar salad in a lettuce-lined salad bowl or lettuce-lined individual bowls.

Serves 4
GRAMS OF SATURATED FAT PER SERVING: 1.0

This low-fat, low-calorie potato salad is made with a zesty yoghurt-horseradish dressing. Keep the skins on the potatoes for extra vitamins and fibre.

Potato Salad

500g/1lb potatoes, preferably new
Dressing:
175g/6oz low-fat natural yoghurt
2 teaspoons creamed horseradish
lemon juice
1 tablespoon finely chopped parsley

1. Cook unpeeled potatoes (whole) in a pan of boiling slightly salted water until tender. Drain. Cut potatoes into large dice while still hot. Allow to cool.
2. Mix dressing ingredients in a bowl then carefully toss in potatoes.
3. Garnish with extra chopped parsley.

Serves 4
GRAMS OF SATURATED FAT PER SERVING: Trace

Caesar Salad

75g/3oz sliced wholemeal bread
1 cos lettuce
8 anchovy fillets, drained and halved lengthways
2 tablespoons olive oil
1 clove garlic, crushed
grated rind and juice of 1 lemon
25g/1oz grated Parmesan cheese
freshly ground black pepper

1. Preheat oven to 200°C/400°F/Gas Mark 6.
2. Remove the crusts from the bread. Cut into 2.5cm/1 inch squares. Bake in oven for 15 to 20 minutes until golden and crisp.
3. Wash and dry the lettuce. Tear into bite-size pieces. Place

the lettuce and bread croutons in large bowl. Arrange the anchovies in a lattice pattern over the salad.
4. To make dressing, mix oil, garlic, lemon rind and 3 tablespoons juice, the Parmesan and pepper to taste in a small bowl. Toss the dressing into the salad at the dinner table.

Serves 4
GRAMS OF SATURATED FAT PER SERVING: 2.5

Bean and Leaf Salad

175g/6oz mixed dried beans (e.g. kidney, black butter, cannellini or flageolet), soaked overnight
600ml/1 pint light stock
1 bunch watercress, trimmed
1 head chicory, trimmed
Dressing:
2 tablespoons sunflower oil
2 tablespoons lemon juice
1 clove garlic, crushed
1 tablespoon chopped fresh parsley
1½ teaspoons dried marjoram

1. Rinse the beans well under fresh water and place together in a saucepan with the stock. Bring to the boil and cook rapidly for 10 minutes. Cover the saucepan with a lid and cook very gently for about one and a half hours or until the beans are tender. Drain well and cool.
2. Separate the salad leaves, wash and drain well. Arrange the leaves in an attractive pattern on a round serving dish. Cover with cling film and refrigerate.
3. Place the oil, lemon juice, garlic and chopped herbs in a bowl and whisk until well blended. Pour the dressing over the beans, stir well to coat evenly.

4. Pile the beans into the centre of the salad leaves and garnish with sliced spring onions or chopped chives.

Serves 4
GRAMS OF SATURATED FAT PER SERVING: 1.0

This healthy salad can be varied by using different raw vegetables, herbs and spices. Serve in a white bowl or dish for added attractiveness.

Lentil and Rice Salad

250g/8oz whole lentils, previously soaked
125g/4oz long-grain brown rice
1 red pepper, chopped
2 stalks celery, chopped
4 spring onions, chopped
2 tablespoons finely chopped fresh parsley
50g/2oz raisins, chopped
Dressing:
3 tablespoons olive oil
1 tablespoon lemon juice
1 garlic clove, crushed
salt and freshly ground black pepper to taste

1. Cook the lentils in plenty of boiling water for about 30 to 40 minutes or until they are tender. Meanwhile, in another pan cook the rice in plenty of boiling water for 35 minutes until just tender. Drain the lentils and rice thoroughly and leave to cool.
2. Gently mix the vegetables, parsley and raisins with the rice and lentils in a large bowl.
3. Mix the dressing ingredients together and toss into the lentil-rice mixture.

Serves 4
GRAMS OF SATURATED FAT PER SERVING: 1.5

This colourful salad is a good choice for lunch boxes. It is refreshing and crisp and 'travels' well if carried in airtight containers.

Fruity Coleslaw

Dressing:
3 tablespoons sunflower oil
2 teaspoons lemon juice
2 teaspoons pure unsweetened apple juice
½ teaspoon mild mustard
 a little salt and freshly ground black pepper
Salad:
1 red dessert apple, cored
1 orange
50g/2oz each black and green grapes, halved and seeded
125g/4oz white cabbage, finely shredded
1 bunch watercress, chopped

1. Whisk together the dressing ingredients. Slice the apple thinly into the dressing and toss thoroughly until coated.
2. Remove the peel and pith from the orange, slice, then cut into quarters. Add to the bowl with all the remaining ingredients, toss well and transfer to a salad bowl.

Serves 4
GRAMS OF SATURATED FAT PER SERVING: 1.5

Cherry Tomato Salad

500g/1lb cherry tomatoes
2 tablespoons olive oil
2 tablespoons chopped fresh basil
2 tablespoons lemon juice
salt and freshly ground black pepper

125g/4oz pitted black olives
basil leaves to garnish

1. Wash and stem tomatoes. Cut any large ones in half.
2. To make the dressing, whisk together the oil, basil, lemon juice and a little salt and pepper. Stir into the tomatoes with the olives. Garnish with fresh basil leaves.

Serves 4
GRAMS OF SATURATED FAT PER SERVING: 1.5

Salad Dressings

French Dressing

150ml/¼ pint olive oil
5 tablespoons white wine vinegar
salt and freshly ground black pepper
½ teaspoon prepared mustard

1. Place all the ingredients in a screw-topped jar and shake well.

Variations:
Use red wine vinegar instead of white wine vinegar.

Add one clove of garlic, peeled and crushed, and one tablespoon of ground tumeric.

Add one tablespoon chopped fresh herbs.

Add one tablespoon toasted sesame seeds.

Serving size: 2 TABLESPOONS
GRAMS OF SATURATED FAT PER SERVING: 3.5

Mayonnaise

1 egg yolk
½ teaspoon English mustard powder
½ teaspoon caster sugar
1 tablespoon white wine vinegar
200ml/⅓ pint sunflower oil
4 tablespoons natural yoghurt
salt and freshly ground black pepper

1. Place the egg yolk in a medium bowl. Whisk in the mustard, sugar and vinegar.
2. Add the oil, in a thin stream, beating all the time until very thick and smooth. Fold in the yoghurt and season with a little salt and pepper.
3. Cover with damp greaseproof paper or cling-film and refrigerate. Mayonnaise will keep at least 2 weeks in the refrigerator.

Variations:
Use one tablespoon whole grain mustard in place of mustard powder.

Add 1 to 2 tablespoons chopped fresh herbs, e.g. parsley, chives, dill.

Add the grated rind and juice of 1 small lemon.

Serving size: 1 TABLESPOON
GRAMS OF SATURATED FAT PER SERVING: 1.5

Creamy Blue Cheese Dressing

150ml/¼ pint natural yoghurt or low-fat soft cheese
1 clove garlic, crushed, optional
1 tablespoon lemon juice

25g/1oz blue cheese, crumbled
freshly ground black pepper

1. Place all the ingredients in a bowl and mix well. Alternatively, put all the ingredients in a blender and blend to a smooth consistency.

Serving size: 1 TABLESPOON
GRAMS OF SATURATED FAT PER SERVING: 0.5

California Green Goddess Dressing

2 tablespoons tarragon vinegar
2 tablespoons homemade mayonnaise (recipe p.265)
125g/4oz natural yoghurt
1 tablespoon anchovy paste
1 tablespoon lemon juice
1 clove garlic, crushed
2 tablespoons finely chopped fresh parsley
1 tablespoon finely chopped fresh chives

1. Put all ingredients in a bowl or blender and mix well until a smooth consistency. Chill for 2 hours in the refrigerator.

Serving size: 1 TABLESPOON
GRAMS OF SATURATED FAT PER SERVING: 1.0

Walnut Yoghurt Dressing

50g/2oz ground walnuts
1 clove garlic, crushed
1 teaspoon sunflower oil
1 teaspoon lemon juice
150ml/¼ pint natural yoghurt
salt
50g/2oz cucumber, peeled and finely chopped

1. Beat together the walnuts, garlic, oil and lemon juice.
   Gradually stir in the yoghurt. Season with a little salt.
   Cover and refrigerate until required. Just before serving
   stir the cucumber into the yoghurt mixture.

Serves 6
GRAMS OF SATURATED FAT PER SERVING: 0.5

Vegetables

These chips have a fraction of the fat and calories of
ordinary chips.

Oven-baked Chips

4 medium potatoes
1 tablespoon sunflower oil
salt to taste, optional

1. Preheat the oven to 230°C/450°F/Gas Mark 8.
2. Cut potatoes into lengthwise strips about 1.25cm/½ inch
   thick and place them in a bowl of ice-cold water to crisp.
   Drain and pat chips dry with kitchen paper.
3. Return the chips to bowl and add the oil. Mix well with
   the hands to distribute the oil evenly over the chips. Place
   on a baking sheet and bake in oven for 35 to 40 minutes
   or until crisp and golden. Sprinkle with a little salt if
   desired and serve immediately.

Serves 4
GRAMS OF SATURATED FAT PER SERVING: 0.5

French Beans with Mushrooms

250g/8oz French beans, topped and tailed

250g/8oz button mushrooms
grated rind and juice of 1 lemon
1 tablespoon pine nuts or flaked almonds
salt and freshly ground black pepper

1. Preheat the oven to 180°C/350°F/Gas Mark 4.
2. Cook the beans in boiling salted water for 5 minutes. Drain and rinse under cold water.
3. Place the beans and mushrooms in a lightly greased ovenproof dish. Stir in the lemon rind and juice, pine nuts or almonds and a little salt and pepper. Bake in the oven for about 35 to 45 minutes. The beans should still retain some bite.

Serves 4
GRAMS OF SATURATED FAT PER SERVING: 0.5

Braised Celery

1¼ kg/2½ lb celery
1 tablespoon sunflower oil
1 bay leaf
300ml/½ pint chicken stock
salt and freshly ground black pepper

1. Preheat the oven to 220°C/425°F/Gas Mark 7.
2. Wash the celery then cut into 5cm/2 inch lengths, reserving any leafy tops for garnish.
3. Heat the oil in a large flameproof casserole. Sauté the celery and bay leaf for 2 minutes. Add the stock and a little salt and pepper. Bring to the boil and cover tightly. Cook in oven for 20 minutes. The celery should retain some bite.

Serves 4
GRAMS OF SATURATED FAT PER SERVING: 0.5

Baked Tomatoes

12 small, firm tomatoes, about 1kg/2lb in total weight
2 tablespoons white wine vinegar
salt and freshly ground black pepper

1. Preheat the oven to 180°C/350°F/Gas Mark 4.
2. Make a small cross in the bottom of each tomato. Place stalk end down in a shallow ovenproof dish. Pour over the vinegar and enough water to come 5 mm/¼ inch up the sides of the dish. Season with a little salt and pepper.
3. Bake for 15 to 20 minutes. Test with a skewer after 15 minutes. They should be just cooked but not too soft. Garnish with fresh marjoram or mint sprigs.

Serves 4
GRAMS OF SATURATED FAT PER SERVING: 0

Stir-frying is a healthy, attractive way of serving vegetables. A large, heavy frying pan will do if you do not own a wok.

Oriental Stir-Fry Vegetables

500g/1lb broccoli
1 small cauliflower
1 tablespoon sesame oil
1 tablespoon sunflower oil
175g/6oz carrots, sliced
2 teaspoons finely grated ginger root
2 teaspoons soy sauce
1 teaspoon sesame seeds

1. Cut broccoli and cauliflower into florets. Slice the tender parts of stems into diagonal pieces. Discard any tough or 'woody' stems. Set aside.
2. Just before serving, heat a wok or large frying pan over

high heat for 30 seconds. Swirl in the oils and count to 20. Add the vegetables and ginger. Stir continuously for about 2 to 3 minutes or until the broccoli turns a very vivid green.
3. Stir in the soy sauce and sesame seeds and serve immediately.

Serves 4
GRAMS OF SATURATED FAT PER SERVING: 1.0

CAKES AND BISCUITS

Dried prunes soaked in cold tea gives this teabread a delectable moist quality and rich flavour, highlighted with a touch of spice. It will keep well for 2 to 3 days in an airtight container.

Cinnamon Banana Teabread

175g/6oz dried pitted prunes
175ml/6fl oz cold tea
125g/4oz plain wholemeal flour
1 tablespoon baking powder
2 teaspoons ground cinnamon
50g/2oz wholemeal breadcrumbs, toasted
75g/3oz soft brown sugar
2 large bananas
120ml/4fl oz sunflower oil

1. Preheat the oven to 180°C/350°F/Gas Mark 4.
2. Place the prunes in a bowl with the cold tea, and leave to soak for 1 hour.
3. Lightly oil a deep 20cm/8 inch square cake tin and line with non-stick baking parchment.
4. Mix together in a bowl the flour, baking powder, cinnamon and all but 1 tablespoon each of the breadcrumbs and sugar.
5. Drain the prunes (reserving the soaking liquid), and roughly chop. Stir into the dry ingredients with 250g/8oz mashed banana. Whisk together the reserved soaking liquid, oil and eggs. Beat into the mixture until thoroughly combined. Turn into the prepared tin.
6. Thinly slice the remaining banana into the reserved breadcrumbs and sugar. Sprinkle over the cake mixture.
7. Bake for about 1 to 1¼ hours, or until the cake springs back when lightly pressed. Cool on a wire rack.

Serves 12
GRAMS OF SATURATED FAT PER SERVING: 1.0

The natural sweetness of carrots combines well with raisins and dates to produce a taste and texture that will make this cake mandatory for special occasions.

Carrot Fruit Cake

125g/4oz soft brown sugar
6 tablespoons clear honey
175g/6oz carrots, finely grated
125g/4oz seedless raisins
50g/2oz stoned dates, chopped
½ teaspoon ground mace
125g/4oz sunflower margarine
150ml/¼ pint water
1 egg, beaten
125g/4oz plain white flour
125g/4oz plain wholemeal flour
2 teaspoons baking powder
Topping:
200g/7oz low-fat soft cheese or natural quark
2 tablespoons clear honey
1 teaspoon lemon juice
1 tablespoon chopped walnuts

1. Preheat the oven to 180°C/350°F/Gas Mark 4.
2. Mix together the sugar, honey, carrots, raisins, dates, mace, margarine and water in a saucepan. Bring to the boil. Simmer gently for 5 minutes. Turn into a mixing bowl and leave until cold.
3. Beat in the egg. Mix together the flours and baking powder and fold into the fruit mixture until thoroughly combined.
4. Lightly oil a 23cm/9 inch cake tin. Line with non-stick

baking parchment. Turn the mixture into a prepared tin and level the surface.
5. Bake for 55 to 60 minutes, or until firm. Cool on a wire rack.
6. Beat together all the topping ingredients except the walnuts. Spread evenly over the surface of the cooled cake. Sprinkle over the walnuts.

Serves 8
GRAMS OF SATURATED FAT PER SERVING: 4.5

Figgy Nut Scone Round

125g/4oz wholemeal self-raising flour
125g/4oz flour, sieved with 1 teaspoon baking powder
50g/2oz white vegetable fat
25g/1oz castor sugar
125g/4oz dried figs, chopped
7 to 8 tablespoons semi-skimmed milk
Topping:
semi-skimmed milk to glaze
15g/½oz chopped walnuts mixed with 1 dessertspoon demerara sugar

1. Preheat the oven to 200°C/400°F/Gas Mark 6.
2. Mix together the flours and baking powder. Rub in the white fat and stir in the sugar and figs. Add enough milk to give a soft but not sticky dough. Turn mixture onto a floured surface and knead lightly. Roll out to a 20cm/8 inch circle and place on a greased baking tray.
3. Score the scone into 8 pieces. Brush top with milk and sprinkle with the topping mixture.
4. Bake for 20 to 25 minutes until well-risen and golden brown.

Serves 8
GRAMS OF SATURATED FAT PER SERVING: 1.5

Banana Raisin Loaf

75g/3oz sunflower margarine
75g/3oz light brown sugar
1 egg
150g/5oz wholemeal self-raising flour
¼ teaspoon bicarbonate of soda
125g/4oz raisins
2 small ripe bananas, mashed
50g/2oz walnuts, chopped

1. Preheat the oven to 180°C/350°F/Gas Mark 4.
2. Cream the margarine and sugar together until light and fluffy. Beat in the egg, stir in the flour and bicarbonate of soda, then add the raisins, bananas and chopped walnuts. Spoon the mixture into a greased greaseproof-lined ½kg/1lb loaf tin.
3. Bake on the middle shelf of the oven for approximately 50 to 60 minutes. Turn out and cool on a wire tray. Decorate with sliced banana.

Serves 8
GRAMS OF SATURATED FAT PER SERVING: 2.5

This cake has a delicate flavour of citrus and spice. Serve it plain or with a tropical fruit salad.

Spiced Honey Ring

125g/4oz sunflower margarine
75g/3oz soft brown sugar
3 tablespoons clear honey
2 eggs
175g/6oz self-raising wholemeal flour
1 teaspoon mixed spice
½ teaspoon ground ginger

finely grated rind of 1 lemon
1 tablespoon honey to glaze
lemon zest to decorate

1. Preheat the oven to 160°C/325°F/Gas Mark 3.
2. Cream together the margarine, sugar and honey. Add the eggs, dry ingredients and lemon rind and beat for 2 to 3 minutes. Place in a greased and floured 20cm/8 inch ring mould and bake on middle shelf for 40 to 45 minutes.
3. Turn out and cool on wire rack. To serve, glaze with honey and decorate with lemon zest.

Serves 8
GRAMS OF SATURATED FAT PER SERVING: 3.5

These fudge brownies have less than half the saturated fat of traditional ones made with butter and chocolate. Nevertheless, we do warn you that one is usually not enough!

Fudge Brownies

125g/4oz sunflower margarine
50g/2oz cocoa or carob powder (available at health food shops)
125g/4oz brown sugar
2 eggs, beaten
50g/2oz plain white flour
1 teaspoon baking powder

1. Preheat the oven to 180°C/350°F/Gas Mark 4.
2. Melt the margarine, cocoa or carob powder and sugar slowly in a saucepan. Remove promptly from heat. Add the remaining ingredients into the mixture and stir until smooth. Spread the mixture into a greased and floured 7 x 11 inch/18 x 28cm tin.
3. Bake in the centre of oven for 25 to 30 minutes. The cake

should be slightly soft in the centre as it will firm up as it cools.

4. Loosen the cake at the sides with a knife but allow to cool in the tin. Cut the cake into 12 squares.

GRAMS OF SATURATED FAT PER BROWNIE 2.5

The sesame seeds create a delicious crunchy coating on these cookies.

Sesame Seed Cookies

50g/2oz white vegetable fat
65g/2½oz self-raising flour
40g/1½oz castor sugar
2–3 drops vanilla essence
sesame seeds, to coat cookies
glacé cherries, to decorate, optional

1. Preheat the oven 180°C/350°F/Gas Mark 4.
2. Place white fat, flour, sugar and vanilla essence in a mixing bowl and mix with a fork to form a firm dough. Turn out onto a lightly floured surface and knead until smooth. Using a teaspoon, divide mixture into small balls and press each out into a saucer of sesame seeds to coat each cookie on one side. Place the flattened rounds on 2 baking sheets and decorate (if wished) with a piece of glacé cherry.
3. Bake on the middle shelf for 15 to 20 minutes. Cool on a wire tray.

Makes about 15
GRAMS OF SATURATED FAT PER COOKIE: 0.5

Lemon and nutmeg digestives have a crisp, light texture with a delicate flavour of lemon and nutmeg. They are ideal with coffee or with fresh fruit salads. If you don't have fine oatmeal, put coarse oatmeal in the food processor or blender.

Lemon and Nutmeg Digestives

175g/6oz self-raising wholemeal flour
50g/2oz fine oatmeal
a little salt
grated rind of 1 lemon
¼ teaspoon grated nutmeg
75g/3oz sunflower margarine
25g/1oz soft brown sugar
2 to 4 tablespoons skimmed milk
grated nutmeg to decorate

1. Preheat the oven to 190°C/375°F/Gas Mark 5.
2. Mix together the flour, oatmeal, salt, lemon rind and nutmeg. Rub in the margarine until the mixture resembles breadcrumbs. Stir in the sugar. Add the milk and mix to a firm dough.
3. Turn onto a floured surface and roll out thinly. Stamp out 24 rounds with a 6cm/2½ inch plain cutter. Place on a non-stick baking sheet and prick with a fork. Brush with water and sprinkle with grated nutmeg.
4. Bake for 15 to 20 minutes. Cool on a wire rack.

Makes 24
GRAMS OF SATURATED FAT: 1 per 3 biscuits

Malted Oat Squares

120ml/4fl oz sunflower oil
3 tablespoons malt extract
50g/2oz soft brown sugar
250g/8oz rolled oats
2 tablespoons sesame seeds, toasted

1. Preheat the oven to 180°C/350°F/Gas Mark 4.
2. Place the oil, malt extract, and sugar in a saucepan and heat gently, stirring all the time. Add the rolled oats and toasted sesame seeds and mix quickly and thoroughly until well blended. Press the mixture evenly into a lightly oiled 20cm/8 inch square shallow cake tin.
3. Bake for 20 to 30 minutes in oven until golden brown and firm to the touch. Cool in the tin for 2 minutes then cut into squares. Cool completely before carefully removing from the tin.

Makes 16
GRAMS OF SATURATED FAT PER SQUARE: 1.0

DESSERTS

You can certainly enjoy elegant, mouth-watering desserts on a healthier diet. In this pavlova recipe, vary the fruit toppings to suit the season and your preferences.

Passion Fruit Pavlova

3 egg whites
175g/6oz soft brown sugar
2 teaspoons cornflour
2 teaspoons white wine vinegar
¼ teaspoon vanilla essence
Topping:
250g/8oz low-fat soft cheese
150ml/¼ pint natural low-fat yoghurt
2 tablespoons clear honey
1 banana, thinly sliced
2 nectarines, sliced
2 ripe mangoes, peeled and sliced
2 passion fruit

1. Preheat the oven to 150°C/300°F/Gas Mark 2.
2. Whisk the egg whites until stiff then gradually whisk in the sugar until the meringue is very stiff. Whisk in the cornflour, vinegar and vanilla essence.
3. Pile the meringue on to a baking sheet lined with non-stick baking parchment and spread into a 20cm/8 inch round. Hollow the centre slightly and bake for 1½ hours.
4. Cool, then remove the paper and place the pavlova on a serving dish (it will crack slightly but this is a characteristic of a pavlova).
5. Mix the cheese with the yoghurt and honey then fold in the banana. Pile onto the meringue and decorate with the nectarine and mango. Halve the passion fruit and scoop out the pulp. Scatter over the top.

Serves 6
GRAMS OF SATURATED FAT PER SERVING: 2.0

Make the most of summer or frozen fruits in a pudding that is suitable for a formal dinner party. Serve plain or with our soft cheese cream (page 291).

Raspberry Liqueur Pudding

500g/1lb blackcurrants, fresh or frozen
500g/1lb raspberries, fresh or frozen
150ml/¼ pint medium white wine
50ml/2fl oz Crême de Cassis
2 tablespoons soft brown sugar
250g/8oz sliced white or wholemeal bread
mint sprigs or raspberry leaves to garnish

1. Thaw the fruit if necessary. Place in a saucepan with the wine and Crême de Cassis. Bring slowly to the boil, stir in the sugar and remove from heat. Cool.
2. Remove the crusts from the bread. Use one slice to cover the base of a 1½ litre/2½ pint pudding basin. Spoon over a little of the fruit mixture. Continue layering the fruit with all but 2 tablespoons of the fruit mixture, ending with a slice of bread.
3. Place a small plate on top of the mixture. Weight down and refrigerate overnight.
4. To serve, loosen the sides of the pudding with a palette knife. Invert onto a serving plate. Brush over the reserved juices to completely stain the bread. Decorate with whole fruit and mint sprigs or raspberry leaves.

Serves 6
GRAMS OF SATURATED FAT PER SERVING: Trace

Gingered Apricot Compote

125g/4oz dried apricots
1kg/2lb rhubarb, trimmed
25g/1oz preserved stem ginger, drained and thinly sliced
1 teaspoon ground ginger
50g/2oz soft brown sugar

1. Cover the apricots with cold water and leave to soak overnight.
2. Preheat the oven to 180°C/350°F/Gas Mark 4.
3. Cut the rhubarb into 2.5cm/1 inch lengths. Place the rhubarb with both gingers in a medium-sized, ovenproof dish. Stir in the soaked apricots with 150ml/¼ pint of the soaking liquid and the sugar. Cover tightly with the foil.
4. Bake for about 30 minutes. Serve hot with custard made with skimmed milk or low-fat natural yoghurt.

Serves 4
GRAMS OF SATURATED FAT PER SERVING: 0

Peaches with Kiwi Fruit

1½kg/3lb ripe peaches
6 tablespoons kirsch
6 tablespoons sparkling mineral water
1 tablespoon clear honey
3 kiwi fruit
2 passion fruit
toasted flaked almonds to decorate, optional

1. Halve, stone and thickly slice the peaches. Pour over the kirsch, water and honey and stir well. Cover and place in the refrigerator to chill for 20 minutes.
2. Peel and thickly slice the kiwi fruit. Halve the passion

fruit and scoop out the pulp. Stir into the peaches.
Decorate with toasted flaked almonds if wished.

Serves 6
GRAMS OF SATURATED FAT PER SERVING: Trace

Pears in port is a perfect ending to a filling meal.

Pears in Port

1 orange
100ml/4fl oz port wine
250ml/8fl oz red grape juice
4 firm dessert pears
2 teaspoons arrowroot

1. Pare away the rind of the orange and cut into thin
   needleshreds. Squeeze the juice from the orange.
2. Place the port in a small saucepan with the grape juice,
   orange needleshreds and juice. Cover and bring to the boil.
3. Peel the pears, leaving on the stalks, and place in the
   saucepan. Baste them with the juice, cover the pan and
   simmer gently for 20 minutes until the pears are tender.
   Cool in the liquid.
4. Arrange the pears on a serving dish. Mix the arrowroot
   with a little of the cooking liquid, then pour back into
   the rest of the liquid and bring to the boil, stirring.
   Simmer until thickened and clear. Leave to cool. Spoon
   over the pears and chill before serving.

Serves 4
GRAMS OF SATURATED FAT PER SERVING: 0

This very simple, but super low-fat dessert provides lots of
taste without the added sugar.

Baked Bananas or Peaches in Orange Juice

4 bananas or peaches, peeled and cut into thick slices
grated rind and juice of 2 oranges
25g/1oz flaked almonds, toasted, or muesli

1. Preheat the oven to 180°C/350°F/Gas Mark 4.
2. Place fruit in ovenproof dish. Pour over orange juice with
   rind. Cover and bake for 15 to 20 minutes until fruit is
   just tender. Sprinkle with toasted almonds or muesli.
   Serve with low-fat natural yoghurt if liked.

Serves 4
GRAMS OF SATURATED FAT PER SERVING: 0.5

Fruit Pancakes

125g/4oz plain flour, sieved
1 egg, beaten
300ml/½ pint semi-skimmed milk
sunflower oil for frying
Filling:
250g/8oz-tin pineapple in natural juice, chopped
150ml/¼ pint pure orange juice
2 teaspoons arrowroot mixed with a little of the orange juice
2–3 teaspoons kirsch, optional
2 large oranges, peeled, segmented and chopped
25g/1oz walnuts, chopped

1. To make the batter, place the flour in a bowl, add egg
   and gradually stir in half the milk, beating thoroughly.
   Stir in the remaining milk.
2. Heat a little oil in a small non-stick frying pan and pour
   in a tablespoon of batter, tipping pan to spread it. Cook
   until underside is golden, turn over and cook other side.
   Turn out. Repeat until remaining batter is used up,

(makes about 8 pancakes). Use rounds of greaseproof paper between the pancakes to prevent sticking. Keep the pancakes warm.

3. For the filling, mix together the pineapple juice and orange juice into a saucepan with the arrowroot mixture. Stirring over a medium heat, slowly bring the sauce to a boil and cook until it is thick and smooth. Add the kirsch, if used. Pour a little of the sauce over the fruit and nuts to coat. Fill the pancakes with the fruit mixture and fold into four. Place on a warmed serving dish. Serve the pancakes with the sauce.

Serves 4
GRAMS OF SATURATED FAT PER SERVING: 2.0

Wholemeal flour and porridge oats can be used in fruit crumbles to boost the fibre value. Sugar can also be kept to a minimum by using natural fruit juice to sweeten the fruit.

Almond Plum Crumble

500g/1lb firm plums, halved and stoned
300ml/½ pint pure unsweetened orange juice
pinch grated nutmeg
75g/3oz wholemeal flour
75g/3oz plain white flour
50g/2oz sunflower margarine
50g/2oz flaked almonds

1. Preheat the oven to 200°C/400°F/Gas Mark 6.
2. Place the plums in a saucepan with the orange juice and nutmeg. Bring to the boil and simmer for 2 minutes. Spoon the fruit mixture into an ovenproof pie dish.
3. Place the flours in a bowl and rub in the margarine until it resembles breadcrumbs. Stir in the sugar and almonds.

Sprinkle over the fruit to cover completely. Bake for 25 to 30 minutes or until golden brown. Serve with sweet tofu cream (page 290) or low-fat natural yoghurt.

Serves 6
GRAMS OF SATURATED FAT PER SERVING: 2.0

Cherry and Blackcurrant Crumble

350g/12oz canned cherries, stoned
2 teaspoons arrowroot
125g/4oz blackcurrants
125g/4oz plain wholemeal flour
50g/2oz porridge oats
1 teaspoon mixed spice
75g/3oz sunflower margarine
50g/2oz soft light brown sugar
25g/1oz blanched almonds, chopped

1. Preheat the oven to 180°C/350°F/Gas Mark 4.
2. Drain the cherries, reserving the juice. Place the fruit in an ovenproof dish.
3. In a saucepan, blend the arrowroot with 150ml/¼ pint of the cherry juice and heat until thickened. Pour over the fruit.
4. Mix together the flour, oats and spice and rub in the margarine. Stir in the sugar and almonds, and spoon over the fruit. Bake for 25 to 30 minutes.

Serves 6
GRAMS OF SATURATED FAT PER SERVING 2.5

Traditional English sponge puddings are quite high in saturated fat. Here is a leaner version with an irresistible taste-combination of orange, hazelnuts and spice.

Hazelnut Sponge Pudding

3 large oranges
125g/4oz hazelnuts
75g/3oz soft brown sugar
2 teaspoons mixed spice
50g/2oz sunflower margarine
1 egg
25g/1oz self-raising wholemeal flour
50g/2oz self-raising white flour
1 teaspoon icing sugar to decorate

1. Preheat the oven to 190°C/375°F/Gas Mark 5.
2. Grate the orange rinds and reserve. Remove all skin and pith from the oranges using a serrated knife. Cut between the membranes to release the segments and reserve.
3. Brown the hazelnuts under a hot grill. Place in a tea towel and rub off the skins. Roughly chop the nuts. Mix half the nuts with 25g/1oz sugar and mixed spice.
4. Cream together the margarine and remaining sugar until very pale and fluffy. Gradually beat in the egg. Fold in the flours, remaining nuts and half the orange rind.
5. Reserve 8 orange segments for garnish. Place the remainder in a shallow 600ml/1 pint baking dish with the nuts, sugar and mixed spice mixture. Spoon over the creamed mixture and scatter over the reserved orange segments and remaining rind. Bake for 35 minutes or until well risen and golden. Dust with icing sugar and serve with nutmeg custard (page 290).

Serves 4
GRAMS OF SATURATED FAT PER SERVING: 3.5

Wholemeal Apple and Blackberry Pie

75g/3oz plain wholemeal flour
75g/3oz plain white flour

1 teaspoon baking powder
2 tablespoons oat bran
75g/3oz white vegetable fat
Filling:
500g/1lb dessert apples, peeled, cored and sliced
250g/8oz blackberries
3 tablespoons clear honey

1. Preheat the oven to 200°C/400°F/Gas Mark 6.
2. Place the flours, baking powder and oat bran in a bowl. Rub in the white fat until the mixture resembles breadcrumbs. Gradually add the water and mix to a firm dough. Chill for 15 minutes.
3. Mix the apples and blackberries together then place in a 900ml/1½-pint pie dish and drizzle over the honey.
4. Turn the dough onto a floured surface and knead lightly. Roll out thinly to a round about 5cm/2 inches larger that the pie dish. Cut off a narrow strip all round and use to cover the dampened rim of the pie dish, then brush with water.
5. Lift the pastry onto a rolling pin and place over the fruit, sealing the edges well. Trim and flute the edges and make a hole in the centre. Brush with water and bake for 30 to 40 minutes. Serve hot or cold.

Serves 6
GRAMS OF SATURATED FAT PER SERVING: 2.5

Typical cheesecake is unbelievably high in saturated fat. One slice can use up an entire allotment on the Basic plan. This version tastes rich and has a fraction of the fat.

Baked Cherry Cheesecake

125g/4oz sunflower margarine
125g/4oz light brown sugar

500g/1lb low-fat soft cheese
2 eggs, separated
50g/2oz ground almonds
50g/2oz semolina
175g/6oz fresh morello cherries, stoned and halved or
125g/4oz canned pitted cherries
1 teaspoon icing sugar

1. Preheat the oven to 190°C/375°F/Gas Mark 5.
2. Cream together the margarine and sugar until very pale and fluffy. Beat in the cheese and the egg yolks until smooth and thoroughly combined. Gradually fold in the ground almonds, semolina and cherries.
3. Whisk the egg whites until stiff but not dry and gently fold into the mixture with a metal spoon or spatula.
4. Lightly oil the base and sides of a deep 20cm/8 inch round, loose-based flan tin. Spoon in the mixture and bake for about 45 to 50 minutes or until golden brown and firm to the touch.
5. Leave to cool in the tin for about 1 hour. (The cheesecake will sink slightly.) Carefully ease out of the tin and slide onto a flat serving plate. Dust with icing sugar and decorate with whole cherries.

Serves 8
GRAMS OF SATURATED FAT PER SERVING: 6.5

Water ice is an interesting alternative to ice cream that provides lots of vitamin C and is fat free.

Blackcurrant Water Ice

300ml/½ pint water
75g/3oz sugar
250g/8oz blackcurrants
1 teaspoon lemon juice
2 fresh egg whites

1. Heat water and sugar together in a pan, stirring until sugar has dissolved. Bring to the boil and simmer gently for 10 minutes. Cool.
2. Meanwhile simmer blackcurrants gently in a little water for 10 minutes until tender. Sieve and make up purée to 300ml/½ pint with water. Cool. Add lemon juice and sugar syrup and pour into ice tray. Freeze for about an hour until nearly firm.
3. Whisk egg whites until stiff. Turn half-frozen mixture into chilled bowl. Whisk until smooth. Fold in egg whites, return mixture to ice tray and freeze until firm. Take out of freezer 5 minutes before serving.

Strawberry or Raspberry Water Ice
Use fruit raw, rub through sieve and make purée up to 300ml/½ pint with water. Continue as above, but use a little less sugar.
Note: Return any unused water ice immediately to the freezer.

Serves 4
GRAMS OF SATURATED FAT PER SERVING: 0

Dessert Toppings

Transform pure, unsweetened juice into a light custard topping.

Orange Custard

2 tablespoons cornflour
450ml/¾ pint pure unsweetened orange juice
1 tablespoon soft brown sugar
150ml/¼ pint low-fat natural yoghurt

1. Mix the cornflour to a smooth paste with a little of the orange juice.

2. Bring the remaining juice to the boil. Remove from heat and whisk in the cornflour mixture and sugar. Return to the boil, stirring all the time until thickened. Remove the pan from heat.
3. Whisk the yoghurt into the mixture. Serve warm or chilled.

Serves 4
GRAMS OF SATURATED FAT PER SERVING: Trace

Nutmeg Custard

2 tablespoons cornflour
600ml/1 pint skimmed milk
1 tablespoon soft brown sugar
½ teaspoon grated nutmeg

1. Mix the cornflour to a smooth paste with a little of the milk.
2. Heat the remainder of the milk to boiling point. Stir in the cornflour, sugar and nutmeg. Simmer until thickened.

Serves 6
GRAMS OF SATURATED FAT PER SERVING: Trace

Tofu, or soy bean curd whips up to make smooth, delicious low-fat cream. Try this sweet tofu cream on your pies, crumbles or fruit compotes.

Sweet Tofu Cream

250g/8oz tofu, drained
1 tablespoon clear honey
2–3 drops real vanilla extract

1. Place the tofu, honey and vanilla in a blender or food processor and blend until smooth.
2. Chill well before serving.

Variation:
Add 2 teaspoons of lemon juice instead of vanilla.

Serves 4
GRAMS OF SATURATED FAT PER SERVING: 0.5

This soft cheese cream makes an ideal substitute for whipped cream. It is perfect with most desserts.

Soft Cheese Cream

250g/8oz low-fat soft cheese or quark
1 tablespoon clear honey or sieved icing sugar
2–3 drops real vanilla essence

1. Blend together the soft cheese or quark, honey or icing sugar and vanilla in a bowl.
2. Chill well before serving.

Serves 4
GRAMS OF SATURATED FAT PER SERVING: 2.5
Made with very low-fat fromage frais or quark: *Trace*

SHEILA MOTTLEY

TOUGH COOKIE

The less-than-virtuous tale of a thalidomide mum.

Sheila Mottley's first child, was one of the last and most severely deformed thalidomide babies. When she insisted on keeping Janette, her husband walked out. This is her moving story, which recalls a hard and colourful life spent keeping her family together, and becoming a grandmother, against all odds.

'It took me five minutes before I could draw the covers back. It was the hardest thing I'd ever had to do in my life till then. My baby opened her eyes and I thought, "Poor little sod, as well as everything else wrong with you, you're cross-eyed!" But it was at that moment that I knew how tightly we were bound together, Janette and me . . . That's when my real fight started.'

'A terrific book by a very strong and humorous woman – I couldn't put it down until the last page'
Pauline Collins

Post·A·Book

A Royal Mail service in association with the Book Marketing Council & The Booksellers Association.

Post-A-Book is a Post Office trademark.

ANDREW TYLER

STREET DRUGS

Alcohol

Amphetamine

Barbiturates

Cannabis

Cocaine

Hallucinogens

Heroin

Nitrites

Solvents

Tobacco

Tranquillisers

Xanthines

Prescribed, trafficked or stolen, drugs are swallowed, smoked, sniffed and injected at all levels of society. Patterns of use and abuse change and change again. Yet accurate information and level-headed advice are hard to come by.

Instead we are bombarded by a succession of panic headlines as scare follows scare. Even medical opinion reverses: yesterday's wonder prescription is today's killer. Fact and fiction are muddled. The law and government policies either limp along behind reality or become sidetracked by moral crusades. History is ignored and lessons never learned.

Street Drugs is a much-needed guide to the whole range of drugs – legal and illegal – in use today. Effects and side-effects, trade names and street names, history and geography, methods and fashions, benefits and dangers, are all clearly described.

Street Drugs is for drug workers, drug users, teachers, parents, for everyone who needs or wants to know about drugs and drug taking.

HODDER AND STOUGHTON PAPERBACKS

MORE NON-FICTION TITLES AVAILABLE FROM HODDER AND STOUGHTON PAPERBACKS

All these books are available at your local bookshop or newsagent, or can be ordered direct from the publisher. Just tick the titles you want and fill in the form below.

Prices and availability subject to change without notice.

HODDER AND STOUGHTON PAPERBACKS, P O Box 11, Falmouth, Cornwall.

Please send cheque or postal order for the value of the book, and add the following for postage and packing.

UK including BFPO – £1.00 for one book, plus 50p for the second book, and 30p for each additional book ordered up to a £3.00 maximum.

OVERSEAS INCLUDING EIRE – £2.00 for the first book, plus £1.00 for the second book, and 50p for each additional book ordered.
OR Please debit this amount from my Access/Visa Card (delete as appropriate).

Card Number ☐☐☐☐☐☐☐☐☐☐☐☐☐☐☐☐☐☐

AMOUNT £ ....

EXPIRY DATE ....

SIGNED ....

NAME ....

ADDRESS ....